Practical TSO/ISPF
for Programmers and the
Information Center

Related books in the Wiley *Practical* series:

Practical MVS JCL, James G. Janossy (1987)

Practical VSAM For Today's Programmers,
James G. Janossy and Richard E. Guzik (1988)

Practical TSO/ISPF for Programmers and the Information Center

James G. Janossy
DePaul University

WILEY

John Wiley & Sons
New York · Chichester · Brisbane · Toronto · Singapore

Library of Congress Cataloging in Publication Data:

Janossy, James G. (James Gustav), 1947–
    Practical TSO/ISPF : for programmers and the information center /
James G. Janossy.
        p. cm.
    ISBN 0-471-63357-7
        1. Time-sharing computer systems. 2. ISPF Dialog Manager
(Computer program) I. Title.
    QA76.53.J36   1988
    005.2'25—dc19   88-95
                                                                CIP

Printed in the United States of America

10   9   8   7   6   5   4   3   2   1

omne tulit punctum
qui miscuit utile dulci

══ PREFACE ══

This book is designed to help newcomers to the TSO/ISPF environment rapidly become proficient in creating and editing programs, submitting jobs, and seeing results. If there is one word that best describes this book, it is "focus." This book is focused on the elements of TSO/ISPF that deliver the benefit of a reliable interactive working environment to personnel day-in, day-out.

TSO/ISPF, the Time Sharing Option, provides the tools for a person to allocate the data sets that house source code and job control language statements, and to compose and modify those statements. TSO/ISPF also provides the means to submit JCL for execution, and to see the output of a job online without having to await paper print. Anyone who interacts with an IBM mainframe running MVS, IBM's premier business data processing operating system, finds it necessary to use TSO or a third-party product similar to it.

TSO has progressed from a simple line editor to a product that offers powerful full-screen editing features and a host of facilities. But while the product has become ever more laden with features, a serious gap has existed in the technical literature concerning it. Of course, vendor manuals are available and describe all aspects of TSO. Yet manuals lack a focus sorely needed by most programmers and end users who must develop and maintain a proficiency in mainstream TSO/ISPF features simply to get their work done.

This book is geared toward giving readers the information needed to effectively use TSO/ISPF. Part 1 groups together five chapters that provide rapid familiarization with unique aspects of the IBM terminal device family, logging on and off, the ISPF main menu, and the initial setup often needed for new accounts. Included here also is a concise overview of partitioned data sets, the unique storage mechanism used to house TSO source code and job control language libraries without a subdirectory mechanism. This part of the book can be assimilated within a few hours, and a newcomer to the environment rapidly given access to TSO/ISPF.

Chapters 6 through 10 are arranged with examples of the most common way TSO/ISPF is used: for the composition of program language code, and the composition and submission of job control language to process it. A newcomer to the TSO/ISPF environment can progress through these chapters actually performing these processes "hands-on" in a self-paced tutorial manner. Reference charts and examples depict a natural flow of actions taken by personnel to accomplish their editing and job submission work.

Chapter 9 provides coverage of the way to view the output of jobs online, using either the Spool Display and Search Facility (SDSF) or TSO/ISPF itself. Chapter 10, at the end of Part 2, highlights a collection of valuable productivity-boosting features and techniques for TSO/ISPF usage, often difficult for personnel to find within large reference works.

TSO/ISPF interactive utilities have replaced, for most programmer and end-user tasks, the use of old 1960s batch utilities. Part 3 provides Chapters 11 through 15, each devoted to one of the TSO/ISPF major interactive utility functions. These chapters are direct and to the point, with illustrations of the most convenient means to make the utilities work for you.

The items in the appendixes were carefully selected to fill gaps in literature arising from modern-day developments. Appendixes on program function key usage and the emulation of IBM terminals with ASCII terminals and microcomputers are especially valuable to people in an educational environment or those accessing a mainframe over a dial-up line. Included here is the job control language to perform a reorganization of a partitioned data set with many space and allocation change options, often overlooked with a raw execution of the IEBCOPY utility. The appendixes include a common-sense treatment of TSO CLISTs, command lists aimed at today's specialized usage of this facility. Concluding the appendixes is a compendium of problem resolution guidance built up from my experience and that of several of my colleagues.

I'd like to thank Steve Samuels, director of the DePaul Computer Career Program, Joel Bernstein and Cyndee Llewellyn, instructors in the CCP, and Dawne Tortorella, director of Academic Computing Services for DePaul University, who reviewed the manuscript and made many valuable suggestions concerning content and presentation. Dr. Helmut Epp, chairman of the Department of Computer Science and Information Systems of DePaul, was a source of encouragement and support in this effort.

Tom Vari of the City of Chicago Datacenter helped in achieving a consistent emphasis by his reading of the manuscript and comments on its content, for which I am grateful. John Whaley, management analyst and consultant, reviewed the manuscript and suggested changes that aided in achieving clarity and consistency.

I would also like to thank Margaret Goldstein of the International Business Machines Corporation, by whose knowledge of the organization and its technical resources this book has benefitted, and to IBM itself, for allowing me to reproduce proprietary illustrations of 3270 and 3191 display stations and keyboards.

This is a practical book. I wrote it for students of the DePaul University Computer Career Program, an intensive curriculum that enrolls postgraduate newcomers to computers and sends them off seven months later with the COBOL, MVS JCL, and CICS skills needed to join the ranks of professional business data processing programmers. These people have programming and careers on their minds, not trivia. TSO/ISPF is, to them, just a means to a programming end. This book is, simply put, intended to be a guide to squeezing the maximum benefit out of TSO/ISPF in the minimum amount of time, so you, too, can get on with using it to your advantage.

JAMES G. JANOSSY

Chicago, Illinois
October 1988

Need to find information quickly? Try the summary index at the end of this book. It's keyed to the pictographs such as this that exist as easily located landmarks on various pages:

```
┌─────┐
│ 0.3 │
│     └──────┐
│  PF  KEYS  │
└────────────┘
```

SUMMARY
CONTENTS

1	INTRODUCTION TO TSO/ISPF	3
2	LOGGING ON AND OFF	9
3	THE ISPF MAIN MENU	19
4	TSO 0: ISPF PARMS—A ONE-TIME SETUP TASK	25
5	PARTITIONED DATA SETS	35
6	A PRACTICAL TSO/ISPF GUIDE	45
7	TSO 2: CREATING AND EDITING	49
8	TSO 2: ADVANCED EDITING AND JOB SUBMISSION	73
9	VIEWING JOB OUTPUT ONLINE	95
10	TSO/ISPF HINTS AND CONVENIENCE FEATURES	111
11	TSO 3.1: PDS LIBRARY MEMBER UTILITY	127
12	TSO 3.2: PARTITIONED DATA SET UTILITIES	137
13	TSO 3.3: COPY/MOVE UTILITY	149

14   TSO 3.4: DATA SET LIST UTILITY   159

15   HARDCOPY PRINT   167

APPENDIXES

A   3270 TERMINAL PF KEYS, SPECIAL KEYS, PA KEYS   173

B   EMULATING IBM TERMINALS WITH ASCII
     TERMINALS AND MICROCOMPUTERS   183

C   PARTITIONED DATA SET REORGANIZATION JCL   187

D   TSO COMMAND LISTS (CLISTs)   195

E   OBTAINING PDS REORGANIZATION JCL AND CLISTs
     ON DISKETTE FOR UPLOADING   217

F   TSO/ISPF COMMAND EXPLANATION AND
     SYNTAX REFERENCE   219

G   TSO/ISPF HORROR STORIES WITH HAPPY ENDINGS   235

H   TSO STATISTICS, TSO 3.5 "RESET," AND
     PDS DIRECTORY INTERNALS   243

     DETAILED INDEX   265

     SUMMARY INDEX   269

=== CONTENTS ===

PART I   GETTING STARTED WITH TSO/ISPF

1   INTRODUCTION TO TSO/ISPF   3

The Environment, 3

Terminals for TSO/ISPF, 4

Special Keys, 4
    Enter / Return (Newline) / Print /
    Reset / Alt / End

Program Function Keys, 8

2   LOGGING ON AND OFF   9

Different Logon Sequences, 9

RACF Security, 11
    RACF Password for TSO Access / Changing the RACF
    Password When First Logging On / Changing an
    Unexpired RACF Password

The READY Prompt, 14

Logging Off, 15

Resolving Common Logon Problems, 16
    Reestablishing Contact After an Interruption /
    Interference When Logging On (TSO or CICS)

3   THE ISPF MAIN MENU   19

Overall Picture of TSO/ISPF Functions, 19

The Core of TSO/ISPF, 23

4 TSO 0: ISPF PARMS—A ONE-TIME SETUP TASK 25

TSO 0.1: Terminal Setup, 25

Completing Setup and Using the = Transfer
Feature, 28

TSO 0.2: Log and List Defaults, 28
   Log Data Set / List Data Set / Print JOB Statement

TSO 0.3: PF Key Definition, 31

5 PARTITIONED DATA SETS 35

Organizing Data Set Storage, 35

Partitioned Data Sets for Source Code and JCL, 36

Working With Partitioned Data Sets, 38
   Creating a PDS / Viewing a PDS Directory / PDS
   Reorganization

Load Module Library: A Special Partitioned
Data Set, 41

PART 2 CREATING AND EDITING CODE AND JCL

6 A PRACTICAL TSO/ISPF GUIDE 45

A Quick Overview of Source Code Entry and
Compilation, 46

Program Correction, 47

Testing of Program Load Modules, 48

TSO/ISPF: The Workbench, 48

7 TSO 2: CREATING AND EDITING 49

Starting the Edit, 49
   The Partitioned Data Set Member List / Scrolling
   Through a PDS Member List / A Road Map to Edit
   Screen Geography

Using the Edit Screen, 56
   A Guide to Edit-Line Commands / Hints / Cancelling
   the Edit Without Creating a Member

Ending the Edit, 70

Accessing Sequential and Non-TSO/ISPF Data Sets, 71

Warning: Monitor Partitioned Data Set Space! 72

8   TSO 2: ADVANCED EDITING AND JOB SUBMISSION   73

Primary (Command Line) Edit Commands, 73

Editing Profile, 74
    Important Profile Parameters / RECOVERY for Automatic
    Edit Resumption / Creating Additional Editing Profiles

Working Primary Editing Commands, 77

9   VIEWING JOB OUTPUT ONLINE   95

TSO 3.8: Outlist Facility, 95
    When to View Output / Viewing Output / Requeueing
    Held Output to Print / Checking Job Status / Print
    Carriage Control Field / A Common Outlist Problem
    for Newcomers

SDSF: Spool Display and Search Facility, 101
    Accessing SDSF / An SDSF Example / Printing Output
    with SDSF / Viewing Print on the Output Queue / Split
    Screen and Output Viewing

10   TSO/ISPF HINTS AND CONVENIENCE FEATURES   111

Flexible Entry of a Transfer, 111

Direct Logoff with =X, 112

Flexible Scrolling with Command Line Override, 112

TSO: Passthrough Command, 113

CANCEL: Cancelling Submitted Jobs, 114

STATUS: Checking Job Status, 114

LISTCAT: A List of Your TSO/ISPF Data Sets, 115

SEND: Sending a Message, 116

KEYS: Redefining PF Keys Anywhere, 118

EXEC: Executing a CLIST from Your Own Library, 119

Stacking Command Line Entries, 120

TSO Tutorial and PANELID, 120

PART 3   TSO/ISPF GENERAL UTILITY FUNCTIONS

11   TSO 3.1: PDS LIBRARY MEMBER UTILITY   127

TSO 3.1: Browse, Print, Rename, and Delete, 127

Miscellaneous TSO 3.1 Options, 131

Data Set Information: *I* / Compress Data Set: *C* / Print a
PDS Index (Directory) Listing: *X* / Print Entire Library
(PDS): *L* / Short Rendition of Data Set Information: *S*

Hints, 135
Partitioned Data Set Housekeeping / Operations on
Non-ISPF Data Sets

12   TSO 3.2: PARTITIONED DATA SET UTILITIES   **137**
Allocate a New Data Set: *A*, 137
Rename an Entire Data Set: *R*, 143
Delete an Entire Data Set: *D*, 143
PDS Space Usage and Reorganization: *Ƅ*, 145
Catalog a Data Set: *C*, 147
Uncatalog a Data Set: *U*, 148
Data Set Information (Short): *S*, 148

13   TSO 3.3: COPY/MOVE UTILITY   **149**
Copy a Member or Data Set: *C*, 151
Move a Member or Data Set: *M*, 153
The Member List During Copy/Move, 153
End of the Copy/ Move Operation, 156
Hints for Copy/Move, 156
Promotion Utility: *P*, 157

14   TSO 3.4: Data Set List Utility   **159**
The Data Set List, 159
TSO 3.4 Controlling Fields, 161
Function Selection from the Data Set List, 162
TSO 3.4 Lesser-Used Options, 164

15   Hardcopy Print   **167**
Screen Printing, 167
Member or Data Set Printing With TSO 3.1, 167
TSO 3.6: Hardcopy Utility, 168
Job Control Language or CLISTS for Printing Items, 171

APPENDIXES

A   3270 TERMINAL PF KEYS, SPECIAL KEYS, PA KEYS   173

Program Function Keys, 173
    Program Function Key Meanings / Additional Function
    Key Commands

Program Access Keys, 181

**B   EMULATING IBM TERMINALS WITH ASCII
TERMINALS AND MICROCOMPUTERS   183**

C   PARTITIONED DATA SET REORGANIZATION JCL   187

Background, 187

Using the PDS Reorganization PROC, 190

Explanation of the PROC, 191

Reblocking a PDS Changing the Space or
Directory Allocation, 192

What to Do if the Reorganization Run Fails, 193

D   TSO COMMAND LISTS (CLISTs)   195

CLIST Background, 195

Allocating a CLIST Library, 196

CLIST Syntax, 197

A Simple CLIST for Tape Block Size Calculation, 198

A CLIST That Composes Disk Space JCL, 200

A CLIST for Message Sending, 202

A CLIST to Broadcast Messages, 206

Editing Base JCL and Submitting a Job via
a CLIST, 210

**E   OBTAINING PDS REORGANIZATION JCL AND CLISTs
ON DISKETTE FOR UPLOADING   217**

**F   TSO/ISPF COMMAND EXPLANATION AND
SYNTAX REFERENCE   219**

G   TSO/ISPF HORROR STORIES WITH HAPPY ENDINGS   235

**H   TSO STATISTICS, TSO 3.5 "*RESET,*" AND
     PDS DIRECTORY INTERNALS   243**

TSO/ISPF Function 3.5: Altering Member Statistics, 243
  Resetting Member Version Number / Changing the Origin
  ID Field / Difference Between N and R Options / Deleting
  Statistics

Internal Composition of a Partitioned Data
Set Directory, 250
  Listing and Dumping Directory Blocks / Format of
  Directory Block Records / Listing a TSO/ISPF Library
  Directory With a COBOL Program

DETAILED INDEX   265

SUMMARY INDEX   269

PART 1

GETTING STARTED WITH TSO/ISPF

To work effectively with TSO/ISPF you need to know some of the unique capabilities and keys provided by the IBM 3270 family of computer terminals, which are unlike any other terminal devices or microcomputers. But after only brief familiarization with the TSO/ISPF software and hardware environment, it's possible to learn how to log on to TSO and perform initial account setup actions. Chapters 1 and 2 help you accomplish this.

TSO/ISPF provides menu access to all of the functions performed by this interactive programming environment. Chapter 3 introduces the ISPF main menu, and contains a concise overview of the "mainstream" functions that support most programming activities.

Source code and job control language statements are created and housed within a form of file unique to the MVS operating system. Chapter 5 provides you with the knowledge you need of partitioned data sets, and shows you how to create and maintain them using TSO/ISPF.

GETTING STARTED
WITH TSQL2

===== 1 =====

Introduction to TSO/ISPF

TSO/ISPF is simply a means to an end. It is the online environment in which source code such as COBOL, PL/I, FORTRAN, fourth-generation languages, or job control language is developed, submitted for processing, and the results seen. While the punched cards of older times were shamed by the programmer's interactive workbenches of UNIX and other minicomputers, TSO/ISPF rivals these in programmer convenience and often exceeds them in ease of use.

THE ENVIRONMENT

TSO—by itself, without the acronym ISPF—is the Time Sharing Option, introduced to the OS/MVS operating system by IBM in the 1970s. In its native mode TSO is command driven and line oriented, in the same manner as microcomputer MS-DOS and VMS of the DEC VAX. Native mode TSO offers only line editing, similar to the primitive EDLIN editor on a PC or "nonkeypad mode" EDT on the VAX. The prompt for terminal operator input under native mode TSO is the word READY, and this primitive form of TSO is sometimes called its "READY" mode.

ISPF stands for Interactive System Productivity Facility, a human-to-machine interface designed to operate within any of IBM's mainframe environments, including VM and DOS/VSE, as well as under MVS. ISPF facilitates the work of programmers and end users by providing labeled "fill-in-the-blank" screens, called "panels," under a simple two-level menu structure. On MVS systems, ISPF is housed "under" TSO, giving rise to the acronym TSO/ISPF, and has evolved from SPF, its earlier name as the Structured Programming Facility.

3

TERMINALS FOR TSO/ISPF

In the modern world, when a programmer in an MVS installation has to compose a program or job control language, edit and modify it, submit it for execution, and view the results, he or she logs on to TSO/ISPF. In order to do this, the programmer uses an IBM terminal of the 3270 equipment family, or an ASCII terminal or PC made to perform like this family by a protocol converter, a communications device that acts as a specialized interface.

Terminals in the IBM 3270 family are called "display stations," and they attach to a controller that acts as a funnel to the mainframe. Memory and circuitry in the terminal and controller, or in the protocol converter, if one is used, allow the terminal to receive a burst of information from the computer, describing an entire screen, and then locally support the manipulation of the screen contents. The 3270s provide several function and control keys not found on ASCII or microcomputer keyboards.

Figure 1.1 is an illustration of the most common IBM 3270 keyboard. Its central portion is similar to an ordinary typewriter keyboard, with additional keys to the left and right. The newest model in the 3270 family, the IBM 3191 terminal, locates some of the additional keys differently and is pictured in Appendix A.

SPECIAL KEYS

IBM 3270 family terminals provide two classes of special keys: terminal control keys and program function, or PF, keys. Appendix A describes all of these in detail; programmers must be aware of the nature of a few of them in order to use TSO/ISPF:

Enter

At the extreme right of the space bar is the *ENTER* key. While this appears to be much like the carriage return key on an ASCII device or microcomputer, *it is different in action from the carriage return.* On a 3270, *ENTER* is not used to position the cursor, it is strictly a signal to the computer that the user of the terminal is finished with work on the screen. The *RETURN* or *NEWLINE* key positions the cursor.

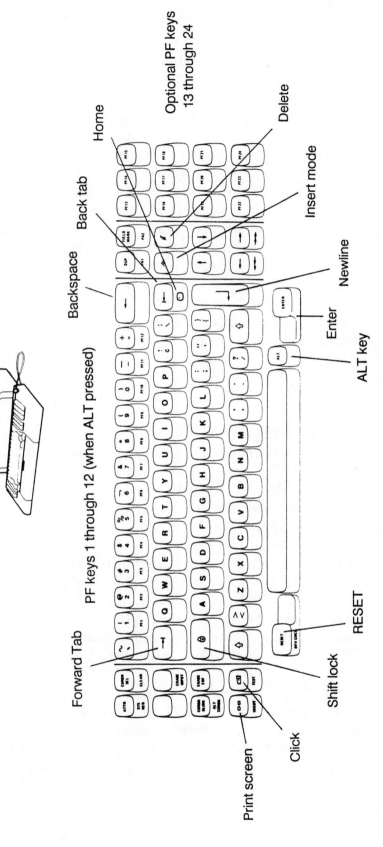

FIGURE 1.1 IBM 3270 computer terminal keyboard; see Appendix A for information on the contemporary IBM 3191 display station and keyboard. (Reprinted with annotations by permission from *IBM 3270 Information Display System 3276 Control Unit Display Station Operator's Guide*, Copyright 1983 by International Business Machines Corporation.)

RETURN (NEWLINE)

A key with no name, the RETURN key is at the right of the letter keys. It is usually labeled with a downward left arrow and is often called the NEWLINE key. It is simply a "tab" key, one that moves the cursor down a line and to the left side of the screen. It is often simulated by protocol converters with the LINE FEED key.

The RETURN key is much like the right and left arrow tabs that are at the ends of the top row of letter keys. All of these keys move the cursor around the screen but do not signal the mainframe that the terminal operator is done with the screen. The terminal appears completely inactive to the mainframe until the ENTER key or one of the PF or PA keys is struck; hitting the RETURN key does not raise the attention of the mainframe. If for an extended period you use only RETURN and the cursor positioning keys, you will be logged off TSO automatically after the installation-defined time limit for mainframe inactivity.

Print

The PRINT key, at the lower left corner of the keyboard, allows a hardcopy of the terminal screen to be printed on a low-speed printing device attached to the same terminal controller as the terminal. The PRINT key is denoted by a small pictograph of a video screen and an arrow pointing to a document symbol.

The pictograph on the PRINT key is very descriptive; the screen print function directs the terminal controller to send a copy of the screen information to a local printing device. If no printing device is attached to the same terminal controller, this function is not available. If PRINT is available and is pressed, but the local printer is busy, not working, or has failed in operation, the DEV CNCL or "device cancel" key must be pressed to unlock the keyboard. The DEV CNCL key is the ALT key and RESET key pressed at the same time.

Non-3270 terminals emulating 3270s do not usually provide a hardware print key. But microcomputers such as PC compatibles using the MS-DOS operating system provide a "Prt Sc" key that delivers exactly the same functionality as the 3270 PRINT key. Microcomputer printers are relatively inexpensive and accomplish screen print by transferring characters from the local screen memory directly to a printer. This combination of equipment is frequently specified for terminal usage when single workstations or dial-up access is needed, providing a more economical solution than a local controller.

Reset

To the left of the space bar is the *RESET* key. This is used if the keyboard locks due to invalid entry of data or a terminal problem, conditions accompanied by the display of an X symbol on the bottom line of the terminal screen. Keyboard reset is this key's only use; it is not a "reset" of the screen image or terminal logic and does not affect operation of the terminal's controller or the computer. *RESET* terminates "insert" mode, a text entry facility processed within the 3270 terminal itself.

RESET is also used to clear problems with an attached hardcopy printer, if one is configured with the controller that services the terminal. If print has been sent to that device, but it is busy, not working, or has failed in operation, *RESET* can be pressed with ALT also held down. The *ALT/RESET* combination is called the *DEV CNCL* or "device cancel" key.

Alt

To the right of the space bar is the *ALT* key. This operates similarly to the *SHIFT* key, but it is used, however, in combination with keys on the top row and sides of the keyboard. *ALT* makes the top row of number keys on the 3270 into program function or *PF* keys. For example, pressing number 1 while holding *ALT* down sends a *PF1*, or "program function 1" signal. Thus the number keys actually have three meanings: the numerals, the *SHIFTed* numeral punctuation symbols, and the *ALTed* numeral program function key values. On the newer IBM 3191 terminal *ALT* need not be pressed to access a PF key.

End

TSO/ISPF help screens and manuals often mention pressing the *END* key in order to terminate a process or move from a submenu to the next higher level menu. "*END*" is not actually the name of a key on the keyboard, but a meaning commonly assigned to program function 3, the *PF3* key. *PF3* is one of 12 function keys usually accessed by pressing the *ALT* key and the top row number 3.

PROGRAM FUNCTION (*PF*) KEYS

TSO/ISPF assigns functions to program function or *PF* keys 1 through 12. These keys are accessed on a normal 3270 programming keyboard by pressing the *ALT* key and the top row number keys. *PF1* through *PF9* are the *ALT/1* through *ALT/9* keys. *PF10* is *ALT/0*, *PF11* is *ALT/-*, and *PF12* is *ALT/=*.

The meaning of *PF* keys is not "hardwired" into terminals or even TSO/ISPF; it is changeable by each individual TSO/ISPF user, but defaults to a standard, as described in Appendix A.

In addition to the *PF1* through *PF12* keys, functions associated with *PF13* through *PF24* are mentioned on various TSO/ISPF screens. This extra bank of function keys is supported on IBM newer-model terminals. These keys default to the same functions as *PF1* through *PF12* but can be assigned other meanings.

2

Logging On and Off

Logging on to TSO is much the same as logging on to any minicomputer: after a connection is established, a logon sequence is performed to identify the individual programmer and the account or files to be accessed. Depending on whether or not a given terminal can also access other interactive software, such as CICS, TSO might or might not have to be identified as the online application desired.

DIFFERENT LOGON SEQUENCES

A typical TSO logon command appears as in Figure 2.1. In this case, "BT05686" is a TSO "user id" issued to a programmer. In response to this entry, TSO may request entry of a password. In a school environment, with the "MVS Express" installation of MVS, you might be required to enter "TSO BT05686" or a similar abbreviated form of the logon command, as illustrated in Figure 2.2.

The TSO user id is a character string, also called a "logon identifier." This identifier is established by an installation for a given TSO user. Once established, the person to whom it is issued will be known to TSO by it, and it will be regarded as the highest level qualifier or "front part" of the name of files—data sets—in which the person stores source code and JCL. For example, the data sets of the person who logs on in this manner will typically be something like:

```
BT05686.SOURCE.COBOL    (language source code)
BT05686.SOURCE.CNTL     (job control language)
BT05686.SOURCE.CLIST    (optional TSO command lists)
```

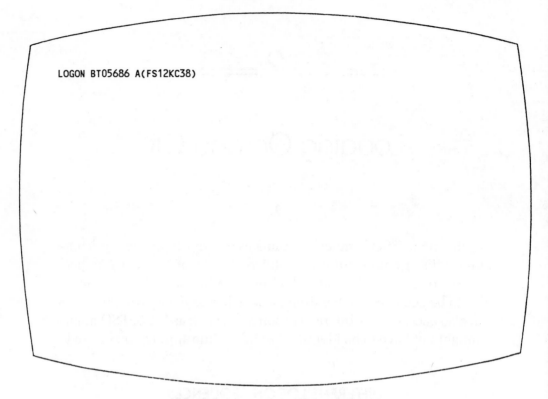

```
LOGON BT05686 A(FS12KC38)
```

FIGURE 2.1   Typical TSO logon screen

or

```
CCPZ04.CSC.PLI          (language source code)
CCPZ04.CSC.CNTL         (job control language)
CCPZ04.CSC.CLIST        (optional TSO command lists)
```

These data sets are not created automatically by TSO/ISPF, however. An installation may create them for new TSO account holders, or may allow newcomers to create or "allocate" them for themselves using JCL or TSO/ISPF function 3.2, as discussed in Chapter 5.

The "A(FS12KC38)" portion of the first logon illustrated is an
"account code" that will be charged with the resources used during
the online TSO session. If an installation requires entry of an account code, its personnel are usually provided with specific infor-

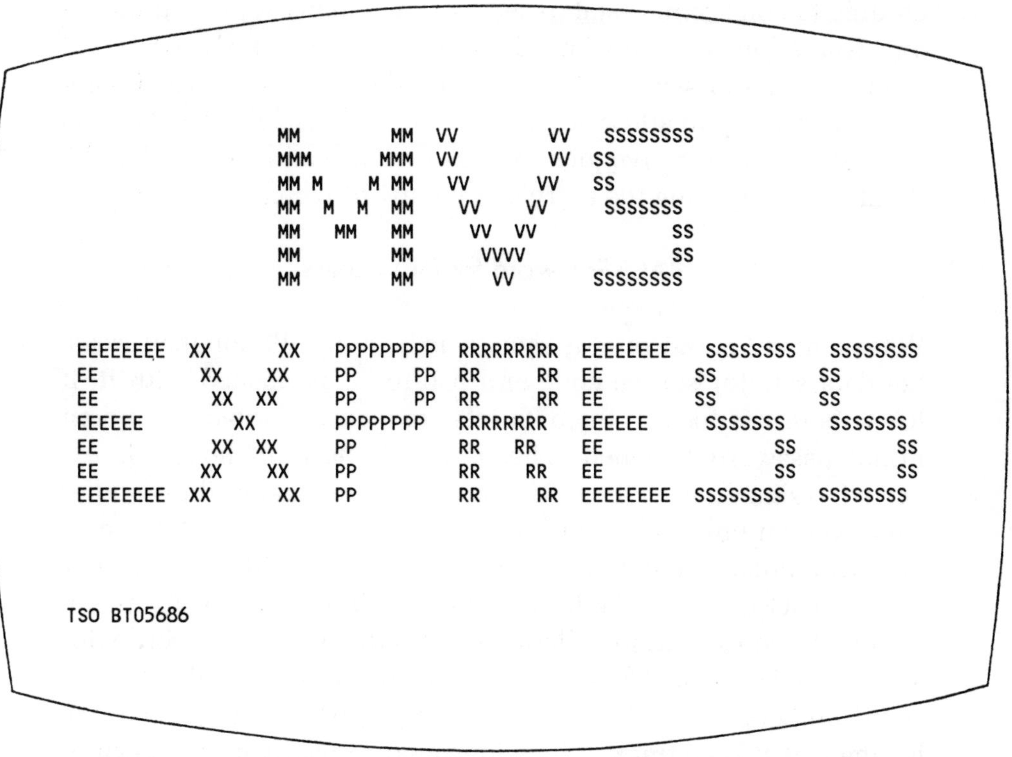

```
                    MM        MM  VV          VV    SSSSSSSS
                    MMM      MMM  VV          VV    SS
                    MM M    M MM  VV         VV     SS
                    MM  M  M  MM   VV       VV       SSSSSSS
                    MM    MM   MM   VV     VV               SS
                    MM         MM    VVVV                   SS
                    MM         MM     VV          SSSSSSSS


    EEEEEEEE  XX      XX   PPPPPPPP   RRRRRRRR   EEEEEEEE   SSSSSSSS   SSSSSSSS
    EE          XX  XX     PP    PP   RR    RR   EE         SS         SS
    EE          XX XX      PP    PP   RR    RR   EE         SS         SS
    EEEEEE       XX        PPPPPPPP   RRRRRRRR   EEEEEE     SSSSSSS    SSSSSSS
    EE          XX XX      PP         RR  RR     EE               SS         SS
    EE          XX  XX     PP         RR   RR    EE               SS         SS
    EEEEEEEE  XX      XX   PP         RR    RR   EEEEEEEE   SSSSSSSS   SSSSSSSS


    TSO BT05686
```

FIGURE 2.2   TSO logon screen under the "MVS Express" release of the operating system

mation about the format and content of this field at the time the TSO account is issued to them.

In response to the logon sequence, TSO may proceed directly with logon processing, or it may request the entry of a logon password, depending on whether or not an installation is making use of a security access system. Access security is not inherent in TSO itself. Several major security products exist and are marketed to the IBM mainframe community, and nearly all mainframe installations acquire and use such a product. When password entry is required, the password usually does not appear on the screen.

RACF SECURITY

IBM's product for data-set security is called Resource Acquisition Control Facility, or RACF. RACF protects data sets from access according to constraints established by the systems support group of an installation. In many installations all data sets are protected from access, and security is relaxed on them in a controlled manner as necessary to allow access to data sets by selected TSO users and batch or interactive jobs. Access to TSO can be controlled by RACF also, requiring the entry of a password when logging on.

RACF Password for TSO Access

When a new TSO account is established, an installation may create the data sets for source code and JCL to be associated with it. If RACF is in use locally, the data sets are usually protected, and an initial password assigned. The new TSO account holder is expected to sign on with the initial password and change it to another value known only to him or her. From this point onward, the new password must be entered to gain access to TSO and the data sets.

New TSO users can be forced to assign a new password immediately. To do this, an installation creates the initial password with an "expired" status. This makes clever use of RACF; all TSO account holders can be forced to change passwords periodically by having RACF keep track of how long a given password has been in effect. After a specified period of time, a password expires and must be changed. By making initial passwords already expired, a new TSO user must deal with password change immediately.

Changing the RACF Password When First Logging On

Figure 2.3 illustrates the message presented by RACF under TSO when a new TSO account holder is first logging on and the installation has established an expired initial password. The first line has prompted for the entry of the initial password, which is not echoed to the screen. The TSO account holder has entered the initial, that is, the "current," password. In response to it, RACF has sent the message that the current password has expired, and directed:

```
REENTER -
```

The message is deceiving and often confusing. *Do not at this point enter the initial password.* RACF is actually asking for you to enter

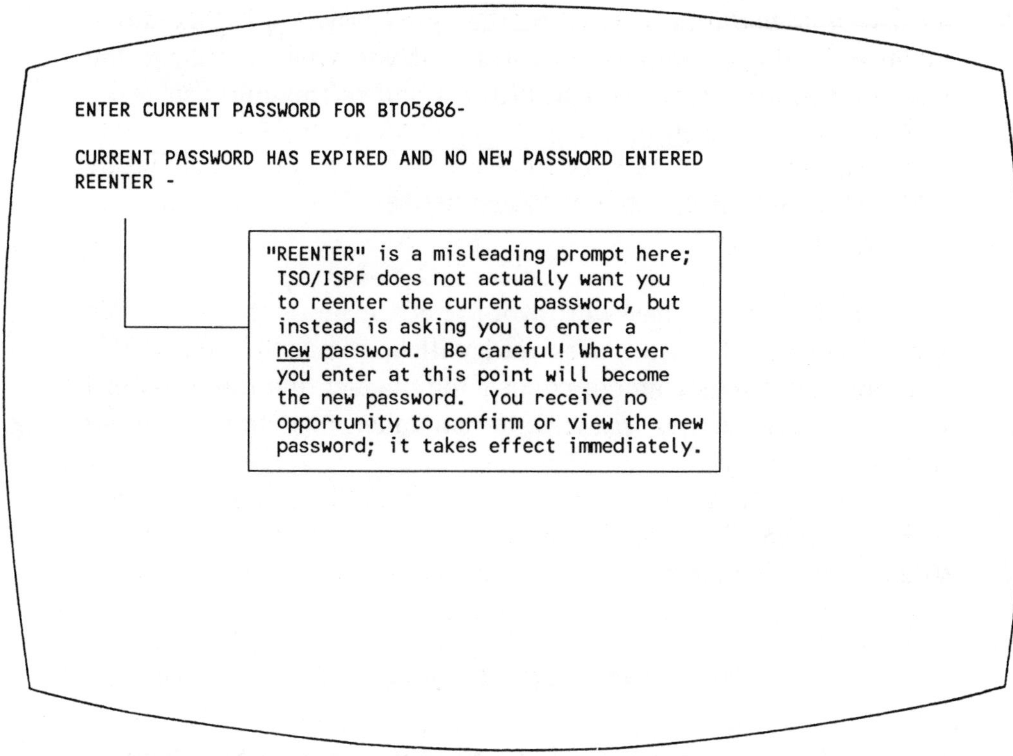

```
ENTER CURRENT PASSWORD FOR BT05686-

CURRENT PASSWORD HAS EXPIRED AND NO NEW PASSWORD ENTERED
REENTER -

                    ┌─────────────────────────────────────┐
          ┌─────────┤ "REENTER" is a misleading prompt here; │
          │         │ TSO/ISPF does not actually want you   │
          │         │ to reenter the current password, but  │
          └─────────┤ instead is asking you to enter a      │
                    │ new password.  Be careful! Whatever   │
                    │ you enter at this point will become   │
                    │ the new password.  You receive no     │
                    │ opportunity to confirm or view the new │
                    │ password; it takes effect immediately. │
                    └─────────────────────────────────────┘
```

FIGURE 2.3   RACF security system message for an expired password

a *new* password. Whatever string of up to eight letters or numbers, starting with a letter, is entered at this time will be accepted as the new password.

RACF does not provide explicit confirmation that it has accepted a new password, and it does not restate the new password to remind you of it. If you do not know what you entered you will not be able to log on again, and you will have to seek the involvement of the installation security coordinator to reestablish a known password.

Changing an Unexpired RACF Password

You may occasionally desire to change a RACF password for TSO access even though the current password has not yet expired. The only opportunity to do this occurs at the time you log on. To change a password, enter the current password, followed immediately by a slash, followed immediately by the new password. For example, if the current password is CARROT and you wish to change the password to BANANA, you would respond in this manner to the RACF password prompt:

```
ENTER CURRENT PASSWORD FOR BT05686-
CARROT/BANANA
```

The current and new password would not appear on the screen. No second entry of the new password will be requested, and RACF will not issue any statement concerning the fact that the password has been changed. You will have to remember what you entered as the new password.

As a suggestion, enter characters with deliberation when you change passwords under RACF. Touch-typing these rapidly leads to password problems if a finger slips and hits a key by mistake.

THE READY PROMPT

Figure 2.4 illustrates a typical screen presented by TSO when its logon processing is complete. This screen is an entry point to the main menu screen of ISPF, but may also be a point from which other specialized online applications within an installation can be accessed, such as Statistical Analysis System, a product of SAS Institute, Inc.; RAMIS, a product of On-Line Software International; MARK-IV from Sterling Software; or IBM's Graphical Data Display Manager (GDDM); among others. In some installations, this screen is bypassed completely, and the ISPF main menu appears immediately.

If the logon completion screen is used in an installation, it may carry messages that the installation desires to broadcast to personnel logging on, such as operational schedules, technical notes, or news and bulletins. If presented with the READY prompt of native mode TSO, you will need to enter "ISPF" in order to access TSO/ISPF. Some installations set TSO to invoke ISPF automatically. In this case, logging on results in the immediate presentation of the main ISPF menu depicted in Figure 3.1. If presented with three asterisks ***, press ENTER; this is the standard TSO indication that a response is needed to continue.

```
LOGON BT05686/BT05686 ACCT(FS12KC38) PROC(TSO001)
IKJ56455I BT05686 LOGON IN PROGRESS AT 15:28:04 ON OCTOBER 22, 1988

        FFFFFFFF    SSSSSSS    DDDDDDD      CCCCCC
        FF         SS         DD    DD    CC    CC       FARNON
        FF         SS           DD    DD  CC              STANDARD
        FFFFF      SSSSS        DD    DD  CC              DATA
        FF              SS    DD    DD    CC              CENTER
        FF              SS    DD    DD    CC    CC        TSO/ISPF
        FF         SSSSSSS    DDDDDDDD      CCCCC

****************************************************************************
SYSTEMS AND PROGRAMMING NEWS AS OF 10/22/88  10:52 AM

    - 3 NEW TEST DISK PACKS, FS0956 FS0958 AND FS0963 ARE INSTALLED
    - THE DOS TO MVS/XA CONVERSION ON 4381 CPU 7 IS NEARING COMPLETION,
        SEE MIKE AGNEW IF TEST JOBS FOR FINAL CONVERSION ARE
        GOING TO NEED ACCESS TO DOS AFTER OCT 30
    - READ/HEED JOB JOB CLASS CHANGE MEMO, CHANGES EFFECTIVE OCT. 25
****************************************************************************

READY
 ispf
```

FIGURE 2.4   TSO screen presented when logon processing has been completed

LOGGING OFF

If the READY prompt appears on the screen, native mode TSO can accept commands. One command among all the others is significant: LOGOFF. Complete logging off from native mode TSO is accomplished with this.

An installation can set up TSO in such a way that exiting from the main ISPF menu automatically logs a person off TSO. Logging off TSO usually results in an explicit message indicating that logoff actions have been completed, such as:

```
IKJ56470I BT05686 LOGGED OFF TSO AT 14:54:50 ON MAY 1, 1988
```

or repeated presentation of the greeting screen depicted in Figure 2.2. At this point, either dim the screen, to prevent burning the message into it, or turn off the terminal, depending on local practice.

RESOLVING COMMON LOGON PROBLEMS

Reestablishing Contact After an Interruption

Disconnection from a TSO session can occur when contact with a mainframe is handled by a minicomputer emulating 3270 terminals, or when a dial-up connection over telephone lines is used. A subsequent attempt to log on before the local "time out" period has elapsed will result in a rejection of the logon because the TSO user id is already in use.

It is possible to reestablish the session during the installation "time out" period by logging on with the RECONNECT specification. RECONNECT is specified after the entries normally made for a logon:

```
LOGON BT05686 A(FS12KC38) RECONNECT
```

If access security is in effect you will be prompted for entry of the current password as if a new logon was being attempted, so that the system can confirm you are the appropriate party to be reconnected to a session.

It is also possible to step through the reconnection process by entering only the first part of a logon sequence, for example, the TSO at the bottom of Figure 2.2. TSO will then prompt for each element of the logon sequence. The word RECONNECT should be entered after the TSO user id or after the account, if an account is required, separated by a space. Figure 2.5 illustrates this prompted reconnection sequence and the message issued by TSO when the reconnection has been completed.

Interference When Logging On (TSO or CICS)

In some installations where terminals are attached to the mainframe through protocol converters and communication switching equipment, a user may become disconnected from his or her terminal session, but the session still remains active as far as the mainframe is concerned. Another user attempting to log on may

```
 IKJ56425I LOGON REJECTED, USERID BT05686 IN USE
 IKJ56400A ENTER LOGON OR LOGOFF-

logon

 IKJ56700A ENTER USERID -

bt05686 reconnect

 IKJ56408I PASSWORD REQUIRED FOR LOGON RECONNECT
 IKJ56714I ENTER CURRENT PASSWORD FOR BT05686-


 IKT00300I LOGON RECONNECT SUCCESSFUL, SESSION ESTABLISHED
***
```

FIGURE 2.5   Prompted sequence of actions to establish a reconnection with TSO after an interruption

then be given the same communication port, with the result that the second user steps into the shoes of the first.

If this occurs to you and you appear to be in someone else's TSO/ISPF session, the cure is simple: just log off, and then log on again. This type of situation is corrected in a timely manner by TSO itself, since an account will be logged off for inactivity within a few minutes. Many types of communication equipment can detect this situation and, if properly programmed by an installation, will automatically terminate a session if a disturbance occurs to the circuit.

If, however, this situation occurs and the session "left hanging" on the mainframe side involves CICS, the primary application-program teleprocessing monitor on IBM mainframes, the situation is more serious. CICS does not have an inherent timeout feature, and a CICS session, if not ended with a logoff, may be left active indefinitely. If you are attempting to log on to TSO and the screen illustrated in Figure 2.6 appears, press the *CLEAR* key (*ALT/cursor select*) to completely clear the screen. Then enter the words:

```
***DFH2312   WELCOME TO CICS/VS  ***  12:40:58




         CCCCCC    IIIII   CCCCCC    SSSSSS         VVVV VVVV    SSSSSS
        CCCCCCCC   IIIII  CCCCCCCC  SSSSSSS         VVV  VVV    SSSSSSSS
        CCCC CC    III    CCCC CC   SSSS SS         VVV  VVV    SSSS SS
        CCC        III    CCC       SSSS      ***   VVV VVV     SSSS
        CCC        III    CCC       SSSS      ***   VVVVV       SSSS
        CCCC CC    III    CCCC CC   SS SSSS         VVVV   SS   SSSS
        CCCCCCCC   IIIII  CCCCCCCC  SSSSSSSS        VVVV   SSSSSSSS
        CCCCCC     IIIII   CCCCCC    SSSSSS         VVV     SSSSSS
```

FIGURE 2.6 CICS logon screen inadvertently accessed instead of TSO; CLEAR and enter CSSF LOGOFF to exit

```
    CSSF LOGOFF
```

and press the *ENTER* key. This will formally log off CICS and allow normal TSO logon. Note: if you are using an ASCII terminal or microcomputer to emulate a 3270 via a protocol converter such as the IBM 7171, see Appendix A for information about the key that sends the *CLEAR* signal.

It is possible for an incorrectly programmed CICS transaction to loop, in which case it is not possible for the terminal executing it to initiate a logoff. If you encounter such a runaway CICS transaction, denoted by a message somewhere on the screen with the letters "DFH," when attempting to log on to TSO, end your attempt to log on. Call the system console operator, indicating that a CICS transaction must be terminated by operator action. The operator has the ability to determine what transaction is causing the offense, and can terminate CICS if necessary to correct the situation. Then try logging on.

3

The ISPF Main Menu

The TSO/ISPF main menu supplied by IBM is shown in Figure 3.1. This is presented on the screen after entry of ISPF at the READY prompt, or immediately upon successful logon if an installation has chosen to set TSO/ISPF up in such a manner. The main menu is the jumping off point for all TSO/ISPF functions.

An installation can customize the TSO/ISPF main menu, either to add extra utilities and software, or to limit access to a selected group of TSO functions. Selections listed beyond Item 6 on the screen depicted in Figure 3.1 represent functions that a systems support programmer might find useful, utilities outside of the scope of TSO/ISPF that an installation has acquired and integrated with TSO support, or learning items such as the TSO/ISPF tutorial.

The TSO/ISPF main menu depicted in Figure 3.2 illustrates how a school or business installation may tailor the main menu to its own purposes, limiting the items on it to those functions that personnel actually need for applications programming and end-user work.

OVERALL PICTURE OF TSO/ISPF FUNCTIONS

Figure 3.3 graphically depicts the functions of TSO/ISPF. Access to each of the major functional areas is possible from the main menu. The submenu for each functional area, in turn, provides access to screens by which various processes can be performed.

TSO 0, ISPF PARMS is a "setup" function that needs to be accessed only once before you begin using TSO for actual work. It allows individual tailoring of a TSO logon id for the terminal, keyboard, and printing facilities in local use.

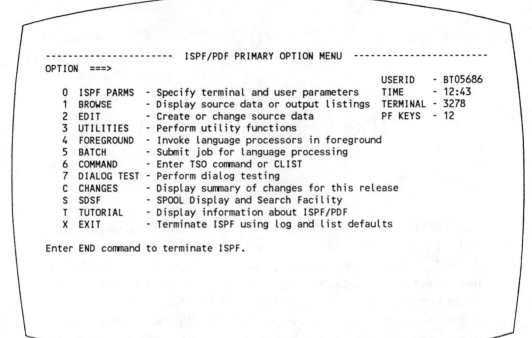

```
---------------------- ISPF/PDF PRIMARY OPTION MENU ----------------------
OPTION ===>
                                                        USERID   - BT05686
     0  ISPF PARMS  - Specify terminal and user parameters  TIME     - 12:43
     1  BROWSE      - Display source data or output listings TERMINAL - 3278
     2  EDIT        - Create or change source data           PF KEYS  - 12
     3  UTILITIES   - Perform utility functions
     4  FOREGROUND  - Invoke language processors in foreground
     5  BATCH       - Submit job for language processing
     6  COMMAND     - Enter TSO command or CLIST
     7  DIALOG TEST - Perform dialog testing
     C  CHANGES     - Display summary of changes for this release
     S  SDSF        - SPOOL Display and Search Facility
     T  TUTORIAL    - Display information about ISPF/PDF
     X  EXIT        - Terminate ISPF using log and list defaults

Enter END command to terminate ISPF.
```

FIGURE 3.1 TSO/ISPF main menu screen

TSO 1, BROWSE is an inquiry function that allows examination of data sets and partitioned data set members, but no ability to change them. It allows viewing records of any length.

TSO 2, EDIT is a very heavily used function. Using it, a programmer can create and modify program source code, and submit job control language for execution. EDIT allows editing of sequential data sets and members of partitioned data sets, but not VSAM data sets. Records of up to 255 bytes in length can be edited.

TSO 3, UTILITIES provides access to eight separate subfunctions, many of which in themselves provide several options. TSO 3 supplants most of the old stable of OS utilities such as IEBPTPCH, IEBGENER, IEHPROGM, IEBUPDTE, and IEHLIST as far as their use in program development is concerned. TSO subfunction 3.8 provides the means to view output, such as the result of a compile, on the screen, avoiding the need for much of the paper output and printing delays that were formerly associated with mainframe programming.

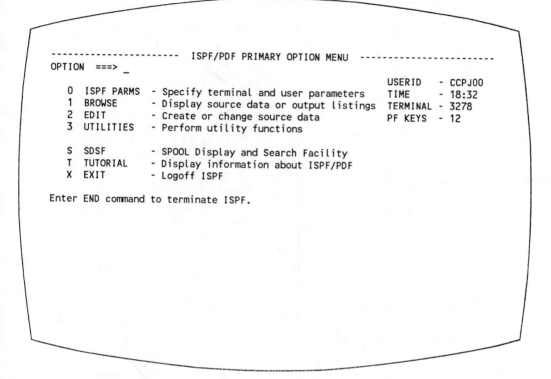

```
-------------------------- ISPF/PDF PRIMARY OPTION MENU ----------------------
OPTION  ===>  _
                                                              USERID   - CCPJ00
      0  ISPF PARMS  - Specify terminal and user parameters   TIME     - 18:32
      1  BROWSE      - Display source data or output listings  TERMINAL - 3278
      2  EDIT        - Create or change source data            PF KEYS  - 12
      3  UTILITIES   - Perform utility functions

      S  SDSF        - SPOOL Display and Search Facility
      T  TUTORIAL    - Display information about ISPF/PDF
      X  EXIT        - Logoff ISPF

 Enter END command to terminate ISPF.
```

FIGURE 3.2   Installation-customized TSO main menu screen

TSO 4, FOREGROUND allows execution of compilers in the "foreground" memory region, "under" TSO rather than under MVS with JCL alone. TSO 4 is not especially popular with many personnel; it is entirely different from the customary JCL-driven compile, link, and run process associated with the mainframe environment. In addition, it uses TSO resources usually needed by other interactive TSO processes, and if heavily used can produce undesirable response time for other programmers.

TSO 5, BACKGROUND is a complement to TSO 4, but is often viewed as unnecessary. It simply generates JCL to compile a program, based on "boilerplate" JCL and option selections set up by the programmer within the function. While it may appear handy, it is usually easier to access a standard compile cataloged procedure, especially when an installation uses different compile and testing JCL for database programs, online programs, and different versions of COBOL and fourth-generation languages.

TSO 6, COMMAND is merely a "passthrough" to native mode

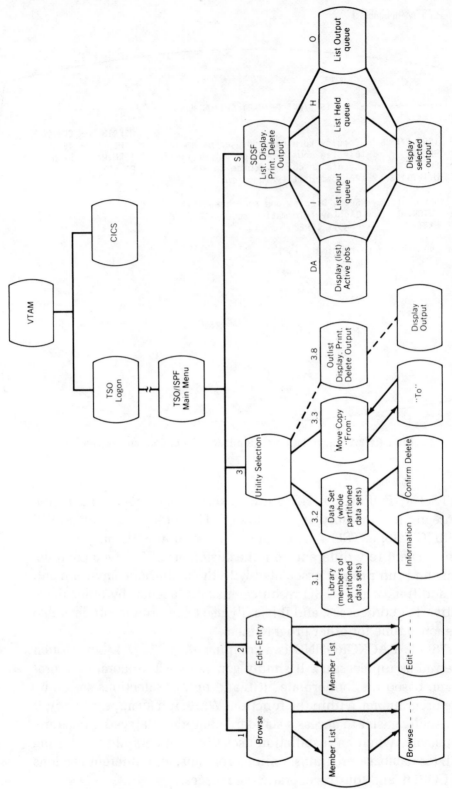

FIGURE 3.3 Functional breakdown of TSO/ISPF

22

TSO. The selection of TSO 6 provides a blank screen on which to enter any raw TSO command. With TSO/ISPF, it is also possible to enter raw TSO commands on the COMMAND line of any screen, as discussed in Chapter 10.

TSO 7, SUPPORT will usually not be visible except to systems programmers. It provides the means to alter TSO/ISPF panels and create new ISPF screens. The panels presented by the main menu selections, collectively called the Program Development Facility, or PDF, were constructed by IBM using facilities of TSO 7.

TSO S, SDSF stands for "Spool Display and Search Facility." It provides facilities to view a greater range of items than does TSO 3.8, allowing access to queues of jobs awaiting execution, jobs executing, and the system master log. SDSF was not designed specifically for programmers and end users but instead for computer console operators formerly limited to paper outputs of the system log, and for systems programmers. If an installation has SDSF it may or may not appear on the main menu, because operators and systems personnel can invoke it outside of TSO.

TSO T, TUTORIAL duplicates the function of the *PF1 HELP* key. *PF1* automatically "homes in" on help screens relevant to the function being performed, whereas you must yourself seek a topic of interest using TSO T.

THE CORE OF TSO/ISPF

As is usually the case with any text editor or set of software tools, an important core of TSO/ISPF provides the most useful functions and the greatest return on time invested in learning. Focusing on this essential core allows a person to become productive rapidly.

What delivers the goods in TSO? When you have executed TSO function 0, ISPF PARMS, once in order to complete TSO account setup, the most useful functions of TSO are 1, 2, and 3, with TSO 2 edit paramount in importance. And within TSO function 3, dealing with utilities, subfunctions 1, 2, and 3 are the most important. In fact, if this is all of TSO/ISPF that you know, you are proficient in the use of the product. Every other feature of TSO/ISPF is peripheral to the work of application programmers and end users. These parts of TSO/ISPF provide full functionality:

| 2 |
| EDIT |

Create and edit source code and JCL
Submit JCL for execution
Create and modify test data

| 3.8 |
| OUTLIST |

View output of compiles and jobs
Requeue output to print
Delete output without printing

or

| SDSF |
| SPOOL |

View output of compiles and jobs
Requeue output to print
Delete output without printing

| 3 |
| UTILITIES |

3.1: Print, rename, or delete members
3.2: Allocate, rename, delete data sets
3.3: Move or copy members or data sets
3.4: Data set list utility (access to functions via data
     set lists)

| 1 |
| BROWSE |

Examine members or data sets with
records of length greater than 255 bytes

If you are like most programmers and end users—with plenty to
do already, and interested in TSO as a tool and not as an end in
itself—you will find that knowing these functions well gives you
the skills you need.

4

TSO 0: ISPF PARMS—
A One-Time Setup Task

```
┌─────────┐
│    0    │
├─────────┤
│ISPF PARM│
└─────────┘
```

When a TSO account is first established by an installation, certain elements of definition must be completed one time by the party to whom the account is assigned, prior to doing any significant work using TSO.

The TSO/ISPF main menu provides the ability to select function 0 to access the setup functions. Figure 4.1 illustrates the screen that appears when TSO 0 setup is selected from the main menu. The first three setup functions must usually be completed by any new TSO user.

```
┌─────────┐
│   0.1   │
├─────────┤
│TERMINAL │
└─────────┘
```

TSO 0.1: TERMINAL SETUP

Terminal setup may be selected from the TSO 0 screen by entering its number, 1, on the OPTION line and pressing ENTER. This provides access to settings that must match the hardware characteristics of the terminal used to access TSO. Figure 4.2 shows the 0.1 setup screen.

TERMINAL TYPE can be entered according to the types shown to the right of the entry field. The most common terminal type in use is the IBM 3278, with a standard keyboard similar to a typewriter. If you are using an IBM 3270 model different from this, enter that selection. The entry is accomplished by pressing the TAB or NEWLINE key to jump the cursor to the first enterable field. The cursor will tab to enterable fields only. Do not press the ENTER key

25

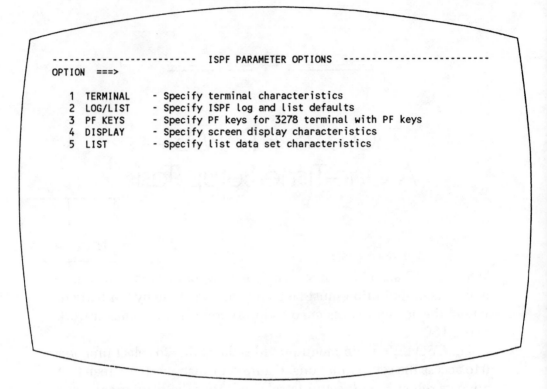

```
------------------------ ISPF PARAMETER OPTIONS ------------------------
OPTION  ===>

    1  TERMINAL    - Specify terminal characteristics
    2  LOG/LIST    - Specify ISPF log and list defaults
    3  PF KEYS     - Specify PF keys for 3278 terminal with PF keys
    4  DISPLAY     - Specify screen display characteristics
    5  LIST        - Specify list data set characteristics
```

FIGURE 4.1   TSO 0 account setup submenu screen

after the field entry; ENTER is pressed only when the entire screen is complete.

NUMBER OF PF KEYS reflects the fact that different IBM terminals have either 12 or 24 special function keys. Most commonly 12 such keys exist, accessible by pressing the number keys across the top of the keyboard while holding down the *ALT* key. If your terminal has a special keypad above or to the right of the letter keys, you may be able to select 24 at the NUMBER OF PF KEYS on the terminal setup screen. If TSO detects additional function keys on the terminal you are using, it may change your selection of 12 to 24 automatically during an ISPF session.

INPUT FIELD PAD refers to the characters that will automatically fill unentered fields on each screen as the screen is presented. If you would like to see how this works, enter a symbol such as "*" or "%" in this specification; a letter will not be acceptable. As soon as the ENTER key is pressed, you will see the COMMAND line

```
------------------------ TERMINAL CHARACTERISTICS -------------------------
COMMAND ===>

TERMINAL TYPE      ===> 3278     (3277  - 3275/3277 terminal)
                                 (3277A - 3275/3277 with APL keyboard)
                                 (3278  - 3276/3278/3279/3290 terminal)
                                 (3278A - 3276/3278/3279 APL keyboard)
                                 (3278T - 3276/3278/3279 TEXT keyboard)
                                 (3290A - 3290 with APL keyboard)

NUMBER OF PF KEYS ===> 12        (12 or 24)

INPUT FIELD PAD    ===> N        (N - Nulls) (B - Blanks) (Special Characters
                                    must not be the same as COMMAND DELIMITER)

COMMAND DELIMITER ===> ;         (Special character for command stacking)

SCREEN FORMAT      ===> DATA     (Select one of the following:)
 (3278 Model 5 only)             (DATA - Format based on data width)
                                 (STD  - Always format 24 lines by 80 chars)
                                 (MAX  - Always format 27 lines by 132 chars)

 (3290 Only)                     (PART - Format using hardware partitions.
                                    Effective the next ISPF invocation.)
```

FIGURE 4.2   TSO 0.1 terminal setup screen

entry field fill with the character specified. Change the pad character to N or B after this, experimenting with other values. Nulls, the default, are good pad characters since they are not transmitted; blanks are also acceptable but slow transmission time.

COMMAND DELIMITER is the character that is used to separate optional multiple commands entered on the COMMAND line. The installation default is usually the most acceptable for use given the particular terminals in the installation. This character is employed to separate multiple commands placed on the COMMAND line of any screen, except commands following the logoff command, where the "field mark" symbol must be used.

SCREEN FORMAT is usually specified as STD or MAX for programming purposes. Only a special mode of terminal, the high-screen density 3278 Model 5, provides the ability to display dimensions other than 80 characters by 24 lines.

An optional screen format specifier for use with IBM's 3290 terminals may also appear on your terminal setup screen. Unless you are using this device, this value can be ignored.

COMPLETING SETUP AND USING THE = TRANSFER FEATURE

With the completion of these entries, the terminal setup screen is finished. TSO/ISPF setup can be continued either by returning to the function 0 menu using the *END* key—the *ALT/3* or *PF3* key— or by entering =0.2 at the command line and pressing *ENTER*. The = entered in the command line under TSO/ISPF means that you desire to transfer immediately to the indicated function, in this case, to setup screen 0.2. When a TSO user knows, from use and recollection, the identity of the screen to which to transfer, there is no need to get there through the menu screens; the = can go there directly, saving time.

The = transfer capability works throughout all of TSO/ISPF, not just the setup functions. In all cases, the destination for a transfer is formed by the main menu function identifier to the left of a decimal point, and the subfunction value to the right. For example, to transfer from the TSO 2 edit function to the data set utility screen, =3.2 can be entered on the TSO command line. Figure 3.3 on page 22 carries all of the common destination values and you will find it handy as you become familiar with the transfer capability.

The = transfer feature is a favorite of most end users and programmers. Menus allow TSO to be used easily by newcomers. The transfer ability is a "get-me-there-in-a-hurry" feature, especially productive when TSO response time lags on a heavily loaded system, or when using a relatively slow dial-up connection.

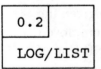

TSO 0.2: LOG AND LIST DEFAULTS

The 0.2 portion of the TSO setup is usually the most problematic for newcomers, since it requires an understanding of what TSO/ISPF is doing, how it performs its "print a screen" or 3.1 "print member" function, and some job control language. Figure 4.3 illustrates this screen.

```
------------------------ LOG AND LIST DEFAULTS ----------------------------
COMMAND ===>

LOG DATA SET DEFAULT OPTIONS              LIST DATA SET DEFAULT OPTIONS
---------------------------               ----------------------------
Process option    ===> D                  Process option   ===> J
SYSOUT class      ===> A                  SYSOUT class     ===> A
Local printer ID ===>                     Local printer ID ===>
Lines per page    ===> 60                 Lines per page   ===> 60
Primary pages     ===> 10                 Primary pages    ===> 50
Secondary pages   ===> 10                 Secondary pages  ===> 10


VALID PROCESS OPTIONS:
  J - Print data set and delete      K - Keep data set (without printing)
  L - Route to local printer, delete  D - Delete data set (without printing)

JOB STATEMENT INFORMATION:    (If option "J" selected)
  ===> //FSBT686A  JOB AK00TSO,'DP2-JANOSSY',CLASS=E,MSGCLASS=A,
  ===> //  MSGLEVEL=(1,1),NOTIFY=BT05686
  ===> //*
  ===> //*
```

FIGURE 4.3   TSO 0.2 log and list disposition setup screen

Log Data Set

The left side of the TSO 0.2 screen deals with a "log" data set that TSO builds as a session progresses. Every time a user logs on, TSO creates and maintains a log into which it writes an entry for every action taken, such as editing a data set or copying a member. Conceivably, the log could be valuable if you wished to document the actions taken for audit trail purposes, or if TSO failed and the recorded sequence of actions performed could help diagnose the cause for failure. Neither of these cases are usually relevant in the applications programming or end-user environments, and the log is typically of no interest.

It is possible to direct TSO to overcome its normal inclination to submit, at the end of the TSO/ISPF session, a batch job to print the log. The columns on the left side of the 0.2 setup screen allow a

TSO user to specify several aspects of the handling of the log data set. All of the specifications for the log become moot if the initial entry is set to D, for delete without printing, which is the setting strongly recommended. Setting the process option for the log data set to K is not desirable; it causes significant waste of disk space and is a practice discouraged or prohibited in some installations.

List Data Set

The right side of the 0.2 setup screen deals with a data set very similar to the log, but called the "list" data set. This data set is created and added to by TSO/ISPF when a screen is printed using a PF key assigned the PRINT function or when function 3.1 is used to print a member.

When TSO prints something using function 3.1, it implies that printing is occurring immediately; in fact, it is not. TSO/ISPF prints something by copying it into the list data set. When the TSO/ISPF session is ended, a batch job is automatically submitted to print the entire aggregation of material that has been heaped into the list data set.

The JOB statement used to submit the job that prints the log and list data sets is at the bottom of the 0.2 setup screen. This is an important point that usually causes newcomers frustration until a correct 0.2 setup is achieved. *Without the correct 0.2 setup, it is impossible to print anything with function 3.1.*

Most often, the list data set is intended to print on the main installation printer, and a "process option" of J is appropriate for it. The SYSOUT class should be indicated as the print class that prints common paper output in the installation, most often A. When J is specified for the process option, no local printer id need be filled in.

If another process option value appears in the center of your 0.2 setup screen, such as L for local printer, the potential exists to indicate the printer id of a device located near your terminals. If an installation permits it, this device can be specified to receive the TSO/ISPF print. The print, however, is often too voluminous to be suited to a dot matrix printer, so caution is advised in using this alternative.

The remaining entries under the list data set deal with the number of lines per page for the print and the quantity of disk space that TSO will allow for housing your listed data. Defaults established by the installation will most likely already appear in these fields, and you need not change them. If no values are present, enter those shown in Figure 4.3.

Print JOB Statement

The 0.2 job statement setup at the bottom of the screen requires the entry of a valid JOB statement image. These JOB statement lines are used by TSO/ISPF by placing them in front of a standard set of JCL, invoking the IEBGENER utility to copy the list data set out to the printer.

Figure 4.3 illustrates a typical JOB statement, but each installation has its own standards and coding for JOB statements. When a person is assigned a TSO account, he or she is given assistance in the 0.2 setup, or provided with an illustration of the JOB statement that is locally suitable for this screen. That JOB statement image is entered by *TABbing* or *NEWLINing* the cursor down to the bottom of the 0.2 screen, and entering it.

Once you have adjusted the entries in the 0.2 screen, and placed an appropriate JOB statement image into the bottom of the screen, exit back to the 0 ISPF PARAMETER OPTIONS screen with the *PF3 END* key, then select function 3. If you prefer, you can enter =0.3 on the command line and press *ENTER*. Either way, you will arrive at the 0.3 setup screen.

TSO 0.3: PF KEY DEFINITION

```
┌──────┐
│ 0.3  │
├──────┴──────┐
│    PF KEYS  │
└─────────────┘
```

TSO allows a programmer to define the functions performed by each of the 12 or 24 *PF* keys. The initial settings of the *PF* keys are usually not changed by programmers or end users, however, because the settings chosen by IBM are as good as any for most work and have the advantage of being standardized.

When the 0.3 setup screen is accessed, a screen similar to that shown in Figure 4.4 appears. If you happen to be on a 24 *PF* key terminal—the type with separate *PF* keys above the letters or with a numbered keypad to the right of the typewriter keys—you will initially get the 0.3 screen with the screen shown in Figure 4.4 presenting *PF* keys 13 through 24. Press *ENTER* once to switch the

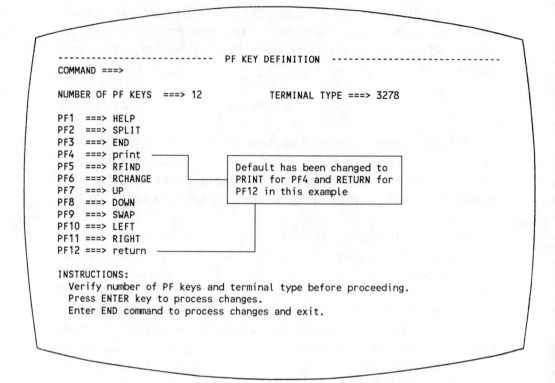

```
---------------------------- PF KEY DEFINITION ----------------------------
COMMAND ===>

NUMBER OF PF KEYS  ===> 12              TERMINAL TYPE ===> 3278

PF1  ===> HELP
PF2  ===> SPLIT
PF3  ===> END
PF4  ===> print  ─────────┐
PF5  ===> RFIND           │     ┌──────────────────────────────┐
PF6  ===> RCHANGE  ───────┘     │ Default has been changed to   │
PF7  ===> UP                    │ PRINT for PF4 and RETURN for   │
PF8  ===> DOWN                  │ PF12 in this example           │
PF9  ===> SWAP                  └──────────────────────────────┘
PF10 ===> LEFT
PF11 ===> RIGHT
PF12 ===> return ─────────────┘

INSTRUCTIONS:
  Verify number of PF keys and terminal type before proceeding.
  Press ENTER key to process changes.
  Enter END command to process changes and exit.
```

FIGURE 4.4   TSO 0.3 program function (PF) key setup screen

screen to *PF* keys 1 through 12. The 0.3 screen shows only 12 key settings at a time. Let's focus on *PF* keys 1 through 12 since these are common to all terminals.

PF keys can be set to emit commands or groups of commands; the customary assignment of *PF* keys is shown in Appendix A. Only a handful of other commands exists for assignment to *PF* keys, including *PRINT-HI, TSO, KEYS, PANELID, PRINTL, PRINTLHI,* and *SPLITV.* We will discuss some of these in the following chapters as they pertain to effective use of TSO/ISPF. The variations on the *PRINT* function are useful only in limited circumstances, and *SPLITV* applies only to the highly specialized 3290 terminal, which permits vertical splitting of the screen.

· To set the *PF* keys to desired functions, tab down the 0.3 screen and type in the function name desired; either uppercase or lowercase letters are satisfactory. On Figure 4.4 *PF4* has been changed from *RETURN* to *PRINT* so that *PF4* will generate a hardcopy of a screen using the list data set. The remainder of the key assignments are normally appropriate as they default.

If you are using a non-IBM ASCII terminal and protocol converter and find that accessing *PF* keys beyond *PF10* is awkward—some terminal emulations require three key strokes to generate *PF11* and *PF12*—you can change the "window left" and "window right" commands to lower-numbered *PF* keys as a convenience. Any one or more commands normally entered on the COMMAND line can be assigned to a *PF* key using the COMMAND DELIMITER value to separate them.

When you have set the *PF* keys to the commands you desire using the TSO 0.3 screen, press *PF3* twice in sequence to return to the main menu. You can now use TSO/ISPF without further regard for the TSO 0 setup functions.

5

Partitioned Data Sets

When IBM developed a presence in the world of computers, it had already existed as a corporation for several decades. One of its main lines of business dealt with mechanical devices to punch, sort, and tabulate 80-column punched cards. When it engineered and built electronic devices to perform similar processing tasks, it was natural to orient them to the same information-storage media. It is therefore no coincidence that program source code statements on IBM mainframes were designed for 80-byte punched cards, as was JCL.

TSO/ISPF is certainly much more capable than a keypunch, but in terms of the storage of program source code and JCL statements, the end result of preparation is the same as with a keypunch. Lines of JCL and source code are stored as 80-byte records. Every statement is a full 80 bytes long, even if it is completely blank. Physical cards, of course, are no longer handled by most installations; instead, the same information, byte for byte, now exists on magnetic storage media such as disk or tape, in "card image" form. All 80 bytes of each card are present, but without the bulk of cards.

ORGANIZING DATA SET STORAGE

Files are known as "data sets" in the IBM mainframe environment. How do we house, organize, access, secure from access, and otherwise manage data sets?

On single-user micros the inventory of files on a given unit of disk media is managed by the diskette or hard disk directory. Un-

35

der sophisticated micro- and minicomputer operating systems such as MS-DOS, UNIX, and VAX VMS, a directory can contain subdirectories, to group related files together. *But there is no provision for subdirectories in MVS.* Instead, file naming and the use of partitioned data sets support all of the processing that occurs on a mainframe under MVS.

PARTITIONED DATA SETS FOR SOURCE CODE AND JCL

The minimum space allocation for a data set under MVS is one track of disk space, which is quite a large amount of space: 19,069 bytes of storage on an IBM 3350 device, and 47,476 bytes on an IBM 3380. If the data set contains only a small amount of information, much space may be wasted by storing it in a file by itself. It can instead be stored along with other like items in a partitioned data set, as one of many members. While the partitioned data set, usually called a "PDS," must consume one track or more, individual members consume a minimum of only one block's worth of space, since each member starts in a new data block.

Source code and job control language is usually stored in partitioned data sets. A partitioned data set is simply a sequential file that was created with two internal parts: its own "directory" and a data area. The directory of a partitioned data set only superficially resembles a subdirectory of VAX VMS, UNIX, or MS-DOS, but it serves a similar purpose. It retains housekeeping information about the subfiles or "members" stored in the data area of the partitioned data set, most particularly, their names and locations within the data area.

Different "versions" of members do not exist in a PDS in an accessible form; only the most recently updated copy of each member is known to the PDS directory and is accessible. Members of a PDS can be treated as if they were data sets in themselves for nearly all purposes. However, a member cannot be further subdivided; it is not entirely correct to think of a PDS in the same way as one might regard a subdirectory on the VAX, under UNIX, or under MS-DOS.

Partitioned data sets are used to house several types of items:

• Programmer-created and -maintained groups of source code and JCL statements

- "Libraries" of items such as copylib members and utility control statements
- Executable "load modules," the MVS equivalent of ".EXE" files

Partitioned data sets appear to MVS as merely another type of data set. A PDS is named in the same way as any other data set:

BT05686.SOURCE.COBOL

or

CCPZ04.CSC.COBOL

Just by seeing this name, it is not possible to tell whether the data set is partitioned or not, but MVS retains information indicating its organization.

In order to deal with a specific member of the partitioned data set, we refer to the member within the data set in this way in JCL:

BT05686.SOURCE.COBOL(PSD183)

or

CSCJGJ.CSC.COBOL(PSD183)

The name within the parentheses—the member name—can be up to eight characters long and must start with a letter.

The creation of a PDS and the management of its internal organization is handled by MVS, as is the retrieval of the group of records within it that represent a member. A programmer in the contemporary MVS environment will typically have at least two PDS's to house the items he or she develops as a part of work activities. Such a PDS, to house source code statements, will carry a final-name portion of COBOL, FORT, PLI, or ASM—whichever is appropriate for the language in use. The other PDS, to house JCL statements, would carry a final-name portion of CNTL, for "control." These standard names cause TSO/ISPF to default automatically to convenient screen presentation formats for each language and JCL. Standard PDS name endings and default editing columns are listed in Figure 5.1.

Record Format	Data set _type_	Numbered (RENUM)	Unnumbered (UNNUM)
Fixed length (RECFM=FB)	PROJECT===> BT05686 GROUP ===> SOURCE TYPE ===> COBOL MEMBER ===>	COLUMNS 007 078	COLUMNS 001 072
Fixed length (RECFM=FB)	PROJECT===> BT05686 GROUP ===> SOURCE TYPE ===> CNTL MEMBER ===>	COLUMNS 001 072	COLUMNS 001 072
Fixed length (RECFM=FB)	PROJECT===> BT05686 GROUP ===> SOURCE TYPE ===> DATA MEMBER ===>	COLUMNS 001 072	COLUMNS 001 072
Variable length (RECFM=V or RECFM=VB)	PROJECT===> BT05686 GROUP ===> SOURCE TYPE ===> CLIST MEMBER ===>	COLUMNS 009 080	COLUMNS 001 072

FIGURE 5.1   Standard partitioned data set names and default editing columns

WORKING WITH PARTITIONED DATA SETS

Creating a PDS

Partitioned data sets for source code and JCL statements are usually created by "allocating" them with TSO/ISPF function 3.2, as described in Chapter 12. A PDS can also be allocated using JCL alone as shown in Figure 5.2. This JCL would be run only once, to create in this case a small partitioned data set suitable for job control language. MVS JCL is discussed in detail in a companion book in this series, *Practical MVS JCL for Today's Programmers* (John Wiley & Sons, 1987).

A member within an existing partitioned data set is created

```
EDIT --- BT05686.SOURCE.CNTL(PDSALLOC) - 01.01 -------------- COLUMNS 001 072
COMMAND ===>                                               SCROLL ===> HALF
****** *************************** TOP OF DATA ******************************
000100 //FSBT686A  JOB AK00TEST,'DP2-JANOSSY',MSGCLASS=X,MSGLEVEL=(1,1),
000200 //   NOTIFY=BT05686
000300 //*******************************************************************
000400 //*                                                              *
000500 //*      PDSALLOC    ALLOCATE A PARTITIONED DATA SET              *
000600 //*      THIS JCL = BT05686.SOURCE.CNTL(PDSALLOC)                 *
000700 //*      (SEE PRACTICAL MVS JCL, CHAPTERS 2 AND 8 FOR MORE        *
000800 //*      INFORMATION ON PARTITIONED DATA SETS AND DISK SPACE,     *
000900 //*      ISBN 0-471-83648-6, JOHN WILEY & SONS, 1987.)           *
000900 //*                                                              *
001000 //*******************************************************************
001100 //STEPA     EXEC  PGM=IEFBR14
001200 //ALLO1        DD  DSN=BT05686.SOURCE.COBOL,
001300 //   UNIT=SYSDA,
001400 //   DISP=(NEW,CATLG,DELETE),
001500 //   DCB=(RECFM=FB,LRECL=80,BLKSIZE=3840),
001600 //   SPACE=(TRK,(10,5,12))
001700 //
****** *************************** BOTTOM OF DATA ***************************
```

FIGURE 5.2 MVS job control language to allocate a partitioned data set for use by TSO/ISPF as a library

simply by beginning to edit it using TSO function 2, as described in Chapter 7. Members can also be established by copying card-image data into an existing PDS using a utility such as IEBGENER or TSO function 3.3.

A member of a PDS is most often deleted using TSO/ISPF function 3.1. Either the IDCAMS or IEHPROGM utility can also be employed for this purpose. A PDS member cannot, however, be deleted using JCL alone, without one of these utilities.

Viewing a PDS Directory

The directory portion of a PDS may contain information concerning each member of the data set, including its creation date, date last modified, current size in records, initial size in records, and the number of lines that have been modified since its creation. When TSO/ISPF has been used to create members in a PDS containing source code or JCL, the directory entry may also contain the TSO/ISPF logon id of the originator. The member entries are maintained in the PDS directory in alphabetical order, even when members are added or renamed.

Figure 5.3 is an illustration of PDS housekeeping information as displayed using TSO/ISPF. The screen illustrated here is called a "member list" and can be obtained when a member is to be edited or TSO/ISPF utility function performed. While it is similar to a file listing produced in response to a "DIR" system command under VAX VMS or MS-DOS, it is more convenient. Many of TSO/ISPF's functions allow selection of a PDS member for processing using the cursor as a pointer in the member list, making it unnecessary to manually enter a member name.

PDS Reorganization

Partitioned data sets provide source code and JCL storage convenience but they have certain upkeep requirements. As members in a PDS are updated by writing them back to the data set, they are placed into available data space following the last member of the PDS, and the PDS directory is updated to reflect the new location of the member. The space in the data set occupied by older copies of the member is essentially "dead," and not accessible or reusable until the PDS is reorganized.

Both batch and online ways exist to reorganize a PDS. The batch means makes use of JCL to invoke the utility program, IEBCOPY, that accomplishes the reorganization, as discussed in detail in Appendix C. Since the net effect appears to be the "squeezing" of active members to the top of the PDS data area, it is often called "compression" when initiated online from TSO/ISPF with utility function 3.1.

If not reorganized periodically to reclaim unusable space, a partitioned data set containing members being edited with TSO/ISPF will eventually exhaust its capacity to sustain the addition of more members or the housing of updated members. If this occurs, a system completion code, or error code, of E37 is received when an attempt is made to save another member or modified member in the PDS. This is a serious problem and often causes the loss of the updates to the member since it was last successfully saved.

The TSO/ISPF 3.2 "data set information" function can be used

```
UTILITIES --- BT05686.SOURCE.COBOL -------------------------------------------
COMMAND ===>                                               SCROLL ===> PAGE
  NAME          VER.MOD  CREATED    LAST MODIFIED   SIZE  INIT   MOD    ID
ACCT1401        01.05   86/06/19   87/06/22 10:43   1093  1086    22  BT05686
ACCT1403        01.15   86/02/16   87/11/28 12:17    455   336   191  BT05686
ACCT1408        01.07   85/04/14   87/11/23 10:24    948   838    27  BT05103
ACCT1435        01.03   86/03/04   88/05/01 19:41    457   457    10  BT05686
ACCT1441        01.02   86/04/17   88/04/09 14:42    127   127    22  BT05686
ACCT1442        01.06   86/01/28   88/04/09 13:15     28     9    28  BT05103
FINC1753        01.01   86/02/22   87/12/06 16:47    488   488    19  BT05686
FINC1763        01.07   85/02/09   87/12/07 10:32    455   257     2  BT05686
FINC1810        01.03   86/05/11   87/12/07 12:21    453   453    63  BT05103
FSBT3708        01.08   87/01/19   88/08/07 18:09   1433  1431    14  BT05686
FSBT3719        01.43   88/06/07   88/08/22 10:04   1092   669     7  BT05686
HGRA0227        01.12   87/07/18   88/07/04 09:25    898   897    68  AM16054
HGRA0232        01.17   86/12/13   87/07/05 13:30    419   282    44  AM16054
HGRA0239        01.82   86/01/09   88/07/15 13:16   1405    56    11  BT05686
PSD183          01.08   86/12/08   87/05/06 10:27    233   233     9  BT05686
SRGN5570        01.11   86/01/29   87/05/22 16:41    306   213   156  BT05686
SRGN5573        01.05   85/07/26   87/05/31 18:23   2428  2396    13  BT05686
SRGN5577        01.05   87/10/21   88/06/23 15:13   1161  1184   287  BT05686
SRGN5580        01.08   87/09/29   88/06/18 17:27   1089  1089    92  BT05686
SRGN6222        01.23   85/04/07   86/06/18 17:03     60   669    16  BT05103
**END**
```

FIGURE 5.3   TSO/ISPF partitioned data set member list

to monitor the condition of a PDS and recognize that a reorganization is needed, as illustrated in Chapter 12.

LOAD MODULE LIBRARY: A SPECIAL PARTITIONED DATA SET

The body of machine language statements resulting from a compile
and linkage edit of source code is called a load module. A load
module is not composed of records in the usual sense; it represents
the variable-length groups of working storage and machine instructions that when loaded to memory can be "run" as a program. An
MVS load module is required to be a member of a partitioned data
set. Load modules cannot be freestanding files; under MVS there is
no separate file analogous to the ".EXE" file of the VAX or MS-DOS
environments.

While the contents of a load module may be examined using

TSO 1, the browse function, they are not created directly by TSO/ISPF; they may be created by JCL edited and submitted via TSO/ISPF. Load modules are usually created by compile and linkage edit cataloged procedures in an installation as either new or replacement members of a permanent partitioned data set that exists specifically to house them.

The execution of program load modules, one after another, is orchestrated by job control language. Production systems are made up of JCL job streams, each job stream containing several steps. Each step executes a load module; steps follow one another in the order coded in a job stream. The JCL making up job streams is usually created with the TSO 2 edit function and submitted via TSO.

PART 2

CREATING AND EDITING
CODE AND JCL

The core of TSO/ISPF functionality resides in TSO 2, the edit. In the chapters presented in this part, you will learn how to use the edit function to create and modify source code and job control language statements. Chapter 6 provides a brief overview of how the facilities of TSO/ISPF are used in combination by a programmer or end user, and you can follow this brief chapter as a tutorial guide to the other chapters here.

Chapter 7 provides knowledge about TSO 2 elementary editing features called edit-line commands, and a concise reference summary of commands. Edit-line commands deal with text manipulations internal to a member being edited.

Chapter 8 covers advanced editing features used to bring information external to a member being edited into it, to change various features of the edit session, and to submit jobs from edit to the computer system for execution.

Chapter 9 describes the two means available under TSO/ISPF to view the output of completed jobs without awaiting paper print. Both the TSO 3.8 outlist facility and the optional Spool Display and Search Facility are discussed.

The focus of these chapters is productivity. Concluding this section is Chapter 10, which highlights practices and techniques that transcend several individual TSO functions to deliver speed and convenience to you.

6

A Practical TSO/ISPF Guide

Approaching TSO/ISPF as a programmer or end-user workbench makes sense. The next four chapters of this book are devoted to this theme and are designed to guide your use of TSO/ISPF in these processes:

- Creating and editing an item of source code or JCL using the TSO 2 edit function
- Using TSO "primary editing" commands to submit job control language to execute a compiler or compiled program
- Viewing the output of a compile or program execution using the TSO 3.8 OUTLIST or SDSF functions

These activities make up the bulk of day-to-day usage of TSO/ISPF by tens of thousands of mainframe applications programmers and end users. In a brief chapter rounding out this part of *Practical TSO/ISPF*, you will find several pithy hints about convenience features that can speed your work but which personnel often find it hard to "discover" on their own.

Before we begin delving into the specifics of source code and JCL creation using TSO/ISPF, let's take a quick look at the general process followed by the majority of programmers and end users when they interact with TSO/ISPF.

A QUICK OVERVIEW OF SOURCE CODE ENTRY
AND COMPILATION

In order to start work on a new program, a programmer usually selects the TSO 2 EDIT function from the main menu, names a new member of his or her source code partitioned data set, and starts with a blank editing screen. The actions needed to do this are described in Chapter 7.

Instead of keying in new code or JCL from scratch, an older body of text is often available for use as a pattern. Standard parts of COBOL, PL/I, FORTRAN, or assembler programs can provide a head start on keying of a new program, or job control language already written for another purpose can guide the keying of new JCL. The COPY command can be used during an edit session to copy in such "boilerplate" to provide a base for the new program or JCL. COPY is a TSO/ISPF "primary editing command," illustrated and discussed in Chapter 8.

TSO/ISPF function keys can be used to navigate through the item being edited, sliding the "window" provided by the TSO/ISPF screen forward and backward. Edit-line commands, illustrated in Chapter 7, provide the means to move, copy, and delete lines of the base material.

Blank lines can now be inserted where needed for the keying of new statements. Additional edit-line commands, illustrated in Chapter 7, provide the text manipulation facilities needed to do this. At some point, efforts will undoubtedly concentrate on the entry of entirely new lines at the end of the material. New blank lines at the end of the item being edited can be acquired to house them.

When source code entry is completed, the entire member can be given a fresh set of line numbers—if line numbers are being used—using the RENUM command, discussed in Chapter 8. Then, pressing the *PF3 END* function key, the edit session is concluded and the member is automatically saved to disk.

If the program is written in a traditional language such as COBOL, PL/I, FORTRAN, or assembler, it is then necessary to enter the TSO 2 EDIT function once again, this time specifying a CNTL job control library in which JCL for a compile, linkage edit, and run exists. While we won't discuss JCL here, a contemporary source of information on it exists in a companion book in this series, *Practical MVS JCL For Today's Programmers* (John Wiley & Sons, 1987). Using the TSO/ISPF edit facility, the compile, linkage edit, and run JCL is tailored to process the source code just written, and to draw it into processing from the partitioned data set in which it resides. Then, using the SUBMIT primary editing command discussed in Chapter 8, the job control language is submitted directly from TSO/ISPF for execution.

If the program developed for submission was written in a fourth-generation language the process of run submission may differ slightly from the foregoing description, depending on the language and environment. In general this process will also be conducted within the TSO 2 edit function, but the language source code statements may exist within the CNTL data set as an "instream" part of the job control language submitted for execution.

We can examine job output without waiting for paper document printing. When our job finishes, the NOTIFY parameter on its JOB statement causes a message to be generated and sent to us. We can then use the TSO 3.8 OUTLIST facility or SDSF, selected from the main menu, to examine the results of the run online.

PROGRAM CORRECTION

Most programmers encounter at least some syntax errors in a first compile or two, and find that corrections and program recompilation are necessary. These steps are easy to perform working from a listing of the program "ordered" using the TSO 3.8 or SDSF functions, described in Chapter 9.

The TSO 2 EDIT function is used to make program corrections, once again employing the editing and text manipulation facilities described in Chapters 7 and 8. The same compile, linkage edit, and run JCL used earlier is then submitted again, either from the edit function, or using a faster means, the TSO passthrough command, described in Chapter 10. The output of the compiler is again viewed using TSO 3.8 or SDSF. The cycle of correction and recompilation continues until a successful compilation is achieved.

If compile, linkage edit, and run JCL is being used, it is possible to see whether the program is operating successfully with only the submission of this JCL, because the JCL not only compiles and linkage edits the program, it runs it. If compile and linkage edit JCL is used, the cycle of correction, editing, and job resubmission leads up to the submission of separate JCL that executes a program load module. The former mode of operation is more typical of a student learning environment, while compile/linkage edit and separate execution are typical of the working environment.

TESTING OF PROGRAM LOAD MODULES

In many instances programmers use job control language for compile/linkage edit, creating permanent program load modules. A second set of JCL is then required to submit modules for execution. The TSO 2 EDIT function is used to create and submit this JCL. After execution, either the TSO 3.8 OUTLIST or SDSF is used to view the job outputs. Incorrect output makes it necessary to step back to the correction and editing of the source code, the submission of JCL to recompile and linkage edit it, and the submission of the JCL to again execute the program load module for another test.

TSO/ISPF: THE WORKBENCH

Because TSO function 2, the edit function, is a self-contained world that even includes the TSO/ISPF job submission facilities, most of the scenario just described takes place within it. These actions comprise the great majority of those performed by programmers and end users in the information center on a day-in, day-out basis.

Although we have pictured here the steps surrounding the development of COBOL, PL/I, FORTRAN, or assembler programs, these actions are much the same even when the program being developed deals with a database management system such as IMS or IDMS, CICS online processing, a combination of these, or higher-level languages such as Easytrieve, MARK-IV, SAS, SPSS, or any of several others. The job control language and cataloged procedures used to process these programs differ, but even CICS online screen map encoding and assembly follow essentially the same steps.

This is the modus operandi of the data-processing world of IBM mainframes under MVS and TSO/ISPF. It is a productive and easy-to-use environment in which to put source code together, compose job control language, submit jobs, and see results online.

7

TSO 2: Creating and Editing

```
┌─────────┬─────────┐
│    2    │         │
├─────────┴─────┬───┤
│               │EDIT│
└───────────────┴───┘
```

The real workhorse of TSO/ISPF is function 2, the "edit" facility. It is with this main menu selection that members of partitioned data sets housing source code and JCL are created and updated. Since jobs can be submitted for execution directly from edit, it is typical for programmers and end users to spend the bulk of their time within TSO 2 EDIT.

TSO 2 EDIT can manipulate partitioned data set members and sequential data sets, but not VSAM data sets. It can handle fixed-length, variable-length, and undefined record formats of up to 255 bytes in length, with no difference in the edit process.

The edit function can create new members only within existing data sets. In order to work with a partitioned data set to create or modify members within it, you must first allocate the data set, a one-time action. Your installation may have allocated your data sets for you; if this is not the case, skip ahead to Chapter 12, TSO/ISPF function 3.2, and see how to do it. Partitioned data sets for TSO libraries can also be allocated using JCL, as illustrated in Figure 5.2 of Chapter 5.

STARTING THE EDIT

To gain access to the TSO edit function, select option 2 from the main menu and press the *ENTER* key. You will be presented with a screen as illustrated in Figure 7.1, called the "Edit–Entry Panel." This screen lets you indicate the partitioned data set and member, or the sequential data set, that you wish to edit.

When starting to edit an item, you do not specify whether you wish to change an existing member or create a new one. If you

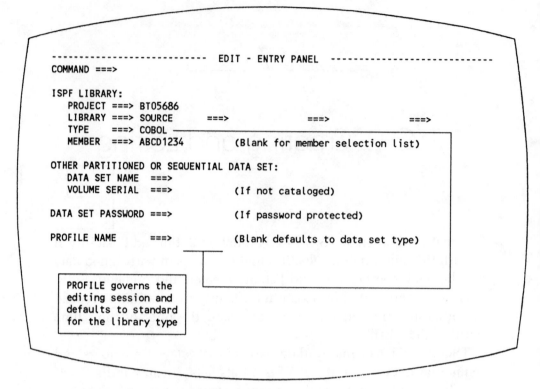

```
--------------------------- EDIT - ENTRY PANEL ----------------------------
COMMAND ===>

ISPF LIBRARY:
   PROJECT ===> BT05686
   LIBRARY ===> SOURCE      ===>              ===>            ===>
   TYPE    ===> COBOL
   MEMBER  ===> ABCD1234         (Blank for member selection list)

OTHER PARTITIONED OR SEQUENTIAL DATA SET:
   DATA SET NAME   ===>
   VOLUME SERIAL   ===>          (If not cataloged)

DATA SET PASSWORD ===>          (If password protected)

PROFILE NAME       ===>          (Blank defaults to data set type)


   PROFILE governs the
   editing session and
   defaults to standard
   for the library type
```

FIGURE 7.1   TSO 2 edit entry screen

name a member that exists, TSO assumes you wish to modify it and provides full screen access to it. If you name a member that does not exist, TSO assumes that you wish to create it and presents a blank screen on which you can begin entry.

Let's say that you have been assigned TSO logon id BT05686, and that your installation naming convention provided for your COBOL library to be named:

    BT05686.SOURCE.COBOL

Let's further suppose that you are going to create a member named ABCD1234 within this library. Fill in the fields on the edit entry panel as shown in Figure 7.1. Note that the additional three fields on the LIBRARY line are not filled in; they are a part of a library management facility proposed by IBM but not used in many installations.

In response to this entry, you will be greeted with a screen that

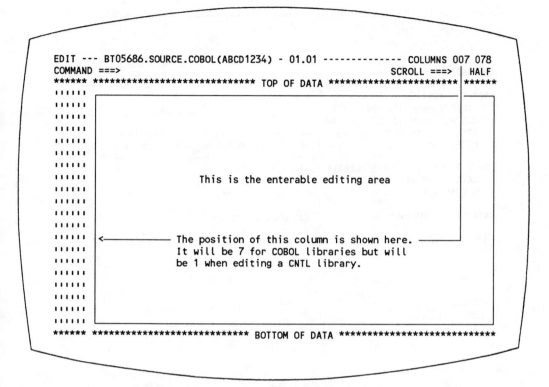

```
EDIT --- BT05686.SOURCE.COBOL(ABCD1234) - 01.01 ------------- COLUMNS 007 078
COMMAND ===>                                             SCROLL ===>  HALF
****** *************************** TOP OF DATA ************************** ******
''''''
''''''
''''''
''''''
''''''
''''''
''''''
''''''               This is the enterable editing area
''''''
''''''
''''''
''''''
''''''  <-------------- The position of this column is shown here. -------
''''''                  It will be 7 for COBOL libraries but will
''''''                  be 1 when editing a CNTL library.
''''''
''''''
''''''
''''''
****** *************************** BOTTOM OF DATA *****************************
```

FIGURE 7.2   TSO 2 edit screen for creation of new member

appears nearly blank, as in Figure 7.2. This screen, called the edit screen, turns the terminal into a word processor specifically attuned to the entry and manipulation of source code and JCL statements. When creating a new member, the screen functions as a clean slate upon which you can enter the source code or job control language you wish to compose.

The Partitioned Data Set Member List

It is possible to get to the edit screen in another way, besides naming a partitioned data set member as illustrated in Figure 7.1. You might on occasion forget the specific spelling of the name of an existing member that you want to edit; wouldn't it be handy to see a list of members in the PDS, from which you could point to a member to select it? TSO/ISPF provides exactly this. To get a member list, just enter the PDS name but leave the member name field blank, as on Figure 7.3, and press the ENTER key. In response, TSO/

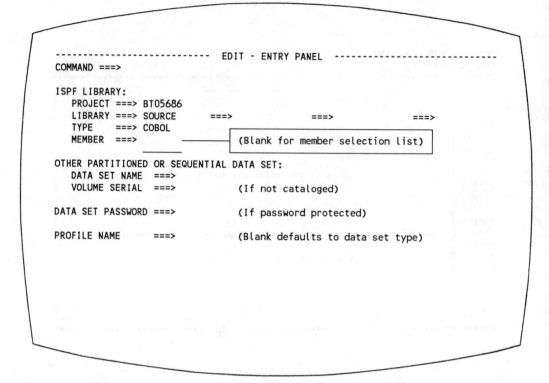

```
------------------------------- EDIT - ENTRY PANEL ----------------------------
COMMAND ===>

ISPF LIBRARY:
   PROJECT ===> BT05686
   LIBRARY ===> SOURCE        ===>              ===>            ===>
   TYPE    ===> COBOL
   MEMBER  ===>         ———————— (Blank for member selection list)

OTHER PARTITIONED OR SEQUENTIAL DATA SET:
   DATA SET NAME   ===>
   VOLUME SERIAL   ===>           (If not cataloged)

DATA SET PASSWORD ===>           (If password protected)

PROFILE NAME      ===>           (Blank defaults to data set type)
```

FIGURE 7.3   TSO 2 edit entry screen filled out to request library member list

ISPF will present a member list as shown in Figure 7.4. A partitioned data set member list shows the contents of the partitioned data set directory; since the directory entries are maintained in alphabetical order, this is the order in which members appear.

To begin editing a member without having to enter its name, run the cursor down the left side of the member list using the *NEW-LINE* key and enter an S for "select" in front of a member name. Then press the *ENTER* key. Editing of the member will commence, without your having to key in its name. In Figure 7.4, we have done this, selecting for editing a member named FSBT3708.

Scrolling Through a PDS Member List

When a partitioned data set has more than 20 members in it, the member list screen cannot show all of the member entries at one

```
UTILITIES --- BT05686.SOURCE.COBOL -----------------------------------------
COMMAND ===>                                                SCROLL ===> PAGE
    NAME          VER.MOD  CREATED    LAST MODIFIED   SIZE  INIT  MOD   ID
  ACCT1401         01.05  86/06/19  87/06/22 10:43    1093  1086    22 BT05686
  ACCT1403         01.15  86/02/16  87/11/28 12:17     455   336   191 BT05686
  ACCT1408         01.07  85/04/14  87/11/23 10:24     948   838    27 BT05103
  ACCT1435         01.03  86/03/04  88/05/01 19:41     457   457    10 BT05686
  ACCT1441         01.02  86/04/17  88/04/09 14:42     127   127    22 BT05686
  ACCT1442         01.06  86/01/28  88/04/09 13:15      28     9    28 BT05103
  FINC1753         01.01  86/02/22  87/12/06 16:47     488   488    19 BT05686
  FINC1763         01.07  85/02/09  87/12/07 10:32     455   257     2 BT05686
  FINC1810         01.03  86/05/11  87/12/07 12:21     453   453    63 BT05103
S FSBT3708         01.08  87/01/19  88/08/07 18:09    1433  1431    14 BT05686
  FSBT3719         01.43  88/06/07  88/08/22 10:04    1092   669     7 BT05686
  HGRA0227                                                           7    68 AM16054
  HGRA0232      ┌────────────────────────────────────────────┐      2    44 AM16054
  HGRA0239      │ Move cursor down the left side of screen    │      6    11 BT05686
                │ with the TAB key, place S in front of the   │      3     9 BT05686
  SRGN5570      │ member you wish to edit, and press the      │      3   156 BT05686
  SRGN5573      │ ENTER key to begin editing a member         │      6    13 BT05686
                └────────────────────────────────────────────┘
  SRGN5577         01.05  87/10/21  88/06/23 15:13    1161  1184   287 BT05686
  SRGN5580         01.08  87/09/29  88/06/18 17:27    1089  1089    92 BT05686
  SRGN6222         01.23  85/04/07  86/06/18 17:03      60   669    16 BT05103
  **END**
```

FIGURE 7.4   TSO library member list screen

time. Two TSO/ISPF *PF* keys are used to move forward and backward in a member list or item being edited:

- *PF8* will scroll ahead in the member list.
- *PF7* will scroll backward in the member list.

The number of lines of movement forward or backward is dictated by the value in the field labeled SCROLL ===> at the top right of the screen. This field can be set to PAGE for a full screen of movement, or HALF for a half screen of movement, or to an integer number of lines, such as 15. Both HALF and a line value of 15 are handy settings since these provide overlap from one screen to another. SCROLL can also contain the abbreviation CSR for "cursor," in which case the *PF8* movement will bring the line on which the cursor is positioned to the top of the screen.

If the screen is presenting names in the member list and you want to return up the hierarchy to the edit entry panel, press the *PF3* key. If you are positioned in a member list and wish to go to the beginning or end of the list, put MAX at the COMMAND ===> field:

```
COMMAND  ===>  MAX
```

and press either *PF8* or *PF7*. These keys work exactly the same way within the edit function itself.

A Road Map to Edit Screen Geography

Figure 7.5 is an edit screen annotated with a few terms relevant to TSO. While definitions are sometimes tedious, the few associated with this screen are common-sense and it helps to know them.

The *command line* COMMAND ===> is where the cursor appears when you reach the edit screen. It is also where the cursor goes if you press the *HOME* key, *ALT/left tab*. TSO/ISPF commands can be entered here, including the SUBMIT command to submit to the "card hopper" for execution a set of job control language being edited.

The *message area* normally displays the record columns or positions on which the display is positioned, but will occasionally display an information or error message from TSO/ISPF. For a partitioned data set ending with the name COBOL, and with a member containing COBOL line numbers in columns 1 through 6, this defaults to columns 7 through 78 as illustrated in Figure 7.5. For other types of data sets, such as CNTL, PLI, or ASM, this defaults to columns 1 through 72. These figures change in response to pressing the *PF11* "right window" and *PF12* "left window" function keys, which move the display window right and left the number of columns indicated in the SCROLL field.

The *line number area* is a trifle confusing because while you can enter things into it, it *does not* indicate information contained on the records being edited. This area shows line numbers that can be referenced in TSO commands; these line numbers may or may not be within the lines being edited. The numbers in the line number

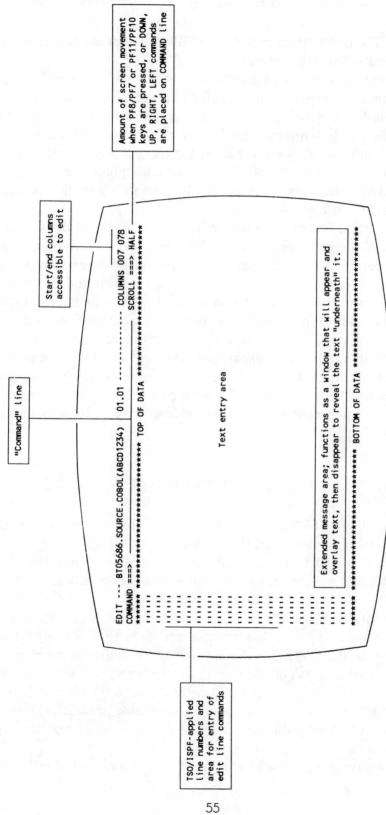

FIGURE 7.5 "Road map" of TSO 2 edit screen geography

55

area can be overwritten to tell TSO/ISPF to insert, delete, move, or copy lines within the member.

The *extended message area* is actually a screen overlay that appears only for special actions such as the submission of a job with the SUBMIT command. When extended messages are sent by TSO/ISPF, the last few lines of the display are replaced with messages and TSO/ISPF's "hit the ENTER key to proceed" abbreviation, three asterisks ***. When the ENTER key is subsequently pressed, the messages are removed, and the display previously on this portion of the screen is restored.

The *system communication area* is the 25th line of the display, outside of the area used by TSO/ISPF. On a real 3270 terminal this lies underneath a bright, hardware-supplied horizontal border at the bottom of the screen. Various symbols appear and disappear from this area as communication occurs between the terminal and the computer, to indicate the status of that communication. Error codes, including a "thunderbolt" indicating disconnection from the computer, may also appear here. On some 3270-type terminals the symbols are replaced by plain text messages. On ASCII devices that mimic 3270s via a protocol converter, this line often does not appear because most such devices support only 24 lines of screen display.

USING THE EDIT SCREEN

Editing under TSO/ISPF is simple: you merely move the cursor around using the tab keys, the *NEWLINE* key, the space bar, or the four directional arrow keys, and enter whatever text you like with the letter and number keys. The full screen serves as a slate of 20 lines. All text entry actions are rapid because none of the cursor movements requires the intervention of the computer; these are handled locally by the 3270 terminal and its controller. Only when a *PF* key or the ENTER key is pressed is transmission made from the terminal and its control unit to the mainframe. TSO is usually set by an installation to automatically log off a terminal that has been inactive for a period of minutes. *You must press ENTER or a PF key occasionally during editing in order not to be regarded by the system as inactive and logged off!*

The entry area for material is framed by the row of asterisks at the top of the screen containing the words TOP OF DATA. If you mistakenly place something in an area such as this, or in the space between the line numbers and the text entry area, the terminal will beep, the keyboard will lock, and a warning indication will appear in the system communication area. These areas are not enterable. Press the *RESET* key, to the left of the space bar, in order to unlock the keyboard if this happens.

Try the entry of some text. Notice that unless you have set your terminal to capital letters only, what you enter appears in lower-case letters. After entering a few lines, press the *ENTER* key. The unused lines at the bottom of the screen are removed, and what you entered has been changed into uppercase letters. The "enter it in lowercase, I'll change it to uppercase" mode is the default for TSO and shows what you have done on the screen since your last transmission to the computer.

If you have now entered a screen full of text in trying out TSO/ISPF, you have probably run out of available lines on the display. Let's learn a few more "edit-line" commands to gain more room for entry.

TSO/ISPF edit-line commands provide the means to insert lines, delete lines, and move lines within a member. All edit-line commands are entered by overwriting the line numbers at the left side of the screen, and then pressing either *ENTER* or a *PF* key.

To acquire more lines at any point on a screen, overwrite the line number just before that point with the letter I and a value representing the number of blank lines to be inserted *after* it. While it is not necessary, it is best to follow this with a space, so that what you entered is easy to see. Figure 7.6(a) illustrates an edit screen filled with material, and into which we wish to insert a few lines.

After entering the insert command, press the *ENTER* key. Figure 7.6(b) illustrates the result. The indicated number of lines are created immediately following the line on which the command was entered; the following lines are moved down. You can now proceed to enter information on the new blank lines.

What if more lines are needed because the bottom of the screen has been reached? You can press the *ENTER* key to obtain one additional blank line, but that can be a slow process. Instead, set the SCROLL field in the upper right corner of the screen to HALF. Then enter the insert command on a line near the bottom specifying a value of 10 or so, and press the *PF8* "scroll forward" function key.

```
EDIT --- BT05686.SOURCE.COBOL(FSBT3708) - 01.01 ------------- COLUMNS 007 078
COMMAND ===>                                                   SCROLL ===> HALF
****** ***************************** TOP OF DATA ******************************
000100  IDENTIFICATION DIVISION.
000200  PROGRAM-ID.     FSBT3708.
000300  AUTHOR.         J JANOSSY.
000400  INSTALLATION.   FARNON STANDARD.
000500  DATE-WRITTEN.   JAN 1988.
000600  DATE-COMPILED.
000700 *REMARKS.        LAST UPDATE 05-22-88  JJ   ORIG 01-19-88   JJ
000800 *
000900 *                THIS PROGRAM UPDATES A SEQUENTIAL MASTER FILE
001000 *                WITH TRANSACTION DATA. A REFERENCE FILE IS
001100 *                LOADED DYNAMICALLY AT RUN TIME, PROVIDING THE
001200 *                INFORMATION FOR ONE OF THE TRANSACTION EDITS
001300 *                AND THE APPLICABLE TRANSACTION RATE. A REPORT
I4 400 *                OF VALID AND INVALID TRANSACTIONS IS PRODUCED.
001500 *                FOLLOWS SOFTWARE ENGINEERING MODEL FOR UPDATE.
001600 *                ADAPTED FOR TRAINING. IDENTICAL TO "PSD186"
001700 *                ON PAGES 395-405 OF COMMERCIAL SOFTWARE
001800 *                ENGINEERING, ISBN 0-471-81576-4, JOHN WILEY
****** ***************************** BOTTOM OF DATA ***************************
        ┌──────────────────────────────────────────────────────────────┐
        │ Entry of I followed by nn indicates Insertion of nn lines     │
        └──────────────────────────────────────────────────────────────┘
```

FIGURE 7.6a Requesting the insertion of additional lines while editing

```
EDIT --- BT05686.SOURCE.COBOL(FSBT3708) - 01.01 ------------- COLUMNS 007 078
COMMAND ===>                                                   SCROLL ===> HALF
****** ***************************** TOP OF DATA ******************************
000100  IDENTIFICATION DIVISION.
000200  PROGRAM-ID.     FSBT3708.
000300  AUTHOR.         J JANOSSY.
000400  INSTALLATION.   FARNON STANDARD.
000500  DATE-WRITTEN.   JAN 1988.
000600  DATE-COMPILED.
000700 *REMARKS.        LAST UPDATE 05-22-88  JJ   ORIG 01-19-88   JJ
000800 *
000900 *                THIS PROGRAM UPDATES A SEQUENTIAL MASTER FILE
001000 *                WITH TRANSACTION DATA. A REFERENCE FILE IS
001100 *                LOADED DYNAMICALLY AT RUN TIME, PROVIDING THE
001200 *                INFORMATION FOR ONE OF THE TRANSACTION EDITS
001300 *                AND THE APPLICABLE TRANSACTION RATE. A REPORT
001400 *                OF VALID AND INVALID TRANSACTIONS IS PRODUCED.
''''''
''''''    ┌──────────────────────────────────────────────────────────┐
''''''    │ These lines have been inserted, ready for entry.         │
''''''    │ TSO/ISPF will give them line numbers when used.          │
          └──────────────────────────────────────────────────────────┘
001500 *                FOLLOWS SOFTWARE ENGINEERING MODEL FOR UPDATE.
001600 *                ADAPTED FOR TRAINING. IDENTICAL TO "PSD186"
001700 *                ON PAGES 395-405 OF COMMERCIAL SOFTWARE
```

FIGURE 7.6b TSO/ISPF response to line insertion request

You will get the additional lines and also see the screen move forward, giving you access to those several new lines.

A Guide to Edit-Line Commands

All TSO/ISPF edit-line commands are entered in the same way, with the terminal user's overwriting the line numbers on a line being edited. Edit-line commands include the letter D for deletion, C for copy, M for moving, and X for excluding lines—that is, temporarily making lines invisible. These commands can operate on either single lines or "blocks" of lines.

Blocks of lines are marked for deleting, copying, moving, or exclusion with two characters, such as DD, CC, MM, or XX at the beginning of the group of lines and at its end. Copying or moving also requires the destination of the block to be indicated, by putting a letter A for "after this line" or B for "before this line" at some place in the item *outside* the block of lines marked. Figure 7.7 shows the full set of commonly used TSO/ISPF edit-line commands. For each of these commands two terminal screens are depicted, illustrating the entry of the command and the effect it produces. Figure 7.7 is a capsule summary and a working reference to TSO/ISPF primary edit commands.

No better way exists to develop a proficiency in the use of a text editor such as the TSO/ISPF 2 EDIT than to try it out and put it through its paces. Create a member in a COBOL or CNTL library, and use the features discussed up to this point to put a program or even just a narrative paragraph in it. Manipulate the text experimenting with inserting lines, deleting lines, copying lines, moving lines, and excluding lines, using Figure 7.7 as your guide.

Hints

Edit-line commands are processed from the top of text to the bottom, and more than one set of edit-line commands can be entered at one time prior to pressing the ENTER key. If any errors in edit-line commands are detected, none of the commands are performed, and all are highlighted to make them more apparent. A brief message concerning the error detected will be displayed in the upper right corner of the screen. You can move forward and backward in the item with the PF8 and PF7 keys to see the highlighted commands without losing the highlighting.

TSO/ISPF edit action desired	Edit line area	What happens when ENTER or a PF KEY is pressed:
LINE INSERT	****** ****** Inn --	"nn" blank lines are created immediately following. See Figures 7.6(a) and (b).
LINE DELETE	D ----	line is deleted
BLOCK DELETE	DD --- ----- ----- DD ---	Block of lines is deleted. Note that the range can span more than one screen of material; PF8 scroll forward or PF7 scroll backward can be done after placement of first "DD" and before placement of second "DD." See Figures 7.8(a) and (b).
LINE COPY	C ---- ----- ----- A ----	Line is copied to a point immediately after one noted with "A". If "B" is used instead of "A" the copy is to a point immediately before the line noted. "C" and "A" can be separated by many screens.
BLOCK COPY	CC --- ----- CC --- ----- A ----	Block of lines is copied to a point immediately after one noted with "A". If "B" is used instead of "A" the copy is to a point immediately before the line noted. "CC/CC" and "A" can be separated by many screens. See Figures 7.9(a) and (b).
LINE MOVE	M ---- ----- ----- A ----	Line is moved to a point immediately after one noted with "A". If "B" is used instead of "A" the copy is to a point immediately before the line noted. "M" and "A" can be separated by many screens.
BLOCK MOVE	MM --- ----- MM --- -----	Block of lines is moved to a point immediately after one noted with "A". If "B" is used instead of "A" the copy is to a point immediately before the line noted. "MM/MM" and "A" can be separated by many screens. See Figures 7.10(a) and (b).

Command	Code	Description
LINE REPEAT	`R---` `A---`	Line is repeated nn times, immediately following
BLOCK REPEAT	`RRnn -` `----- ` `RR ---`	Block is repeated nn times, immediately following. See Figures 7.11(a) and (b).
BLOCK SHIFT LEFT	`((nn -` `----- ` `(( ---`	Contents of block is shifted nn columns left
BLOCK SHIFT RIGHT	`))nn -` `----- ` `)) ---`	Contents of block is shifted nn columns right. Useful if COBOL source code has inadverdently been entered starting in column 1 instead of 7; use nn of 6. See Figures 7.12(a) and (b).
LINE EXCLUDE	`X ----` `----- `	Line is removed from view, replaced on screen with a line indicating that it is hidden. Visibility is restored when RESET is placed on COMMAND line and ENTER key is pressed. BLOCK EXCLUDE command (below) is more useful.
BLOCK EXCLUDE	`XX ---` `----- ` `----- ` `XX ---`	Block is removed from view, replaced on screen with a line that tells how many lines are not shown. Useful when editing widely separated parts of same member. Restore excluded lines to visibility by putting RESET on COMMAND line, and pressing ENTER. See Figures 7.13(a) and (b).
COLUMN RULER	`----- ` `COLS -` `----- `	A column ruler is displayed above this line. It remains in this place in the member but does not become a part of it. Many column rulers can be displayed in the same member. All are removed with the RESET command on the COMMAND line. See Figures 7.14(a) and (b).

SAMPLE field underscored with ****** represents line number field on TSO edit screen. Line numbers remaining in this in this field do not need to be erased when executing an edit line command, but they are not shown in these examples.

Copyright 1988 James G. Janossy -- Figure 7.7 in PRACTICAL TSO/ISPF FOR PROGRAMMERS AND THE INFORMATION CENTER (Wiley, 1988)

FIGURE 7.7   Summary of useful TSO/ISPF edit-line commands

```
EDIT --- BT05686.SOURCE.COBOL(FSBT3708) - 01.01 ------------- COLUMNS 007 078
COMMAND ===>                                                  SCROLL ===> HALF
****** **************************** TOP OF DATA ******************************
000100  IDENTIFICATION DIVISION.
000200  PROGRAM-ID.     FSBT3708.
000300  AUTHOR.         J JANOSSY.
000400  INSTALLATION.   FARNON STANDARD.
000500  DATE-WRITTEN.   JAN 1988.
000600  DATE-COMPILED.
000700 *REMARKS.        LAST UPDATE 05-22-88  JJ    ORIG 01-19-88   JJ
000800 *
DD 900 *                THIS PROGRAM UPDATES A SEQUENTIAL MASTER FILE
001000 *                WITH TRANSACTION DATA. A REFERENCE FILE IS
001100 *                LOADED DYNAMICALLY AT RUN TIME, PROVIDING THE
001200 *                INFORMATION FOR ONE OF THE TRANSACTION EDITS
001300 *                AND THE APPLICABLE TRANSACTION RATE. A REPORT
DD 400 *                OF VALID AND INVALID TRANSACTIONS IS PRODUCED.
001500 *                FOLLOWS SOFTWARE ENGINEERING MODEL FOR UPDATE.
001600 *                ADAPTED FOR TRAINING. IDENTICAL TO "PSD186"
001700 *                ON PAGES 395-405 OF COMMERCIAL SOFTWARE
001800 *                ENGINEERING, ISBN 0-471-81576-4, JOHN WILEY
****** **************************** BOTTOM OF DATA ***************************
```

Block of lines marked with DD/DD indicates deletion

FIGURE 7.8a   Requesting deletion of a group of lines ("block delete")

```
EDIT --- BT05686.SOURCE.COBOL(FSBT3708) - 01.01 ------------- COLUMNS 007 078
COMMAND ===>                                                  SCROLL ===> HALF
****** **************************** TOP OF DATA ******************************
000100  IDENTIFICATION DIVISION.
000200  PROGRAM-ID.     FSBT3708.
000300  AUTHOR.         J JANOSSY.
000400  INSTALLATION.   FARNON STANDARD.
000500  DATE-WRITTEN.   JAN 1988.
000600  DATE-COMPILED.
000700 *REMARKS.        LAST UPDATE 05-22-88  JJ    ORIG 01-19-88   JJ
000800 *
001500 *                FOLLOWS SOFTWARE ENGINEERING MODEL FOR UPDATE.
001600 *                ADAPTED FOR TRAINING. IDENTICAL TO "PSD186"
001700 *                ON PAGES 395-405 OF COMMERCIAL SOFTWARE
001800 *                ENGINEERING, ISBN 0-471-81576-4, JOHN WILEY
001900 *                AND SONS, 1985, EXCEPT FOR ADDITION OF THE
002000 *                OUTPUT OF FINISHED-TRANS (BT3708U3). NOTE
002100 *                CHANGE IN TRANSACTION RECORD SIZE AND CONTENT.
002200 *
002300  ENVIRONMENT DIVISION.
****** **************************** BOTTOM OF DATA ***************************
```

Lines 900 through 1400 have been deleted; no "undelete" is possible

FIGURE 7.8b   TSO/ISPF response to block delete request

```
EDIT --- BT05686.SOURCE.COBOL(FSBT3708) - 01.01 -------------- COLUMNS 007 078
COMMAND ===>                                                SCROLL ===> HALF
****** **************************** TOP OF DATA ****************************
000100  IDENTIFICATION DIVISION.
000200  PROGRAM-ID.    FSBT3708.
000300  AUTHOR.        J JANOSSY.
000400  INSTALLATION.  FARNON STANDARD.
000500  DATE-WRITTEN.  JAN 1988.
000600  DATE-COMPILED.
CC 700  *REMARKS.      LAST UPDATE 05-22-88  JJ   ORIG 01-19-88  JJ
000800  *
CC 900  *              THIS PROGRAM UPDATES A SEQUENTIAL MASTER FILE
001000  *              WITH TRANSACTION DATA. A REFERENCE FILE IS
001100  *              LOADED DYNAMICALLY AT RUN TIME, PROVIDING THE
001200  *              INFORMATION FOR ONE OF THE TRANSACTION EDITS
001300  *              AND THE APPLICABLE TRANSACTION RATE. A REPORT
A 1400  *              OF VALID AND INVALID TRANSACTIONS IS PRODUCED.
001500  *              FOLLOWS SOFTWARE ENGINEERING MODEL FOR UPDATE.
001600  *              ADAPTED FOR TRAINING. IDENTICAL TO "PSD186"
001700  *              ON PAGES 395-405 OF COMMERCIAL SOFTWARE
001800  *              ENGINEERING, ISBN 0-471-81576-4, JOHN WILEY
001900  *              AND SONS, 1985, EXCEPT FOR ADDITION OF THE
002000  *              OUTPUT OF FINISHED-TRANS (BT3708U3). NOTE
****** **************************** BOTTOM OF DATA ****************************
```

FIGURE 7.9a Requesting copy of a group of lines to after a designated line ("block copy")

```
EDIT --- BT05686.SOURCE.COBOL(FSBT3708) - 01.01 -------------- COLUMNS 007 078
COMMAND ===>                                                SCROLL ===> HALF
****** **************************** TOP OF DATA ****************************
000100  IDENTIFICATION DIVISION.
000200  PROGRAM-ID.    FSBT3708.
000300  AUTHOR.        J JANOSSY.
000400  INSTALLATION.  FARNON STANDARD.
000500  DATE-WRITTEN.  JAN 1988.
000600  DATE-COMPILED.
000700  *REMARKS.      LAST UPDATE 05-22-88  JJ   ORIG 01-19-88  JJ
000800  *
000900  *              THIS PROGRAM UPDATES A SEQUENTIAL MASTER FILE
001000  *              WITH TRANSACTION DATA. A REFERENCE FILE IS
001100  *              LOADED DYNAMICALLY AT RUN TIME, PROVIDING THE
001200  *              INFORMATION FOR ONE OF THE TRANSACTION EDITS
001300  *              AND THE APPLICABLE TRANSACTION RATE. A REPORT
001400  *              OF VALID AND INVALID TRANSACTIONS IS PRODUCED.
001410  *REMARKS.      LAST UPDATE 05-22-88  JJ   ORIG 01-19-88  JJ
001420  *
001430  *              THIS PROGRAM UPDATES A SEQUENTIAL MASTER FILE
001500  *              FOLLOWS SOFTWARE ENGINEERING MODEL FOR UPDATE.
001600  *              ADAPTED FOR TRAINING. IDENTICAL TO "PSD186"
001700  *              ON PAGES 395-405 OF COMMERCIAL SOFTWARE
001800  *              ENGINEERING, ISBN 0-471-81576-4, JOHN WILEY
```

FIGURE 7.9b TSO/ISPF response to group copy request

```
EDIT --- BT05686.SOURCE.COBOL(FSBT3708) - 01.01 ------------- COLUMNS 007 078
COMMAND ===>                                                  SCROLL ===> HALF
****** **************************** TOP OF DATA ****************************
000100  IDENTIFICATION DIVISION.
000200  PROGRAM-ID.     FSBT3708.
000300  AUTHOR.         J JANOSSY.
000400  INSTALLATION.   FARNON STANDARD.
000500  DATE-WRITTEN.   JAN 1988.
000600  DATE-COMPILED.
MM 700  *REMARKS.        LAST UPDATE 05-22-88  JJ   ORIG 01-19-88  JJ
000800  *
MM 900  *               THIS PROGRAM UPDATES A SEQUENTIAL MASTER FILE
001000  *               WITH TRANSACTION DATA. A REFERENCE FILE IS
001100  *               LOADED DYNAMICALLY AT RUN TIME, PROVIDING THE
001200  *               INFORMATION FOR ONE OF THE TRANSACTION EDITS
001300  *               AND THE APPLICABLE TRANSACTION RATE. A REPORT
A 1400  *               OF VALID AND INVALID TRANSACTIONS IS PRODUCED.
001500  *               FOLLOWS SOFTWARE ENGINEERING MODEL FOR UPDATE.
001600  *               ADAPTED FOR TRAINING. IDENTICAL TO "PSD186"
001700  *               ON PAGES 395-405 OF COMMERCIAL SOFTWARE
001800  *               ENGINEERING, ISBN 0-471-81576-4, JOHN WILEY
001900  *               AND SONS, 1985, EXCEPT FOR ADDITION OF THE
002000  *               OUTPUT OF FINISHED-TRANS (BT3708U3). NOTE
****** **************************** BOTTOM OF DATA *************************
```

FIGURE 7.10a Requesting move of a group of lines to after a designated line ("block move")

```
EDIT --- BT05686.SOURCE.COBOL(FSBT3708) - 01.01 ------------- COLUMNS 007 078
COMMAND ===>                                                  SCROLL ===> HALF
****** **************************** TOP OF DATA ****************************
000100  IDENTIFICATION DIVISION.
000200  PROGRAM-ID.     FSBT3708.
000300  AUTHOR.         J JANOSSY.
000400  INSTALLATION.   FARNON STANDARD.
000500  DATE-WRITTEN.   JAN 1988.
000600  DATE-COMPILED.
001000  *               WITH TRANSACTION DATA. A REFERENCE FILE IS
001100  *               LOADED DYNAMICALLY AT RUN TIME, PROVIDING THE
001200  *               INFORMATION FOR ONE OF THE TRANSACTION EDITS
001300  *               AND THE APPLICABLE TRANSACTION RATE. A REPORT
001400  *               OF VALID AND INVALID TRANSACTIONS IS PRODUCED.
001410  *REMARKS.        LAST UPDATE 05-22-88  JJ   ORIG 01-19-88  JJ
001420  *
001430  *               THIS PROGRAM UPDATES A SEQUENTIAL MASTER FILE
001500  *               FOLLOWS SOFTWARE ENGINEERING MODEL FOR UPDATE.
001600  *               ADAPTED FOR TRAINING. IDENTICAL TO "PSD186"
001700  *               ON PAGES 395-405 OF COMMERCIAL SOFTWARE
001800  *               ENGINEERING, ISBN 0-471-81576-4, JOHN WILEY
001900  *               AND SONS, 1985, EXCEPT FOR ADDITION OF THE
002000  *               OUTPUT OF FINISHED-TRANS (BT3708U3). NOTE
002100  *               CHANGE IN TRANSACTION RECORD SIZE AND CONTENT.
```

FIGURE 7.10b TSO/ISPF response to group move request

```
 EDIT --- BT05686.SOURCE.COBOL(PSD200) - 01.03 --------------- COLUMNS 007 078
 COMMAND ===>                                                  SCROLL ===> HALF
 001800 FILE-CONTROL.
 001900     SELECT DATAFILE  ASSIGN TO UT-S-INDATA1.
 002000     SELECT REPORT1   ASSIGN TO UT-S-OTREPT1.
 002100     SELECT REPORT2   ASSIGN TO UT-S-OTREPT2.
 002200*
 002300 DATA DIVISION.
 002400 FILE SECTION.
+ RR2 00*
 002600 FD  DATAFILE
 002700     LABEL RECORDS ARE STANDARD
 002800     BLOCK CONTAINS 0 RECORDS
 002900     RECORD CONTAINS 80 CHARACTERS.
+ RR 000 01  DATAFILE-REC                   PIC X(80).
 003100/
 003200 WORKING-STORAGE SECTION.
 003300 01  FILLER  PIC X(23)  VALUE  '*WORKING STORAGE START*'.
 003400*
 003500 01  WS-FLAGS.
 003600     12 F1-EOF-FLAG                   PIC X(1)  VALUE 'M'.
 003700        88 F1-EOF-DATAFILE-END                  VALUE 'E'.
 003800*
 003900 01  WS-COUNTERS.
```

FIGURE 7.11a   Requesting two replications of a group of lines ("block repeat")

```
 EDIT --- BT05686.SOURCE.COBOL(PSD200) - 01.03 --------------- COLUMNS 007 078
 COMMAND ===>                                                  SCROLL ===> HALF
 001800 FILE-CONTROL.
 001900     SELECT DATAFILE  ASSIGN TO UT-S-INDATA1.
 002000     SELECT REPORT1   ASSIGN TO UT-S-OTREPT1.
 002100     SELECT REPORT2   ASSIGN TO UT-S-OTREPT2.
 002200*
 002300 DATA DIVISION.
 002400 FILE SECTION.
┌ 002500*
│ 002600 FD  DATAFILE
│ 002700     LABEL RECORDS ARE STANDARD
│ 002800     BLOCK CONTAINS 0 RECORDS
│ 002900     RECORD CONTAINS 80 CHARACTERS.
└ 003000 01  DATAFILE-REC                   PIC X(80).
+ 003010*
 003020 FD  DATAFILE
 003030     LABEL RECORDS ARE STANDARD
 003040     BLOCK CONTAINS 0 RECORDS
 003050     RECORD CONTAINS 80 CHARACTERS.
+ 003060 01  DATAFILE-REC                   PIC X(80).
 003070*
 003080 FD  DATAFILE
 003090     LABEL RECORDS ARE STANDARD
V
```

FIGURE 7.11b   TSO/ISPF response to block replication request

```
EDIT --- BT05686.SOURCE.COBOL(PSD200) - 01.03 --------------- COLUMNS 007 078
COMMAND ===>                                                  SCROLL ===> HALF
001800 FILE-CONTROL.
  ))4 00 SELECT DATAFILE   ASSIGN TO UT-S-INDATA1.  ┐
002000 SELECT REPORT1      ASSIGN TO UT-S-OTREPT1.  │
  )) 100 SELECT REPORT2    ASSIGN TO UT-S-OTREPT2.  ┘  ┌──────────────┐
002200*                                                │ These lines are │
002300 DATA DIVISION.                                  │ four columns too │
002400 FILE SECTION.                                   │ far left and the │
002500*                                                │ ))4 block command│
002600 FD  DATAFILE                                    │ will shift them   │
002700     LABEL RECORDS ARE STANDARD                  │ to the right      │
002800     BLOCK CONTAINS O RECORDS                    └──────────────┘
002900     RECORD CONTAINS 80 CHARACTERS.
003000 01  DATAFILE-REC                  PIC X(80).
003100/
003200 WORKING-STORAGE SECTION.
003300 01  FILLER  PIC X(23)  VALUE  '*WORKING STORAGE START*'.
003400*
003500 01  WS-FLAGS.
003600     12 F1-EOF-FLAG                PIC X(1)  VALUE 'M'.
003700        88 F1-EOF-DATAFILE-END               VALUE 'E'.
003800*
003900 01  WS-COUNTERS.
```

FIGURE 7.12a Requesting four position rightward shift of text

```
EDIT --- BT05686.SOURCE.COBOL(PSD200) - 01.03 --------------- COLUMNS 007 078
COMMAND ===>                                                  SCROLL ===> HALF
001800 FILE-CONTROL.
001900     SELECT DATAFILE   ASSIGN TO UT-S-INDATA1.  ┐
002000     SELECT REPORT1    ASSIGN TO UT-S-OTREPT1.  │
002100     SELECT REPORT2    ASSIGN TO UT-S-OTREPT2.  │
002200*                                               ┘
002300 DATA DIVISION.
002400 FILE SECTION.                         ┌──────────────────┐
002500*                                      │ Lines content now │
002600 FD  DATAFILE                          │ in correct position│
002700     LABEL RECORDS ARE STANDARD        └──────────────────┘
002800     BLOCK CONTAINS O RECORDS
002900     RECORD CONTAINS 80 CHARACTERS.
003000 01  DATAFILE-REC                  PIC X(80).
003100/
003200 WORKING-STORAGE SECTION.
003300 01  FILLER  PIC X(23)  VALUE  '*WORKING STORAGE START*'.
003400*
003500 01  WS-FLAGS.
003600     12 F1-EOF-FLAG                PIC X(1)  VALUE 'M'.
003700        88 F1-EOF-DATAFILE-END               VALUE 'E'.
003800*
003900 01  WS-COUNTERS.
```

FIGURE 7.12b TSO/ISPF response to rightward text shift request

```
EDIT --- BT05686.SOURCE.COBOL(PSD183) - 01.03 --------------- COLUMNS 007 078
COMMAND ===>                                                SCROLL ===> HALF
014100*
014200 2100-WRITE-R1-OUTPUT.
014300     IF R1-LINES-REMAINING IS LESS THAN R1-WANTED-LINE-SPACING
014400        PERFORM 2900-R1-NEWPAGE.
014500     WRITE REPORT1-REC FROM R1-PRINT-SLOT
014600        AFTER ADVANCING R1-WANTED-LINE-SPACING LINES.
014700     COMPUTE R1-LINES-REMAINING =
014800        (R1-LINES-REMAINING - R1-WANTED-LINE-SPACING).
XX 900*
015000 2700-READ-DATAFILE.
015100     READ DATAFILE INTO DATAFILE-INPUT-AREA        ┌──────────────────┐
015200        AT END                                     │ These lines will │
015300           MOVE 'E' TO F1-EOF-FLAG.                │ be hidden from   │
015400     IF F1-EOF-FLAG NOT EQUAL 'E'                  │ view by the XX/XX│
015500        ADD +1 TO WS-DATAFILE-IN-COUNT.            │ block exclude    │
XX 600*                                                  │ commands at left │
015700 2900-R1-NEWPAGE.                                  └──────────────────┘
015800     ADD +1 TO R1-PAGE-COUNT.
015900     MOVE R1-PAGE-COUNT TO R1-PH2-PAGE-NO.
016000     WRITE REPORT1-REC FROM R1-PAGE-HDR1
016100        AFTER ADVANCING PAGE-EJECT.
016200     WRITE REPORT1-REC FROM R1-PAGE-HDR2 AFTER ADVANCING 1 LINES.
```

FIGURE 7.13a Requesting "hiding" or exclusion of a group of lines ("block exclude")

```
EDIT --- BT05686.SOURCE.COBOL(PSD183) - 01.03 --------------- COLUMNS 007 078
COMMAND ===>                                                SCROLL ===> HALF
014100*
014200 2100-WRITE-R1-OUTPUT.
014300     IF R1-LINES-REMAINING IS LESS THAN R1-WANTED-LINE-SPACING
014400        PERFORM 2900-R1-NEWPAGE.
014500     WRITE REPORT1-REC FROM R1-PRINT-SLOT
014600        AFTER ADVANCING R1-WANTED-LINE-SPACING LINES.
014700     COMPUTE R1-LINES-REMAINING =
014800        (R1-LINES-REMAINING - R1-WANTED-LINE-SPACING).
- - - - - - - - - - - - - - - - - - - - - - - - - - - 8 LINES(S) NOT DISPLAYED
015700 2900-R1-NEWPAGE.
015800     ADD +1 TO R1-PAGE-COUNT.              ┌──────────────────────┐
015900     MOVE R1-PAGE-COUNT TO R1-PH2-PAGE-NO. │ ===> RESET will again │
016000     WRITE REPORT1-REC FROM R1-PAGE-HDR1   │ display these lines   │
016100        AFTER ADVANCING PAGE-EJECT.        └──────────────────────┘
016200     WRITE REPORT1-REC FROM R1-PAGE-HDR2 AFTER ADVANCING 1 LINES.
016300     WRITE REPORT1-REC FROM R1-PAGE-HDR1 AFTER ADVANCING 1 LINES.
016400     WRITE REPORT1-REC FROM R1-COL-HDR1  AFTER ADVANCING 4 LINES.
016500     WRITE REPORT1-REC FROM R1-COL-HDR2  AFTER ADVANCING 1 LINES.
016600     MOVE SPACES TO REPORT1-REC.
016700     WRITE REPORT1-REC AFTER ADVANCING 2 LINES.
016800     COMPUTE R1-LINES-REMAINING = (R1-LINE-LIMIT - 10).
016900     MOVE R1-NORMAL-LINE-SPACING TO R1-WANTED-LINE-SPACING.
```

FIGURE 7.13b TSO/ISPF response to line exclusion request

```
EDIT --- CSCJGJ.CSC.COBOL(CHARFUN) -------------------------- COLUMNS 007 078
COMMAND ===>                                                 SCROLL ===> HALF
008800 *
008900 * SQUISH RIGHT
009000 *
009100       MOVE +23 TO W2-SUB.
009200       MOVE ALL '0' TO W2-AREA.
009300       PERFORM 3000-SQUISH-RIGHT
009400          VARYING W1-SUB FROM +22 BY -1
009500             UNTIL W1-SUB < +1.
 cols 0 *
009700 3000-SQUISH-RIGHT.
009800     IF W1-BYTE(W1-SUB) NOT EQUAL SPACE
009900        SUBTRACT +1 FROM W2-SUB
010000        MOVE W1-BYTE(W1-SUB) TO W2-BYTE(W2-SUB).
010100 *
010200 4000-DECIMAL-SCAN.
                                  ┌─────────────────────────────────┐
010400       ADD +1 TO WS-NU     │ The letters "cols" can be placed │
010500       IF W3-SUB = +23     │ in the line number area of any edit │
010600       MOVE W2-SUB TO      │ line and will insert a column ruler │
010700 *                        │ at this point. The ruler does not │
010800 5000-FURTHER-TESTS.       │ become part of the member, and can │
010900       IF W1-BYTE = '?'    │ be removed from display by ===> RESET │
                                  └─────────────────────────────────┘
```

FIGURE 7.14a   Requesting display of a column ruler at a given point while editing

```
EDIT --- CSCJGJ.CSC.COBOL(CHARFUN) --------------------- ┌─ COLUMNS 007 078
COMMAND ===>                                             │  SCROLL ===> HALF
008800 *                                          ┌──────────────────────┐
008900 * SQUISH RIGHT                             │ Column ruler will move │
009000 *                                          │ right and left if the  │
009100       MOVE +23 TO W2-SUB.                  │ PF11/PF10 keys or the  │
009200       MOVE ALL '0' TO W2-AREA.             │ RIGHT and LEFT command │
009300       PERFORM 3000-SQUISH-RIGHT            │ line commands are used │
009400          VARYING W1-SUB FROM +22 BY -1     └──────────────────────┘
009500             UNTIL W1-SUB < +1.
=COLS> ---1----+----2----+----3----+----4----+----5----+----6----+----7----+---
009600 *
009700 3000-SQUISH-RIGHT.
009800     IF W1-BYTE(W1-SUB) NOT EQUAL SPACE
009900        SUBTRACT +1 FROM W2-SUB
010000        MOVE W1-BYTE(W1-SUB) TO W2-BYTE(W2-SUB).
010100 *
010200 4000-DECIMAL-SCAN.
010300     IF W2-BYTE(W2-SUB) EQUAL '.'
010400        ADD +1 TO WS-NUMBER-OF-DECIMALS
010500        IF W3-SUB = +23
010600        MOVE W2-SUB TO W3-SUB.
010700 *
010800 5000-FURTHER-TESTS.
```

FIGURE 7.14b   TSO/ISPF response to request for column ruler display

To remove an edit-line command, blank it out with spaces. To remove all edit-line commands, enter RESET on the command line, and press ENTER.

For commands such as delete D, copy C, move M, and exclude X, it is possible to affect a block of lines by putting the single command letter on a line, immediately followed by a number. The number indicates how many lines, including the one on which the command is entered, will be affected. "Start" and "stop" block versions of the commands, using DD and DD, CC and CC, MM and MM, or XX and XX, are handiest for some commands, but for "delete to end of data," this can save having to traverse to the end to mark it. For example, to delete from a given point to the end of data, place D9999 on a line; the line and up to 9,998 lines following are deleted. If there are not 9,998 lines following, as many lines as do follow are deleted.

Lines can be excluded from screen display, collapsing what is presented, using the X command as illustrated in Figure 7.13(a). Excluding a block of lines is sometimes convenient in working with widely separated parts of a member; the "split screen" mode of TSO/ISPF, described in Chapter 9, cannot be invoked with both parts of the split screen operating on the same member to edit it. Excluded lines can be made visible again by entering RESET on the command line and pressing the ENTER key.

Lines excluded from the display are still eligible for find and change actions. If an excluded line meets a find or change condition, it is made visible again. It is sometimes handy to exclude all lines, then perform a mass find or mass change. Only the lines containing the item sought will be made visible.

Cancelling the Edit Without Creating a Member

If you arrive at an empty edit screen not because you wanted to create a new member, but because you misspelled the name of an existing member, enter CANCEL at the command line where the cursor was initially positioned. This will "bail out" of the edit without saving any indication of the new, empty member. Depending on how your installation has set TSO/ISPF to operate, ending the edit of a new empty member with the *PF3 END* key may or may not place an entry for the member in the directory; CANCEL on the command line always avoids creation of this entry.

EDIT's CANCEL is different from a native mode TSO command

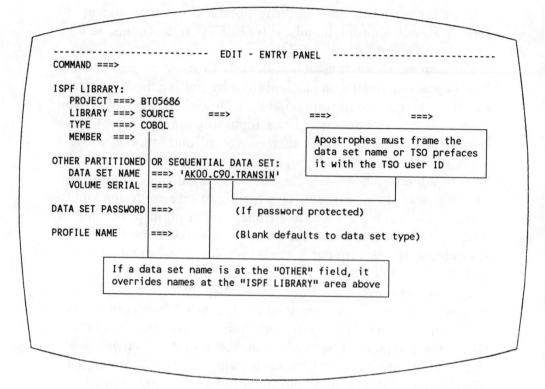

```
----------------------------- EDIT - ENTRY PANEL -----------------------------
COMMAND ===>

ISPF LIBRARY:
    PROJECT ===> BT05686
    LIBRARY ===> SOURCE        ===>              ===>              ===>
    TYPE    ===> COBOL
    MEMBER  ===>                                 ┌──────────────────────────────┐
                                                 │ Apostrophes must frame the   │
OTHER PARTITIONED OR SEQUENTIAL DATA SET:        │ data set name or TSO prefaces│
    DATA SET NAME  ===> 'AK00.C90.TRANSIN'       │ it with the TSO user ID      │
    VOLUME SERIAL  ===>                          └──────────────────────────────┘

DATA SET PASSWORD ===>            (If password protected)

PROFILE NAME      ===>            (Blank defaults to data set type)

        ┌────────────────────────────────────────────────────────┐
        │ If a data set name is at the "OTHER" field, it          │
        │ overrides names at the "ISPF LIBRARY" area above        │
        └────────────────────────────────────────────────────────┘
```

FIGURE 7.15   Filling out the edit-entry panel to edit a non-TSO/ISPF sequential data set

of the same name. The two commands are unrelated, although they are both entered on the command line. CANCEL on the command line during editing stops the edited member from being saved to disk when the edit is ended. CANCEL on the command line outside of edit is the way to cancel a job that has been submitted for execution, as described in Chapter 8.

ENDING THE EDIT

You can leave the editing of an item at any point by pressing the PF3 END key. With the AUTOSAVE profile parameter on, TSO/ISPF will save the edited item for you in its partitioned data set or the sequential data set from which you obtained it. If you do not want to have it saved in its edited form, enter CANCEL on the command line to override TSO/ISPF's intention to save it.

Edit-line commands are only one of two classes of editing commands available. TSO/ISPF also provides "primary edit commands," entered via the command line. We explore primary edit commands, which allow manipulations between the member being edited and members external to it, in Chapter 8.

ACCESSING SEQUENTIAL AND NON-TSO/ISPF DATA SETS

The TSO edit function allows you to edit simple sequential data sets with records from 10 to 255 bytes in length in addition to partitioned data set libraries. The need to do this seldom arises, but browse actions on sequential data sets, for "online dump" purposes, are more common. Since the manner of specifying a sequential data set name is the same for TSO 2 EDIT and TSO 1 BROWSE, it is informative to see an example of it.

The middle portion of the edit-entry panel contains an area labeled OTHER PARTITIONED OR SEQUENTIAL DATA SET, with two entry fields. These fields can be used to enter a sequential data set name that does not conform to the TSO/ISPF PROJECT, LIBRARY, and TYPE format, and a disk volume serial number. For example, suppose you intended to create, edit, or browse a sequential data set named:

    AK00.C99.TRANSIN

that contained test data for a program. You could access the data set for editing by filling out the edit entry panel as shown in Figure 7.15.

In Figure 7.15 the OTHER DATA SET NAME ===> is enclosed within apostrophes. This is necessary because TSO/ISPF prefixes any data set name with the TSO logon identifier, unless we explicitly indicate that this is not applicable. If we specified the OTHER DATA SET NAME ===> without the surrounding apostrophes, it would appear to the system as BT05686.AK00.C99.TRANSIN. The entries in the OTHER fields are temporary and are erased by TSO/ISPF as you transfer between screens, but if present they take precedence over entries in the ISPF LIBRARY fields.

It is possible to enter any data set name in the OTHER fields, even other TSO/ISPF partitioned data set and member names. To access member LFWSTHD1 of a typical installation copylib partitioned data set named SYS1.COPYLIB, the OTHER data set name field can be entered with surrounding apostrophes as:

```
DATA SET NAME ===> 'SYS1.COPYLIB(LFWSTHD1)'
```

To obtain a member list for a partitioned data set indicated in the OTHER field, enter the PDS name without a member name. In the example immediately above, we could obtain a member list of SYS1.COPYLIB by entering it without any member name in the OTHER field as:

```
DATA SET NAME ===> 'SYS1.COPYLIB'
```

The VOLUME SERIAL field of the OTHER field must be filled in only if the data set you want to access is not cataloged. See Chapter 6 of a companion book in this series, *Practical MVS JCL for Today's Programmer* (John Wiley & Sons, 1987), for full information on the MVS system cataloging facility, which is used automatically for TSO/ISPF library partitioned data sets.

WARNING: MONITOR PARTITIONED DATA SET SPACE!

A data set is read into memory when edit starts on it. It is thus possible to edit a partitioned data set member that, due to a lack of space in the partitioned data set, cannot later be saved. When this occurs, TSO/ISPF displays a message containing the standard MVS system completion code for an out-of-space condition, E37. In response, you must enter CANCEL on the COMMAND line and press *ENTER* in order to exit from the edit. Running out of usable space in a partitioned data set storing your source code can result in expending much work editing a member, only to risk losing it.

Keep track of the condition of partitioned data set libraries using the TSO/ISPF "data set information" function TSO 3.1 or TSO 3.2. Delete members no longer needed and reorganize a PDS when it is becoming full, as described in Chapter 11 and Appendix C, to avoid such problems. If the problem does occur, see Appendix G for a panic situation solution that can spare the loss of the work performed on a member.

═══ 8 ═══

TSO 2: Advanced Editing and Job Submission

2
COMMANDS

Edit-line commands offer many facilities for working with a body of source code or job control language. TSO/ISPF also provides a higher level of features known as "primary editing commands," which deal with either the submission of jobs for processing or text external to a member being edited. Primary editing commands are different from edit-line commands. While they are used during EDIT, they are entered on the command line after the label COMMAND ===> and not on the line numbers of the lines being edited.

PRIMARY (COMMAND LINE) EDIT COMMANDS

Two categories of primary edit commands exist. One group is made up of global controlling parameters for the edit session, and dictates things about the format of the editing screen and the columns it displays. The other group consists of actual working commands that are used to locate items within a member, copy or write to other members, submit a job for execution, and so forth.

As a pragmatic observation, fewer than half of the primary editing commands of either the controlling or working categories are useful to applications-programming and end-user personnel. It makes sense to focus on those of greatest utility.

Figure 8.1 lists the primary editing commands. The controlling parameters for edit sessions are noted with an asterisk.

*	AUTOLIST		EXCLUDE	*	RECOVERY
*	AUTONUM		FIND		RENUM
*	AUTOSAVE	*	HEX		REPLACE
	BOUNDS	*	IMACRO		RESET
	BUILTIN		LEVEL		RMACRO
	CANCEL		LOCATE		SAVE
*	CAPS		MODEL		SORT
	CHANGE		MOVE	*	STATS
	COPY	*	NOTE		SUBMIT
	CREATE	*	NULLS	*	TABS
	DEFINE	*	NUMBER		UNNUM
	DELETE	*	PACK		VERSION
	EDIT	*	PROFILE		

FIGURE 8.1   TSO/ISPF primary editing commands, entered on the COMMAND ===> line

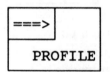

PROFILE

EDITING PROFILE

The global parameters that govern editing sessions are maintained in "edit profiles" retained automatically by TSO/ISPF. The profile for a given edit session is made visible by one of the primary edit commands on the COMMAND ===> line, aptly named PROFILE; it is hidden again by entry of the word RESET on the command line. A profile display is depicted in Figure 8.2.

A default edit profile is created automatically for you by TSO/ISPF for each type of partitioned data set you edit—COBOL, CNTL, PLI, FORT, ASM. If you change settings in your edit profile during a session, the changes are recorded and preserved thereafter for that type of partitioned data set. See Figure 5.1 for default column editing treatment accorded to each partitioned data set type.

Important Profile Parameters

A few profile-stored parameters of special importance are yes/no switches that are set and reset by the entry of their names on the command line, with the word ON or OFF following. Because of their nature, these settings should be verified early in a new TSO/ISPF user's work:

RECOVERY ON—Establishes data set recovery during edit. In case of interruption or logoff due to inactivity during a session, the

```
EDIT --- BT05686.SOURCE.COBOL(INTER) - 01.02 --------------- COLUMNS 007 078
COMMAND ===>                                                SCROLL ===> PAGE
****** **************************** TOP OF DATA ****************************
=PROF> ....COBOL (FIXED - 80)....RECOVERY ON....NUMBER ON COB.............
=PROF> ....CAPS ON....HEX OFF....NULLS OFF....TABS ON STD..................
=PROF> ....AUTONUM ON....AUTOLIST OFF....STATS ON.........................
=TABS> -   -   -                               -
=COLS> ---1----+----2----+----3----+----4----+----5----+----6----+----7----+---
000100 IDENTIFICATION DIVISION.
000200 PROGRAM-ID.    INTER.
000300 AUTHOR.        J JANOSSY.
000400 INSTALLATION.  FARNON STANDARD.
000500 DATE-WRITTEN.  FEB 1988.
000600 DATE-COMPILED.
000700 *REMARKS.        TEST IBM VSCOBOL INTERMEDIATE FIELD PRECISION.
000800 *
000900 ENVIRONMENT DIVISION.
001000 CONFIGURATION SECTION.
001100 SOURCE-COMPUTER.   IBM-4381.
001200 OBJECT-COMPUTER.   IBM-4381.
001300 *
001400 DATA DIVISION.
001500 WORKING-STORAGE SECTION.
001600 *
```

FIGURE 8.2 Requesting and viewing the edit session "profile" currently in effect

restoration of changes and updates up to the point of failure is handled automatically by TSO with RECOVERY ON. The only exception to this is a new member that has never once been SAVEd; only existing members receive RECOVERY ON protection. *Hint: do an explicit SAVE for a new member once, by putting the word SAVE on the command line and pressing ENTER, early in its initial creation edit.*

CAPS ON—Causes lowercase letters entered by the terminal operator to be converted to uppercase by TSO. CAPS OFF turns off this service. There is little need in program and job control language development for CAPS OFF to be set, but it is useful when lowercase letters must be entered into literal strings in program source code.

AUTOSAVE ON—Causes the member being edited to be saved automatically when the edit is ended. Saving can be overridden by placing the command CANCEL on the command line before pressing the *PF3 END* key. If AUTOSAVE is off, you must explicitly enter the SAVE command on the command line to record the changes made to a member during an edit session.

STATS ON—Allows TSO to place statistics such as last date and time of edit, original number of lines, current number of lines, and originating TSO account into the partitioned data set directory entries for members. This provides member lists that are more informative than would be simple lists of member names.

The default for these, with the exception of RECOVERY, is normally ON, and most TSO/ISPF users find this suitable.

RECOVERY for Automatic Edit Resumption

The first time you make use of your COBOL or CNTL partitioned data set you should check the profile and set RECOVERY ON. Be sure to set RECOVERY ON for *each* partitioned data set you have *if you desire the protection of this service.* You will not thereafter need to be concerned with PROFILE; the edit profile will remain in effect for all members of the partitioned data set.

Setting RECOVERY ON incurs increased system overhead and, if widely used within an installation, can adversely affect TSO/ISPF response time and disk space usage. RECOVERY should be set on if you use TSO/ISPF via a dial-up connection or through a minicomputer emulating a TSO controller. Both of these types of connections are subject to disruption independent of the mainframe, increasing the potential for loss of editing work through unintended disconnection. Beyond this, the stability of your mainframe and local TSO/ISPF environment dictates whether RECOVERY should be set on or off.

Creating Additional Editing Profiles

Beyond the default edit profile for a partitioned data set, up to 24 additional edit profiles may be created. To create a profile, enter a name at the PROFILE ===> field on the EDIT - ENTRY panel, then begin editing a member. Put the word PROFILE on the COMMAND ===> line, set the profile parameters as you wish, put RESET on the command line, and press *ENTER*. When you end your editing of the member by pressing the *PF3 END* key, the new profile will be saved automatically by TSO/ISPF for you.

In a subsequent edit session, you can invoke a custom profile by putting its name on the EDIT - ENTRY panel as you designate a member for editing or request a member list; if you leave the PRO-FILE ===> blank, the default profile will be in effect.

The basic edit profiles created by TSO/ISPF are usually well suited to productive editing work, and most professionals conduct their business with little or no concern for the multiple editing profile facility.

WORKING PRIMARY EDITING COMMANDS

A subset of 12 working primary editing commands provides a core of functionality. These can be entered immediately after the label COMMAND ===> at the top of the screen. Rather than listing these important commands in alphabetical sequence, let's consider them in order of utility.

COMMAND ===> *SUBMIT or SUB* for Job Submission

Submits the member being edited for execution. This is relevant only to job control language members, because the submission is that of a batch job to the system input queue. In response to the pressing of the *ENTER* key with SUBMIT or SUB on the command line, the system uses the extended message area of the screen to indicate the job number assigned to the job (Figure 8.3).

It is occasionally necessary to cancel a job once submitted. This can be done using the non-edit CANCEL command, also known as the native mode TSO CANCEL command, citing the job name and assigned number, as described in Chapter 10. Non-edit CANCEL is *not* the same as the primary editing CANCEL.

COMMAND ===> *CANCEL or CAN* to Abandon Edit

Overrides the AUTOSAVE edit profile parameter and allows ending the edit session without saving the member being edited. This is useful if you arrive at a blank screen to start creating a new member when you actually misspelled the name of an existing member that you wanted to edit. If you CANCEL out of the edit, you avoid

```
EDIT --- BT05686.SOURCE.CNTL(PRINT) - 01.06 ---------------- COLUMNS 001 072
COMMAND ===> sub                                           SCROLL ===> PAGE
****** **************************** TOP OF DATA ******************************
000100 //FSBT686A   JOB AKOOTSO,'DP2-JANOSSY',CLASS=E,MSGCLASS=A,
000200 //  MSGLEVEL=(1,1),NOTIFY=BT05686
000300 //*
000400 //*    THIS JCL = BT05686.SOURCE.CNTL(PRINT)
000500 //*
000600 //************************************************************
000700 //*                                                        *
000800 //*    STEP A -- EXECUTE UTILITY PROGRAM IEBGENER TO       *
000900 //*               COPY SOME TEST DATA TO "SYSOUT" TO       *
001000 //*               PRINT IT. (THE FORMAT FOR THIS TEST      *
001100 //*               DATA IS SHOWN ON PAGE 355 OF PRACTICAL   *
001200 //*               MVS JCL, FIGURE 17.13(A).                *
001300 //*                                                        *
001400 //************************************************************
001500 //STEPA      EXEC  PGM=IEBGENER
001600 //SYSPRINT   DD    SYSOUT=*
001700 //SYSUT1     DD    DSN=BT05686.SOURCE.DATA(STATEDAT),
JOB FSBT686A(JOB07820) SUBMITTED
***
```

FIGURE 8.3 Submitting job control language to the input queue for batch processing

the creation of an empty member in your partitioned data set. CANCEL can also be used to omit the saving of a member that you began to edit but do not wish to save in altered form. Pressing either the *PF3 END* key or the *ENTER* key causes processing of the CANCEL command.

Note that the primary editing CANCEL command is different from non-edit CANCEL command, which cancels execution of a submitted job. This is admittedly confusing and it is unfortunate that the designers of TSO chose command words in this manner. The non-edit CANCEL command is described in Chapter 10.

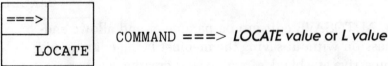

COMMAND ===> *LOCATE value or L value*

Positions the screen to the next line starting with the stated number or characters, as illustrated in Figure 8.4(a). In this case we are ed-

```
EDIT --- BT05686.SOURCE.COBOL(CCPZ002) - 01.03 ------------- COLUMNS 007 078
COMMAND ===> l 25200                                         SCROLL ===> PAGE
008800          15 WS-TIME-HH          PIC 9(02).
008900          15 WS-TIME-MM          PIC 9(02).
009000          15 WS-TIME-SS          PIC 9(02).
009100 *
009200 01 FLAGS.
009300          12 F-EDIT              PIC X(01) VALUE 'G'.
009400          12 F-END               PIC X(01) VALUE 'N'.
009500          12 F-FOUND             PIC X(01) VALUE ' '.
009600 *
009700 01 ATTRIBUTES.
009800          12 BRT-UNPROT-MDT       PIC X(01) VALUE 'I'.
009900          12 BRT-UNPROT-NUM-MDT   PIC X(01) VALUE 'R'.
010000 *
010100 01 RECORD-IO-AREA.
010200          12 CUSTMAST.
010300 *           NOTE: ACCOUNT-NUM IS REDUNDANT SINCE PRIMARY IS AT DISP. 0
010400             15 CUSTMAST-PRIMARY-KEY         PIC X(08) VALUE SPACE.
010500             15 CUSTMAST-NON-KEY-INFO.
010600                18 CUSTMAST-ADDRESS.
010700                   21 CUSTMAST-STREET-DIR     PIC X(01) VALUE SPACE.
010800                   21 CUSTMAST-STREET-NAME    PIC X(15) VALUE SPACE.
010900                   21 CUSTMAST-HOUSE-NUM      PIC 9(05) VALUE 0.
```

FIGURE 8.4a   Requesting LOCATE of a specific line during edit

```
EDIT --- BT05686.SOURCE.COBOL(CCPZ002) - 01.03 ------------- COLUMNS 007 078
COMMAND ===>                                                 SCROLL ===> PAGE
025200          PERFORM 02000-PREPARE.
025300          PERFORM 02100-RECEIVE-MAP-ROUTINE.
025400 *
025500 01100-PROCESS.
025600          PERFORM 02200-SETUP.
025700          PERFORM 02300-SEND-MAP-ROUTINE.
025800          PERFORM 02400-CICS-RETURN-W-TRANSID THRU 02400-EXIT.
025900 *
026000 01200-END.
026100          IF F-END      = 'T'
026200             PERFORM 02500-CICS-TRANSFER      THRU 02500-EXIT.
026300
026400          PERFORM 02600-CICS-SEND-TEXT        THRU 02600-EXIT.
026500          PERFORM 99999-CICS-RETURN           THRU 99999-EXIT.
026600 /
026700 02000-PREPARE.
026800          IF EIBCALEN = 0
026900 *           CONTROL IS FROM CICS OR ANOTHER APPLICATION PGM
027000             MOVE SPACE        TO CA-FULL-COMMON-AREA
027100             MOVE HIGH-VALUES TO CA-ACCEPTED-KEY
027200             MOVE 'U1'         TO SC-FUNCTION-REQ
027300          ELSE
```

FIGURE 8.4b   TSO/ISPF response to line locate request

iting a COBOL program of several hundred lines and want to position the screen so that the display starts at line 25200. Figure 8.4(b) shows the result of LOCATE command use.

If within a member list, LOCATE will position the screen so that the list starts with a stated member or partial member name. If, for example, we are within a member list for a COBOL library, and want to position the display so that it begins with members starting with the letters "HGA," we can use the LOCATE command:

```
COMMAND  ===>  L  HGA
```

After pressing the ENTER key the display jumps forward so that the first member name starting with HGA is at the top of the screen.

LOCATE and FIND have a similarity of purpose; LOCATE seeks and locates a line based on specification of its leading part, such as line number or member name, whereas FIND searches for character-string content in any part of the lines.

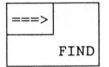

COMMAND ===> *FIND value, F value, F value ALL*

Seeks a character string within a member being edited or within a member list. Figure 8.5(a) illustrates the use of FIND to cause the screen to move to the position in a COBOL program in which the word PROCEDURE occurs. Figure 8.5(b) shows the screen after pressing the ENTER key for this FIND. Surrounding apostrophes are necessary when the value sought is a character string containing special characters such as the hyphen or asterisk; the apostrophes can always be entered to avoid having to recall when they are necessary.

FIND searches the member from the position of the cursor within it forward to the end. If the entire member is to be searched, FIND must be preceded by either a LOCATE 1 or L 1 command, or positioned to the beginning of the member by putting MAX or M on the command line and pressing the PF7 "scroll backward" function key.

One execution of the FIND command finds the value and also loads a buffer with it. Pressing the PF5 REPEAT FIND key will then seek each subsequent occurrence of the value.

FIND with the ALL option is handy in correcting source code

```
EDIT --- BT05686.SOURCE.COBOL(CCPZ002) - 01.03 -------------- COLUMNS 007 078
COMMAND ===> f 'procedure'                                 SCROLL ===> PAGE
****** *************************** TOP OF DATA ****************************
000100  IDENTIFICATION DIVISION.
000200  PROGRAM-ID.    CCPZ002.
000300 *               CICS UPDATE - Z002 - BASIC UPDATE  TEST NUMCHECK
000400 *               VERSION 1   - LAST UPDATE: 02/01/87 ORIGINAL
000500 *               VERSION 2   - LAST UPDATE: 03/02/87 TAV ADDED DELETE LOG
000600 *               VERSION 3   - LAST UPDATE: 03/06/87 TAV PGM CNTL  TE LOG
000700 *               VERSION 4   - LAST UPDATE: 03/07/87 TAV NUMCHECK  TE LOG
000800  AUTHOR.        T VARI.
000900  DATE-WRITTEN.  FEB   1988.
001000  DATE-COMPILED.
001100 *REMARKS:        STYLE: BASIC    - INTRODUCTORY CONCEPTS TAKE
001200 *                                  PRIORITY OVER EFFICIENCY
001300 *                                - SYSTEM DOES     TRANSFER INFO
001400 *               DESIGN: PREPROCESS/PROCESS OR END
001500 *                       PREPROCESS- NO CA (CICS('Z002') OR XCTL'D)
001600 *                               CA    (FROM THIS TRANS('Z002')
001700 *                       PROCESS  - RETURN W/TRANS AFTER SEND
001800 *                       END      - XCTL TO END/ OR RETURN TO CICS
001900 *               MAP I/O :RECEIVE  - FULL RECEIVE
002000 *                                - MAPFAIL IGNORE/HANDLE SHORT
002100 *                       SEND      - FULL SEND
```

FIGURE 8.5a Requesting FIND of a given character string and scrolling to the first line containing it

```
EDIT --- BT05686.SOURCE.COBOL(CCPZ002) - 01.03 -------- CHARS 'PROCEDURE' FOUND
COMMAND ===>                                               SCROLL ===> PAGE
023500 /
023600  PROCEDURE DIVISION.
023700 *   ACCORDING TO INSTALLATION STANDARDS FOR CICS PROGRAM TESTING,
023800 *   AT LEAST THE FIRST EXECUTION OF CODE SHOULD BE UNDER CEDF.
023900 *   THE LAST COMMAND MUST BE A CICS RETURN.
024000 *   (CICS RETURN AFTER MAINLIN IS OPTIONAL)
024100 *   THE FIRST LINE SHOULD BE :
024200        IF EIBAID = DFHPF2 PERFORM 01200-END.
024300 /
024400  00000-MAINLINE.
024500        PERFORM 01000-PREPROCESS.
024600        IF F-END = 'N'
024700            PERFORM 01100-PROCESS
024800        ELSE
024900            PERFORM 01200-END.
025000 *
025100  01000-PREPROCESS.
025200        PERFORM 02000-PREPARE.
025300        PERFORM 02100-RECEIVE-MAP-ROUTINE.
025400 *
025500  01100-PROCESS.
025600        PERFORM 02200-SETUP.
```

FIGURE 8.5b TSO/ISPF response to character-string FIND request

errors from a printed compile because it lets you skip directly to lines containing errors via their content. Here is a particularly expedient way to do this, that not only finds the lines in error, but "pops them out" visibly:

1.   Exclude all the lines in a member using an edit line exclude command such as X9999 on the first line. This excludes the line on which it is coded, and the next 9998 lines.

2.   Do a FIND . . . ALL for the incorrect source code phrase or value.

Excluded lines are processed for FIND or CHANGE; when found, they are made visible. You can then correct them with a minimum of navigation within the member and screen. The RESET primary editing command can be used to restore all excluded lines to view. This technique saves time if you are working on a dial-up line into a remote computer, since it minimizes the amount of screen transmission.

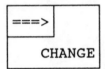

COMMAND ===> *CHANGE 'old' 'new' ALL*

Changes the next occurrence of the "old" value to the "new" value. If the optional word ALL is included on the command, all occurrences of the old value, from the current position in the item onward, are changed to the new value. A bright " == CHG>" message is placed in the line number area of any line on which a change has been made, and the screen display is advanced so that the first of the changed lines is displayed. To process the entire member, make sure that you are positioned at the top of it when you execute the CHANGE command.

Figures 8.6(a) and 8.6(b) depict an editing screen before and after execution of a CHANGE command. In this case, we are positioned at the top of a member within a COBOL library, and desire to change all occurrences of RPT1-PAGECOUNT to RPT1-PGCT.

If there is enough blank area for the replacement text to be housed without affecting the placement of text following, the text following is not moved. This is very considerate treatment by a text editor and helps to preserve the indentation conventions customarily found in source code, even when mass changes are made. On

```
EDIT --- BT05686.SOURCE.COBOL(PSD187) --------------------- COLUMNS 007 078
COMMAND ===> c 'rpt1-pagecount' 'rpt1-pgct' all              SCROLL ===> PAGE
008800 *                                                              008800
008900 * * * * * * * * * * * * * * * * * * * * * * * * * * * * * * *  008900
009000 *                                                              009000
009100  01   RPT1-HOUSEKEEPING.                                       009100
009200       12   RPT1-RECORD-COUNT         PIC 9(5)      VALUE ZERO.  009200
009300       12   RPT1-LINES-REMAINING      PIC S9(2)     COMP-3 VALUE ZERO. 009300
009400       12   RPT1-PAGECOUNT            PIC S9(3)     VALUE ZERO.  009400
009500 *                                                              009500
009600  01   WS-VR-AREA.                                              009600
009700       12   WS-BASE-SALARY            PIC 9(4)V99   VALUE ZERO.  009700
009800       12   WS-OVERTIME               PIC 9(4)V99   VALUE ZERO.  009800
009900       12   WS-GROSS-PAY              PIC 9(4)V99   VALUE ZERO.  009900
010000       12   WS-REG-OT-PAY             PIC 9(4)V99   VALUE ZERO.  010000
010100       12   WS-REG-OT-HR              PIC 9(4)V99   VALUE ZERO.  010100
010200       12   WS-DOUBLE-OT-PAY          PIC 9(4)V99   VALUE ZERO.  010200
010300       12   WS-DOUBLE-OT-HR           PIC 9(4)V99   VALUE ZERO.  010300
010400 *                                                              010400
010500  01   WS-VR-TOTALS.                                            010500
010600       12   WS-TO-BASE-SALARY         PIC 9(5)V99   VALUE ZERO.  010600
010700       12   WS-TO-OVERTIME            PIC 9(5)V99   VALUE ZERO.  010700
010800       12   WS-TO-GROSS-PAY           PIC 9(5)V99   VALUE ZERO.  010800
010900 *                                                              010900
```

FIGURE 8.6a Requesting a mass change ("change all") of a character string during edit

```
EDIT --- BT05686.SOURCE.COBOL(PSD187) ---------------- CHARS 'RPT1-PAGECOUNT' C
COMMAND ===>                                                 SCROLL ===> PAGE
008800 *                                                              008800
008900 * * * * * * * * * * * * * * * * * * * * * * * * * * * * * * *  008900
009000 *                                                              009000
009100  01   RPT1-HOUSEKEEPING.                                       009100
009200       12   RPT1-RECORD-COUNT         PIC 9(5)      VALUE ZERO.  009200
009300       12   RPT1-LINES-REMAINING      PIC S9(2)     COMP-3 VALUE ZERO. 009300
==CHG>       12   RPT1-PGCT                 PIC S9(3)     VALUE ZERO.  009400
009500 *                                                              009500
009600  01   WS-VR-AREA.                                              009600
009700       12   WS-BASE-SALARY            PIC 9(4)V99   VALUE ZERO.  009700
009800       12   WS-OVERTIME               PIC 9(4)V99   VALUE ZERO.  009800
009900       12   WS-GROSS-PAY              PIC 9(4)V99   VALUE ZERO.  009900
010000       12   WS-REG-OT-PAY             PIC 9(4)V99   VALUE ZERO.  010000
010100       12   WS-REG-OT-HR              PIC 9(4)V99   VALUE ZERO.  010100
010200       12   WS-DOUBLE-OT-PAY          PIC 9(4)V99   VALUE ZERO.  010200
010300       12   WS-DOUBLE-OT-HR           PIC 9(4)V99   VALUE ZERO.  010300
010400 *                                                              010400
010500  01   WS-VR-TOTALS.                                            010500
010600       12   WS-TO-BASE-SALARY         PIC 9(5)V99   VALUE ZERO.  010600
010700       12   WS-TO-OVERTIME            PIC 9(5)V99   VALUE ZERO.  010700
010800       12   WS-TO-GROSS-PAY           PIC 9(5)V99   VALUE ZERO.  010800
010900 *                                                              010900
```

FIGURE 8.6b TSO/ISPF response to mass change during edit

```
EDIT --- BT05686.SOURCE.COBOL(PSD187) -------------------- ERROR - CHARS 'FROM'
COMMAND ===> c all 'from' 'fromfromfromfromfromfromfromfrom'  SCROLL ===> PAGE
008500 *                                                          *   008500
==ERR> *          OBTAINED FROM A COPY LIBRARY.  REFERENCE TO THESE  *   008600
008700 *          FIELDS IN THE PROCEDURE DIVISION REQUIRES           *   008700
008800 *          QUALIFICATION SUCH AS "STD-HEADING-INFO OF VR-TOP".* 008800
008900 * * * * * * * * * * * * * * * * * * * * * * * * * * * * * *  *   008900
009000 *                                                               009000
009100 01  VALID-REPORT-HOUSEKEEPING.                                  009100
009200     12  VR-RECORD-COUNT        PIC 9(5)     VALUE ZERO.         009200
009300     12  VR-LINES-REMAINING     PIC S9(2)    COMP-3 VALUE ZERO.  009300
009400     12  VR-PAGE-COUNT          PIC S9(3)    VALUE ZERO.         009400
009500 *                                                               009500
009600 01  WS-VR-AREA.                                                 009600
009700     12  WS-BASE-SALARY         PIC 9(4)V99  VALUE ZERO.         009700
009800     12  WS-OVERTIME            PIC 9(4)V99  VALUE ZERO.         009800
009900     12  WS-GROSS-PAY           PIC 9(4)V99  VALUE ZERO.         009900
010000     12  WS-REG-OT-PAY          PIC 9(4)V99  VALUE ZERO.         010000
010100     12  WS-REG-OT-HR           PIC 9(4)V99  VALUE ZERO.         010100
010200     12  WS-DOUBLE-OT-PAY       PIC 9(4)V99  VALUE ZERO.         010200
010300     12  WS-DOUBLE-OT-HR        PIC 9(4)V99  VALUE ZERO.         010300
010400 *                                                               010400
010500 01  WS-VR-TOTALS.                                               010500
010600     12  WS-TO-BASE-SALARY      PIC 9(5)V99  VALUE ZERO.         010600
```

FIGURE 8.6c Error message returned by TSO/ISPF when a change cannot be made due to insufficient room on the line being changed

the other hand, if enough room does not exist on a line to accommodate the new value, an error message is returned in the line number area, as illustrated in Figure 8.6(c).

The search and replacement values are surrounded with apostrophes. If the ALL specification is omitted, only the first occurrence of the old value will be found and replaced, and the *PF6 REPEAT CHANGE* function key can be pressed to find and change each subsequent occurrence.

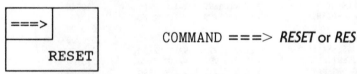

COMMAND ===> *RESET* or *RES*

Allows the removal from the screen of the edit PROFILE, column rulers, ==CHG> messages, and TSO/ISPF messages concerning the lack of member statistics or presence of lowercase letters in the text. RESET also cancels insert mode, if insert mode is on.

```
EDIT --- BT05686.SOURCE.COBOL(PSD192) - 01.64 -------------- COLUMNS 001 072
COMMAND ===> reset                                         SCROLL ===> PAGE
****** **************************** TOP OF DATA ******************************
==MSG> -CAUTION- PROFILE CHANGED TO "NUMBER ON COB" (FROM "NUMBER OFF").
==MSG>         DATA HAS VALID COBOL NUMBERS.
==MSG> -CAUTION- PROFILE CHANGED TO "CAPS OFF" (FROM "CAPS ON") BECAUSE DATA
==MSG>         CONTAINS LOWER CASE CHARACTERS.
==MSG> -CAUTION- DATA CONTAINS INVALID (NON-DISPLAY) CHARACTERS.  USE COMMAND
==MSG>         ===> FIND P'.'        TO POSITION CURSOR TO THESE CHARACTERS.
000100  IDENTIFICATION DIVISION.
000200  PROGRAM-ID.    PROG4.
000300  AUTHOR.        AGNES K ANTKOWIAK.
000400  INSTALLATION.  DEPAUL UNIVERSITY.
000500  DATE-WRITTEN.  MAY 1, 1988.
000600  DATE-COMPILED.
000700 *REMARKS.       THIS PROGRAM READS A FILE OF RECORDS AND PRODUCES
000800 *               A VALID RECORD LISTING AND AN ERROR LISTING THAT
000900 *               IS PRINTED WITH PAGE AND COLUMN HEADINGS.
001000 *
001100  ENVIRONMENT DIVISION.
001200  CONFIGURATION SECTION.
001300  SOURCE-COMPUTER.   IBM-4381.
001400  OBJECT-COMPUTER.   IBM-4381.
001500  SPECIAL-NAMES.     C01 IS PAGE-EJECT.
```

FIGURE 8.7 TSO/ISPF messages placed at top of data set when an edit is started; these may be removed by placing RESET on the command line and pressing ENTER

Figure 8.7 illustrates a TSO/ISPF edit screen received when editing of a member with content not matching the edit profile is begun. The profile in this case apparently specifies "NUMBER OFF," but the member actually has COBOL line numbers, so TSO/ISPF changes the profile to accommodate this. In addition, the member contains both lowercase letters and non-displayable characters. TSO/ISPF posts "information-only" messages at the top of the data area indicating the presence of these rather unusual conditions, some of several potential such conditions. Messages such as these can be eliminated by placing RESET in the COMMAND ===> field and pressing the *ENTER* key.

COMMAND ===> *UNNUM* or *UNN*

Different types of partitioned data sets used as TSO/ISPF libraries can contain actual, in-the-record line numbers in up to three

places, depending on their type. Job control language can contain optional line numbers in columns 73 through 80 of each card image, called "standard" numbers. COBOL source code can contain either or both COBOL line numbers in columns 1 through 6 and standard numbers in columns 73 through 80. Command lists, called CLISTs, may have line numbers in positions 1 through 8.

UNNUM removes all line numbers from a member regardless of of the type of line numbers that exist. The line numbers that appear on the left side of the TSO edit screen do not disappear when this is done, however. Instead, they become relative line numbers that start with 000001 for the first line, and increment upward by 1 for each line. These are not contained in any portion of the record.

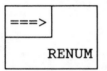

COMMAND ===> *RENUM STD or COB* or *REN STD or COB*

Renumbers the lines of a member. RENUM has two useful parameters, STD or COB, which are relevant only after an UNNUM.

If a COBOL member is UNNUMed, and then a RENUM COB is executed, TSO will apply COBOL line numbers in positions 1 through 6 of each record. For all subsequent work, only RENUM need be executed in order to renumber the COBOL line numbers; once the choice of line number placement is made, it is established and known. Using COBOL line numbers on COBOL members gives an advantage: columns 7 through 78 of source code lines carrying COBOL numbers are presented on the screen by default. This makes it unnecessary to move the cursor long distances to reach the source code A and B margins in columns 8 and 12.

RENUM STD after an UNNUM applies line numbers to columns 73 through 80, of relevance only to job control language statements.

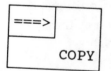

COMMAND ===> *COPY membername*

COPY allows the copying in of a member or part of a member. Membername is the name of a member in the partitioned data set being edited. If the command is given in the form illustrated in Figure 8.8, while in a completely empty edit screen—as is the case when a new member is being created—all of membername is

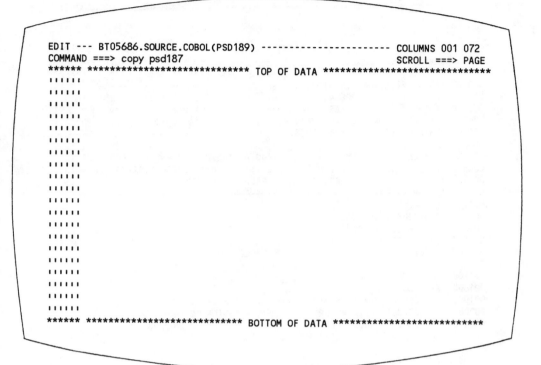

```
EDIT --- BT05686.SOURCE.COBOL(PSD189) --------------------- COLUMNS 001 072
COMMAND ===> copy psd187                                    SCROLL ===> PAGE
****** ***************************** TOP OF DATA ******************************
''''''
''''''
''''''
''''''
''''''
''''''
''''''
''''''
''''''
''''''
''''''
''''''
''''''
''''''
''''''
''''''
''''''
''''''
''''''
''''''
****** **************************** BOTTOM OF DATA ***************************
```

FIGURE 8.8   Requesting copy of a member within the same library to start a new member

brought in. This is a handy way to begin a new program patterning it on an existing one.

If COPY is issued with a member name following, as in Figure 8.9, when editing a member that already has contents, it is necessary to indicate where the incoming text is to be placed. Either an A, for "after," or a B, for "before," must be placed in the line number area of one line in the member being edited.

COPY may be issued on the command line without a member name following, in order to copy in text from a different partitioned data set. Such an operation, bringing in text external to the PDS being edited, is illustrated in Figure 8.10(a). In this case, a second screen, called the EDIT - COPY screen, is presented to allow specification of the source of copied-in text. Figure 8.10(b) illustrates the EDIT - COPY screen. It provides several fill-in fields, and starts with a line at the top identifying the data set into which the copied text will be inserted.

```
EDIT --- BT05686.SOURCE.COBOL(PSD187) - 01.00 -------------- COLUMNS 007 078
COMMAND ===> copy comment                                   SCROLL ===> PAGE
****** **************************** TOP OF DATA ******|**********************
000100  IDENTIFICATION DIVISION.
000200  PROGRAM-ID.    PROG4.                         COMMENT is a member in
000300  AUTHOR.        AGNES K ANTKOWIAK.             the same library, and
000400  INSTALLATION.  DEPAUL UNIVERSITY.             is copied in after the A
000500  DATE-WRITTEN.  MAY 1, 1988.
000600  DATE-COMPILED.
000700 *REMARKS.        THIS PROGRAM READS A FILE OF RECORDS AND PRODUCES
000800 *                A VALID RECORD LISTING AND AN ERROR LISTING THAT
000900 *                IS PRINTED WITH PAGE AND COLUMN HEADINGS.
a 1000 * ─────────────────────────────────────────────────────────────
001100  ENVIRONMENT DIVISION.
001200  CONFIGURATION SECTION.
001300  SOURCE-COMPUTER.   IBM-4381.
001400  OBJECT-COMPUTER.   IBM-4381.
001500  SPECIAL-NAMES.     C01 IS PAGE-EJECT.
001600 *
001700  INPUT-OUTPUT SECTION.
001800  FILE-CONTROL.
001900      SELECT PAYROLL-DATA-FILE      ASSIGN TO P4DATA.
002000      SELECT VALID-REPORT           ASSIGN TO P4VALREP.
002100      SELECT ERROR-REPORT           ASSIGN TO P4ERRREP.
```

FIGURE 8.9 Requesting copy of a member within the same library to a point after a given line in existing member

In an external COPY it is possible to limit the lines of text to be copied in. However, in order to specify the lines to be copied, you need to know the line numbers they carry and must specify whether they are COBOL line numbers (columns 1–6), standard line numbers (columns 73–80), or relative line numbers, the TSO/ISPF-applied line count. This makes an external COPY something for which you must plan, not something possible to do "on the fly" as the thought strikes while editing a member.

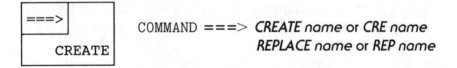

COMMAND ===> *CREATE name* or *CRE name*
REPLACE name or *REP name*

Allows writing out a portion of the member currently being edited to a new member in the same or other partitioned data set. If the

```
EDIT --- BT05686.SOURCE.COBOL(PSD187) - 01.00 -------------- COLUMNS 007 078
COMMAND ===> copy  ┌──────────┐                              SCROLL ===> PAGE
****** ************************** TOP OF DATA ****** │**********************
000100  IDENTIFICATION DIVISION.                     │
000200  PROGRAM-ID.     PROG4.                        │
000300  AUTHOR.         AGNES K ANTKOWIAK.         ┌──┴────────────────────────┐
000400  INSTALLATION.   DEPAUL UNIVERSITY.        │ Leaving off the member name │
000500  DATE-WRITTEN.   MAY 1, 1988.              │ gives you next copy screen   │
000600  DATE-COMPILED.                            └─────────────────────────────┘
000700 *REMARKS.        THIS PROGRAM READS A FILE OF RECORDS AND PRODUCES
000800 *                A VALID RECORD LISTING AND AN ERROR LISTING THAT
000900 *                IS PRINTED WITH PAGE AND COLUMN HEADINGS.
a 1000 *
001100  ENVIRONMENT DIVISION.
001200  CONFIGURATION SECTION.
001300  SOURCE-COMPUTER.    IBM-4381.
001400  OBJECT-COMPUTER.    IBM-4381.
001500  SPECIAL-NAMES.      C01 IS PAGE-EJECT.
001600 *
001700  INPUT-OUTPUT SECTION.
001800  FILE-CONTROL.
001900      SELECT PAYROLL-DATA-FILE      ASSIGN TO P4DATA.
002000      SELECT VALID-REPORT           ASSIGN TO P4VALREP.
002100      SELECT ERROR-REPORT           ASSIGN TO P4ERRREP.
```

FIGURE 8.10a Requesting copy from another library to a point after a given line in existing member ("external copy")

```
--------------------------- EDIT - COPY ----------------------------------
COMMAND ===>
"CURRENT" DATA SET: BT05686.SOURCE.COBOL(PSD187)

FROM ISPF LIBRARY:
   PROJECT ===> BT05677          ┌──────────────────────────────────┐
   LIBRARY ===> SOURCE           │ The copied item can now come from  │
   TYPE    ===> COBOL            │ a different library and partial     │
   MEMBER  ===> comment          │ copies can be designated            │
                                 └──────────────────────────────────┘
FROM OTHER PARTITIONED OR SEQUENTIAL DATA SET:
   DATA SET NAME   ===>
   VOLUME SERIAL   ===>           (If not cataloged)

DATA SET PASSWORD ===>           (If password protected)

LINE NUMBERS (BLANK FOR ENTIRE MEMBER OR SEQUENTIAL DATA SET):
   FIRST LINE      ===> 10
   LAST LINE       ===> 16
   NUMBER TYPE     ===> relative (STANDARD, COBOL, or RELATIVE)

Press ENTER key to copy.
Enter END command to cancel copy.
```

FIGURE 8.10b TSO/ISPF response to external copy request, screen allowing specification of source for the copy

89

destination is to be the same library, the member name is stated. If the destination is another library, the member name is omitted from the command line, causing presentation of a screen to specify the data set and member, very similar to that provided for an external COPY.

The CREATE command is issued in the form illustrated in Figure 8.11. The beginning and ending lines to be copied out must have been marked previously with the characters CC in the line number area. If MM is used to denote the start and end of text in the member being edited, the lines are deleted after being copied out, in effect "moving" them out to the destination.

CREATE will fail if the member named as the destination of the write action already exists. If that is the case, the REPLACE command can be issued instead with exactly the same format. The existing member will be replaced with the material designated to be copied or moved out.

```
EDIT --- BT05686.SOURCE.COBOL(PSD187) - 01.00 -------------- COLUMNS 007 078
COMMAND ===> create psd200                              SCROLL ===> PAGE
****** ***************************** TOP OF DATA ******************************
cc 100   IDENTIFICATION DIVISION.
000200   PROGRAM-ID.    PROG4.
000300   AUTHOR.        AGNES K ANTKOWIAK.
000400   INSTALLATION.  DEPAUL UNIVERSITY.
000500   DATE-WRITTEN.  MAY 1, 1988.
000600   DATE-COMPILED.
000700   *REMARKS.        THIS PROGRAM READS A FILE OF RECORDS AND PRODUCES
000800   *                A VALID RECORD LISTING AND AN ERROR LISTING THAT
000900   *                IS PRINTED WITH PAGE AND COLUMN HEADINGS.
001000   *
001100   ENVIRONMENT DIVISION.
001200   CONFIGURATION SECTION.                  ┌─────────────────────────┐
001300   SOURCE-COMPUTER.    IBM-4381.           │ Marked block is copied  │
001400   OBJECT-COMPUTER.    IBM-4381.           │ out to a new member named│
001500   SPECIAL-NAMES.      C01 IS PAGE-EJECT.  │ PSD200 in the library   │
cc 600   *                                       └─────────────────────────┘
001700   INPUT-OUTPUT SECTION.

001900      SELECT PAYROLL-DATA-FILE      ASSIGN TO P4DATA.
002000      SELECT VALID-REPORT           ASSIGN TO P4VALREP.
002100      SELECT ERROR-REPORT           ASSIGN TO P4ERRREP.
```

FIGURE 8.11   Requesting CREATE of new member in same library housing copy of specified lines of existing member

COMMAND ===> *HEX ON* or *HEX OFF*

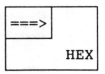

HEX ON changes the display into one which displays the hexa-decimal representation of each line as well as the character representation. Figures 8.12(a) and 8.12(b) show the same screen in normal HEX OFF mode, and with HEX ON.

Within edit, HEX ON allows entry of values that have no printable representation. The hexadecimal presentation of data is enterable and takes precedence over the character display of the data. Replacing the hexadecimal value for a byte actually replaces the byte; the character representation on the screen will change to match the hexadecimal values when ENTER is pressed. This is how unprintable values can be entered for special printing effects, such as rulings and borders on laser printers, and a way that screen attribute control bytes can be generated for CICS programs.

HEX ON is especially useful in TSO 1, the browse, since it can serve as a quick substitute for a paper dump. It is even possible to examine the contents of load modules, composed of undefined-length records, using TSO 1 BROWSE with HEX ON.

COMMAND ===> *SAVE*

Placing the word SAVE on the COMMAND line and pressing the ENTER key, as illustrated in Figure 8.13(a), causes the member being edited to be written out. TSO/ISPF responds with a message confirming that the member has been saved, as indicated in Figure 8.13(b). This is called an explicit SAVE, as opposed to the automatic SAVE performed by TSO/ISPF when the AUTOSAVE edit profile parameter is set on.

If AUTOSAVE, a part of the edit profile, is ON, and RECOVERY is ON, manual saving of a member is not necessary to insure against loss of work. Due to the manner in which members are stored in a partitioned data set, excessive SAVEs are not desirable. Each explicit SAVE causes more of the available PDS space to be consumed, forcing the need for more frequent reorganization.

The first time a new member is created and lines are being entered into it, SAVE should be issued once, early in the session. This

```
EDIT --- BT05686.SOURCE.DATA(RHYME) - 01.01 ---------------- COLUMNS 001 072
COMMAND ===>                                                 SCROLL ===> PAGE
****** **************************** TOP OF DATA ******************************
000001 0123456789
000002 THE TIME HAS COME,
000003 THE WALRUS SAID,
000004 TO TALK OF MANY THINGS.
000005 SAILING SHIPS, AND
000006 SEALING WAX, AND
000007 CABBAGES AND KINGS.
000008 !@#$%^&*()_+){  ":';
000009 abcdefghijklmnop
000010 qrstuvwxyz
****** ************************** BOTTOM OF DATA ****************************
```

FIGURE 8.12a TSO 2 edit screen in normal HEX OFF mode

```
EDIT --- BT05686.SOURCE.DATA(RHYME) - 01.01 ---------------- COLUMNS 001 072
COMMAND ===> hex on                                          SCROLL ===> PAGE
****** **************************** TOP OF DATA ******************************


-------------------------------------------------------------------------------
000001 0123456789
       FFFFFFFFFF4444444444444444444444444    If you change the hex     4444444444
       0123456789000000000000000000000000    representation, the       0000000000
------------------------------------------    character data will       ----------
000002 THE TIME HAS COME,                     change.  This is how
       ECC4ECDC4CCE4CDDC64444444444444444    you can enter values      4444444444
       38503945081203645B00000000000000    for which no keys         0000000000
------------------------------------------    exist on the keyboard     ----------
000003 THE WALRUS SAID,
       ECC4ECDDEE4ECCC64444444444444444444444444444444444444444444444444444444
       38506139420219480000000000000000000000000000000000000000000000000000000
-------------------------------------------------------------------------------
000004 TO TALK OF MANY THINGS.
       ED4ECDD4DC4DCDE4ECCDCE444444444444444444444444444444444444444444444444444
       360313206604158038957280000000000000000000000000000000000000000000000000
-------------------------------------------------------------------------------
```

FIGURE 8.12b TSO 2 edit screen with HEX ON in effect

```
EDIT --- BT05686.SOURCE.COBOL(CSCZ001) - 01.00 ------------- COLUMNS 007 078
COMMAND ===> save ─────────────────────                       SCROLL ===> PAGE
008800        12 FILLER                  PIC X(05)       VALUE  'WSCA'.
008900        12 CA-FULL-COMMON-AREA.
009000           15 FILLER               PIC X(100).
009100  01  CA-LENGTH
009200                          ┌──────────────────────────────────┐
009300 /                        │ Explicit SAVE command copies the │
009400  LINKAGE SECTION.        │ member being edited to disk without │
009500  01  DFHCOMMAREA         │ ending the edit session.  But use of │
009600 *                        │ RECOVERY ON is recommended instead │
009700 *                        │ of repeated usage of SAVE if data │
009800  PROCEDURE DIVISION.     │ loss due to interruption is a concern │
009900 *                        └──────────────────────────────────┘
010000 * TO PREVENT DFHEOF (CICS EGG ON FACE) IT IS MANDATORY TO CODE
010100 * A CICS RETURN AT THE END OF YOUR SOURCE AND TO EXECUTE
010200 * THE PROGRAM(FOR AT LEAST THE FIRST TIME)UNDER CEDF.
010300 * IT IS RECOMMENDED TO CODE A "NON-EXECUTING" RETURN
010400 * AT THE END OF YOUR MAINLINE. IT'S HIGHLY RECOMMENDED TO CODE THE
010500 * FOLLOWING 'SAFETY VALVE'.
010600        IF EIBAID = DFHPF2 EXEC CICS RETURN END-EXEC.
010700 /
010800  00000-MAINLINE SECTION.
010900        PERFORM 01000-PREPROCESS.
```

FIGURE 8.13a   Requesting explicit SAVE of a member being edited

```
EDIT --- BT05686.SOURCE.COBOL(CSCZ001) - 01.00 ---------- ┌──────────────────────┐
COMMAND ===>                                              │ MEMBER CSCZ001 SAVED │
                                                          └──────────────────────┘
008800        12 FILLER                  PIC X(05)       VALUE  'WSCA'.
008900        12 CA-FULL-COMMON-AREA.
009000           15 FILLER               PIC X(100).
009100  01  CA-LENGTH                    PIC S9(04) COMP VALUE
009200                                        +100.
009300 /
009400  LINKAGE SECTION.
009500  01  DFHCOMMAREA                  PIC X(100).
009600 *
009700  PROCEDURE DIVISION.
009800 * TO PREVENT DFHEOF (CICS EGG ON FACE) IT IS MANDATORY TO CODE
009900 * A CICS RETURN AT THE END OF YOUR SOURCE AND TO EXECUTE
010000 * THE PROGRAM(FOR AT LEAST THE FIRST TIME)UNDER CEDF.
010100 * IT IS RECOMMENDED TO CODE A 'NON-EXECUTING' RETURN
010200 * AT THE END OF YOUR MAINLINE. IT'S HIGHLY RECOMMENDED TO CODE THE
010300 * FOLLOWING 'SAFETY VALVE'.
010400        IF EIBAID = DFHPF2 EXEC CICS RETURN END-EXEC.
010500 /
010600  00000-MAINLINE SECTION.
010700        PERFORM 01000-PREPROCESS.
010800        IF F-END = 'N'
010900           PERFORM 01100-PROCESS
```

FIGURE 8.13b   TSO/ISPF response to explicit SAVE request

establishes the member in the partitioned data set directory and allows the RECOVERY option, if ON, to take effect. RECOVERY cannot occur unless the member being edited has an entry in the PDS directory; without this early manual SAVE a new member is at peril of loss due to interruption even with RECOVERY ON.

=9=

Viewing Job Output Online

```
+--------+     +--------+
| 3.8    |     | SDSF   |
|--------+     +--------+
| OUTLIST|        SPOOL|
+--------+     +--------+
```

TSO/ISPF provides two means of examining the output from a job online. One of these is called the TSO 3.8 OUTLIST facility, and the other is SDSF, the Spool Display and Search Facility. Either one or the other is used by programmers and end users to see the results of a job without waiting for paper print. Both provide the means to shunt output to print or to delete it without printing it.

Whether you use TSO 3.8 OUTLIST or SDSF to view output depends on your installation and guidelines established for programmers and end users. If both are present on your computer system and no restrictions apply to their use, SDSF will probably operate consistently faster and prove to be more convenient.

```
              +--------+
              | 3.8    |
              +--------+
              | OUTLIST|
              +--------+
```

TSO 3.8: OUTLIST FACILITY

The outlist facility is a part of TSO/ISPF and is the more limited of the online print viewing mechanisms. In order to view print using TSO 3.8, it must have been sent to a special print output class, usually class X. This is called the "held class," as opposed to class A, which normally prints without the possibility of TSO 3.8 OUTLIST viewing. For example, if compiler output emerging at a DDname of //SYSPRINT is directed in this manner, it prints on paper:

```
//SYSPRINT DD SYSOUT=A
```

In order to hold output so that it can be viewed using TSO 3.8 OUTLIST, we only have to change this coding to:

```
//SYSPRINT DD SYSOUT=X
```

It will remain accessible to the outlist function until we either delete it or requeue it to print.

As a convenience that makes it unnecessary to change many lines of job control language when output is sometimes desired to print, and sometimes desired to be held, MVS JCL allows us to code an asterisk instead of a letter:

```
//SYSPRINT DD SYSOUT=*
```

the asterisk "refers back" to the value on the JOB statement MSGCLASS value. Coding such as this also results in such output being held:

```
//FSBT686A JOB AK00COMP,'DP2-JANOSSY',CLASS=E,
// MSGCLASS=X,
// MSGLEVEL=(1,1),NOTIFY=BT05686
```

If MSGCLASS in this JOB statement is changed to A, all print outputs coded with an asterisk will print. Hardcoded SYSOUT=A parameters within the JCL are not affected by this and always print. MSGCLASS itself dictates where MVS-generated items, such as its reporting on job handling, are printed.

Chapter 12 of a companion book in this series, *Practical MVS JCL for Today's Programmer* (John Wiley & Sons, 1987) provides detailed information on the MVS job control language SYSOUT parameter and its many specialized print options.

When to View Output

The optional NOTIFY parameter on the JOB statement for a job that has been submitted indicates the TSO/ISPF user id that will be notified when the job has completed execution. The message will interrupt your work if you are logged on when it is issued, or will be stored and presented when you next log on:

```
10.12.03 JOB 577 $HASP165 BT05686A ENDED CN(00)
```

or

```
10.45.51 JOB 632 $HASP165 BT05686A ENDED - ABENDED
CN(00)
```

This command line transfer entry will get you directly to the 3.8 screen from any other point within TSO/ISPF:

```
COMMAND  ===>  =3.8
```

After placing =3.8 on the command line, press the ENTER key. Alternatively you can press the PF3 END key, repeatedly if necessary, to get to the main menu, and select 3.8 from it.

Viewing Output

Figure 9.1 is a depiction of the TSO 3.8 screen. It provides five options:

L   Using this you can "list" or see the status of any jobs on the system matching the JOBNAME entered in the middle of the screen. Messages returned by TSO/ISPF in response to option L show your jobs awaiting execution, executing, or fully processed with print yet remaining on the system. JOBNAME is the name immediately following the slashes on the JOB statement.

D   The job matching the JOBNAME and JOBID—JOB number— will be deleted from its held status and not printed.

P   Not normally used, this is one way of causing the job matching the JOBNAME and JOBID to be printed. The R option does the same thing, but allows greater flexibility.

R   Commonly used to shunt held material to print, R "requeues" the material into the print class indicated at the NEW OUTPUT CLASS field. Requeuing a job to class A causes it to be printed.

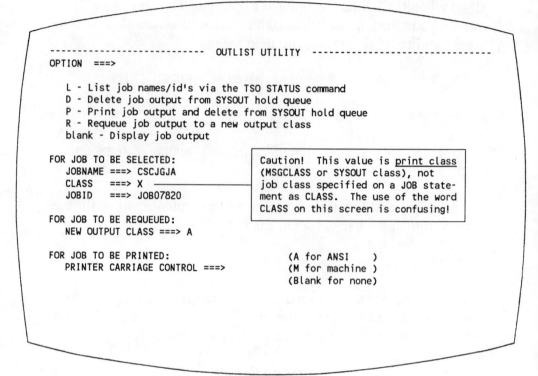

```
------------------------------ OUTLIST UTILITY ------------------------------
OPTION  ===>

    L - List job names/id's via the TSO STATUS command
    D - Delete job output from SYSOUT hold queue
    P - Print job output and delete from SYSOUT hold queue
    R - Requeue job output to a new output class
    blank - Display job output

FOR JOB TO BE SELECTED:            ┌─────────────────────────────────────┐
   JOBNAME ===> CSCJGJA            │ Caution!  This value is print class │
   CLASS   ===> X ─────────────────│ (MSGCLASS or SYSOUT class), not     │
   JOBID   ===> JOB07820           │ job class specified on a JOB state- │
                                   │ ment as CLASS.  The use of the word │
FOR JOB TO BE REQUEUED:            │ CLASS on this screen is confusing!  │
   NEW OUTPUT CLASS ===> A         └─────────────────────────────────────┘

FOR JOB TO BE PRINTED:                        (A for ANSI   )
   PRINTER CARRIAGE CONTROL ===>              (M for machine )
                                              (Blank for none)
```

FIGURE 9.1   TSO 3.8 outlist utility screen for viewing batch job output online

b (blank) The output from the job matching the JOBNAME, print
    CLASS, and JOBID is displayed on the screen.

Using the outlist screen is as simple as tabbing the cursor down
to the JOBNAME field, entering the job name, moving the cursor
down to CLASS and entering X, and moving the cursor down to
the JOBID field, entering the job number in the format JOBnnnnn
or J(nnn), and pressing the *ENTER* key. Figure 9.2 illustrates the
output of a run as it appears on the outlist screen. Carriage control
characters such as plus signs, spaces, zeros, hyphens, and ones do
not cause the same actions on a terminal screen as they do on a
printer, so all material on the screen will appear single-spaced. The
carriage control symbols at the beginning of each line will actually
appear on the screen as you move the display leftward and rightward.

Printed output is usually wider than the 80-character width of
computer terminals. To see the right side of printout, press the

```
OUTLIST LISTING FOR CSCJGJA -------------------------- LINE 000000 COL 001 080
COMMAND ===>                                              SCROLL ===> HALF
******************************** TOP OF DATA *********************-CAPS ON-**
1                         J E S 2  J O B  L O G  --  S Y S T E M  E X P R  --  N
--------- JOB 7820  IEF097I CSCJGJA  - USER CSCJGJ   AND GROUP CSC     ASSIGNED
 15.36.09 JOB 7820  ICH70001I CSCJGJ   LAST ACCESS AT 15:34:10 ON FRIDAY, JULY 8
 15.36.09 JOB 7820  $HASP373 CSCJGJA  STARTED - INIT 4 - CLASS A - SYS EXPR
 15.36.23 JOB 7820  $HASP395 CSCJGJA  ENDED
0------ JES2 JOB STATISTICS ------
- 08 JUL 88 JOB EXECUTION DATE             ┌─────────────────────────────┐
-         72 CARDS READ                    │ Carriage control values in the │
                                           │ first position of printlines may │
-          0 SYSOUT PUNCH RECORDS          │ appear. Use PF11 or the RIGHT  │
-         17 SYSOUT SPOOL KBYTES           │ command to window rightward.   │
-       0.24 MINUTES EXECUTION TIME        └─────────────────────────────┘
       1    //CSCJGJA   JOB 1,'BIN 7 JANOSSY',MSGLEVEL=(1,1),MSGCLASS=X,
            //  NOTIFY=CSCJGJ
            ***
            ***    THIS JCL = CSCJGJ.CSC.CNTL(PRTMUCHO)
            ***
            ***********************************************************
            ***                                                    *
            ***    STEP A -- EXECUTE UTILITY PROGRAM IEBGENER TO    *
            ***               COPY SOME TEST DATA TO "SYSOUT" TO    *
```

FIGURE 9.2   Compile results as viewed online using the TSO 3.8 outlist utility

PF11 scroll right function key (Alt/-). The screen will move rightward the amount indicated in the SCROLL ===> field at the top
of the screen. Pressing PF10 will move the screen leftward again.
Make sure you window right with PF11 when resolving JCL errors;
some are reported in the last part of the printline, not visible in the
first 80 columns of print initially presented by the outlist screen.

TSO/ISPF makes clever use of itself in responding to an outlist
request. It actually takes a temporary copy of the material from the
held queue and invokes the TSO function 1 browse to provide access to it. All of the normal browse manipulations are available,
including the use of PF8 and PF7 for vertical movement and the
FIND and LOCATE commands.

The entries in the several TSO 3.8 OUTLIST fields are retained
by TSO/ISPF when you leave this function. Since programmers
often use the same job name on many runs, this field does not usually have to be changed on the 3.8 screen. Similarly, the held print
class X need not be entered each time the outlist facility is used.

The job number does change, since each job submitted has received a unique number issued by MVS.

The JOB statement for a job contains a parameter named CLASS. This refers to job processing class, not print class. JOBCLASS and print CLASS are different, although each is coded as a single letter, and the letter values are sometimes the same. *The CLASS field on the TSO 3.8 screen refers to print CLASS, not JOBCLASS.*

Requeueing Held Output to Print

After viewing held output with the outlist, press the PF3 END key to end viewing and return to the TSO 3.8 selection screen. If viewing output has been sufficient for your purposes and there is no need to print it, enter D on the command line and press the *ENTER* key. Since the JOBNAME, CLASS, and JOBID fields are retained by TSO/ISPF, merely entering the D to initiate deletion of the material after viewing it is sufficient. The material will be deleted from the MVS output queue and will not print.

If you want to have a printed copy of the material after viewing it, place R on the command line of the TSO 3.8 screen, and make sure that a suitable value is contained in the NEW OUTPUT CLASS field. Normally, an A in the new output class field will be appropriate. The NEW OUTPUT CLASS field is retained by TSO/ISPF, so once entered, it need not be entered again. Pressing the *ENTER* key will now cause the requeuing of the material to the specified output class. Once this is done, the material is not in the held print class and cannot be viewed using the TSO 3.8 outlist facility.

Print directed to the X held queue should be disposed of in a timely manner with either D deletion or R requeueing. Its presence in the held queue depletes the capacity of the system spool, which contains all of the printed output of the computer system.

Checking Job Status

Entering L as the option on the TSO 3.8 outlist screen causes information to be presented about jobs currently on the system carrying job names matching the JOBNAME field. These allow you to determine whether a given job is still executing. This option is handy to use if an output that was specified cannot be found, because TSO 3.8 OUTLIST cannot be used to view the output of a job until it finishes execution.

The L option provides information on all jobs matching the JOB-NAME stated, not just on held output. You can potentially learn of the presence of output on the system with the L option but not be able to examine it with the TSO 3.8 screen if its JCL did not route print output to the held queue, X.

Print Carriage Control Field

The PRINTER CARRIAGE CONTROL field of the TSO 3.8 screen is normally not filled in. This field allows specification of additional carriage control treatment for material being requeued to print with the outlist utility. System and compiler outputs and application program reports already contain carriage control information that will be carried through to print, even though output was held for online viewing.

A Common Outlist Problem for Newcomers

You may initially find that it is impossible to view job output at the TSO 3.8 screen, and be greeted with a message such as this:

```
IKJ56320I NO HELD OUTPUT FOR JOB BT05686A(JOB011763)
IN CLASS A
```

The source of error is the "CLASS A" at the end of the message, which refers to print class. A value in this statement other than X means that JOB class, and not print class, has been entered at the TSO 3.8 screen CLASS field. Held output, viewable with the outlist facility, is almost universally coded as print class X. Change the CLASS field on the TSO 3.8 OUTLIST screen to X and try viewing the output again. It is unfortunate that the MVS JCL terminology relating to class is not clearer and more consistent. CLASS on the JOB statement refers to *job class*, and CLASS on the TSO/ISPF 3.8 screen refers to *print class*, MSGCLASS.

```
SDSF
     SPOOL
```

SDSF: SPOOL DISPLAY AND SEARCH FACILITY

SDSF is not a part of TSO; it was developed in an IBM field division, not its software development center, as a utility for operations personnel to allow viewing the master system log online and to allow issuance of system commands. It is so handy, however, that it has become a feature regularly associated with TSO/ISPF. SDSF may or may not be available in your installation. The features that applications-programming personnel are authorized to access may vary from installation to installation.

SDSF is similar in display presentation to the TSO 3.8 outlist utility but permits viewing any outputs, held or otherwise. SDSF also provides the ability to see partial system allocation/deallocation reports as a job is executed and even the job control language for jobs on the computer system input queue before they begin execution.

Accessing SDSF

SDSF can be selected from the TSO/ISPF main menu or with the transfer feature by entering = S at the command line of any screen. When SDSF is accessed, the SDSF primary option menu depicted in Figure 9.3 is presented.

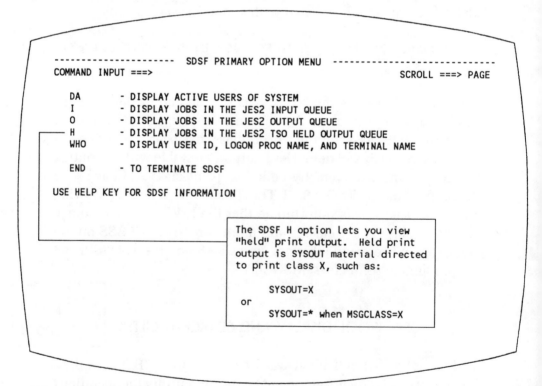

```
-------------------- SDSF PRIMARY OPTION MENU --------------------------------
COMMAND INPUT ===>                                           SCROLL ===> PAGE

    DA        - DISPLAY ACTIVE USERS OF SYSTEM
    I         - DISPLAY JOBS IN THE JES2 INPUT QUEUE
    O         - DISPLAY JOBS IN THE JES2 OUTPUT QUEUE
    H         - DISPLAY JOBS IN THE JES2 TSO HELD OUTPUT QUEUE
    WHO       - DISPLAY USER ID, LOGON PROC NAME, AND TERMINAL NAME

    END       - TO TERMINATE SDSF

USE HELP KEY FOR SDSF INFORMATION


                              The SDSF H option lets you view
                              "held" print output.  Held print
                              output is SYSOUT material directed
                              to print class X, such as:

                                  SYSOUT=X
                              or
                                  SYSOUT=* when MSGCLASS=X
```

FIGURE 9.3   TSO S SDSF primary option menu screen

SDSF lets you monitor the progress of a job from the time it is submitted, through execution; view its output; and then delete or print its output. In order to do this, you need to know whether a job has completed execution, either by keeping track of the job completion notifications from MVS, or by using SDSF itself. To see jobs that have been submitted but have not completed execution, select option I, for "input queue," from the SDSF menu. To see held output from a job that has finished execution, select option H, for "held." To see output directed to the print queue, select option O, for "output."

An SDSF Example

Let's assume you have submitted two jobs a minute or two apart, which have been assigned job number 09371 and 09382, and you have now accessed the SDSF primary option menu. Select I in order to view the input queue, the line of submitted jobs awaiting execution. A screen such as Figure 9.4 will appear.

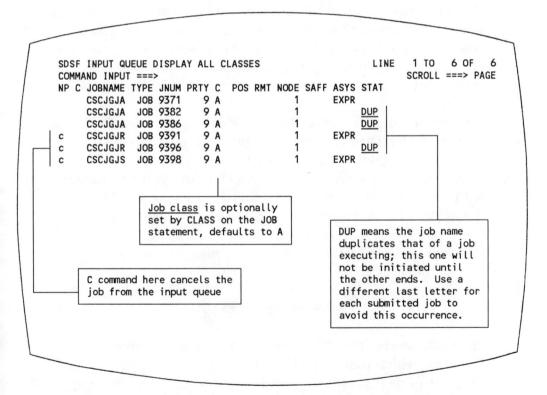

```
SDSF INPUT QUEUE DISPLAY ALL CLASSES                    LINE   1 TO   6 OF   6
COMMAND INPUT ===>                                            SCROLL ===> PAGE
NP C JOBNAME TYPE JNUM PRTY C  POS RMT NODE SAFF ASYS STAT
     CSCJGJA  JOB 9371  9 A        1              EXPR
     CSCJGJA  JOB 9382  9 A        1                   DUP
     CSCJGJA  JOB 9386  9 A        1                   DUP
  c  CSCJGJR  JOB 9391  9 A        1              EXPR
  c  CSCJGJR  JOB 9396  9 A        1                   DUP
  c  CSCJGJS  JOB 9398  9 A        1              EXPR
```

Job class is optionally set by CLASS on the JOB statement, defaults to A

C command here cancels the job from the input queue

DUP means the job name duplicates that of a job executing; this one will not be initiated until the other ends. Use a different last letter for each submitted job to avoid this occurrence.

FIGURE 9.4 SDSF I "input queue" screen listing jobs submitted awaiting execution, and jobs executing

Notice that both of your jobs appear on this screen. One has nothing under the "ASYS" column, and one has an indication such as EXPR. Lack of an indication under ASYS means the job is awaiting execution; an indication in this column means that the job is currently executing.

You can view the material connected with either a job awaiting execution or a job that is executing simply by tabbing the cursor down the I "Input queue" screen and placing an S, for "select," in the column labeled NP. When you press ENTER, you will be presented with the first page of the output as it exists at that point. The output may have intermediate messages on it, only partial outputs, or messages referring to cancellation that will be removed automatically by MVS once the job successfully completes execution. You can move the screen window rightward with the *PF11* key, leftward again with *PF10*, forward with *PF8*, and backward with *PF7*, just as in edit, browse, and the TSO 3.8 OUTLIST facility.

When a job completes execution, it is no longer on the input queue, and is not accessible via the I screen. Instead, if you press *PF3* and return to the SDSF primary option menu, you can select either the H or the O screens. The choice of screen is dictated by whether or not the output has been sent to SYSOUT = X, the **H**eld class, or an **O**utput class such as SYSOUT = A that will automatically print. The H and O screens are nearly identical in layout and use.

Figure 9.5 illustrates the SDSF H held output screen. Each held output will be listed on one line of this screen. To select held output for viewing, tab the cursor down the NP column to the appropriate line, enter an S, and press *ENTER*. You will be presented with the first page of the output, similar to Figure 9.6. Maneuver around within the output listing, moving the screen window rightward with the *PF11* key, leftward again with *PF10*, forward with *PF8*, and backward with *PF7*, just as in edit, browse, and the TSO 3.8 OUTLIST facility.

Printing Output with SDSF

To conclude viewing of held output under SDSF, press the *PF3 END* key, which returns you to the SDSF H held output screen. Output can be disposed of from the held class either by Purging (deleting) it, or Outputting (requeueing) it. The difference in ter-

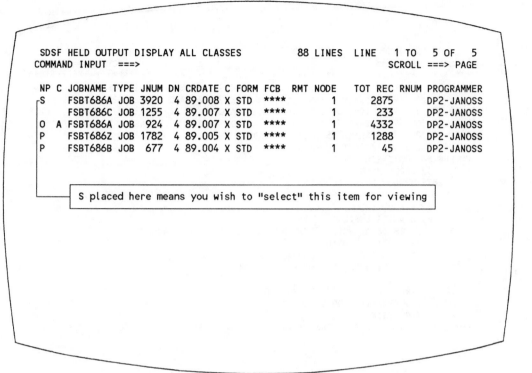

```
SDSF HELD OUTPUT DISPLAY ALL CLASSES            88 LINES  LINE   1 TO   5 OF   5
COMMAND INPUT  ===>                                       SCROLL ===> PAGE

NP C JOBNAME TYPE JNUM DN CRDATE C FORM FCB  RMT NODE    TOT REC RNUM PROGRAMMER
 S    FSBT686A JOB 3920  4 89.008 X STD  ****      1      2875        DP2-JANOSS
      FSBT686C JOB 1255  4 89.007 X STD  ****      1       233        DP2-JANOSS
 O  A FSBT686A JOB  924  4 89.007 X STD  ****      1      4332        DP2-JANOSS
 P    FSBT686Z JOB 1782  4 89.005 X STD  ****      1      1288        DP2-JANOSS
 P    FSBT686B JOB  677  4 89.004 X STD  ****      1        45        DP2-JANOSS
```

┌───┐
│ S placed here means you wish to "select" this item for viewing   │
└───┘

FIGURE 9.5   SDSF H "held output" screen listing completed jobs for which output was designated with print class X

minology between the TSO 3.8 OUTLIST facility and SDSF is unfortunate, but reflects their diverse origins.

To requeue output from the held class to a printing class using SDSF, tab the cursor down the NP column to the appropriate line and place a letter O, for "output," at that point, as illustrated in Figure 9.7. Then tab to the right on the same line to the column labeled C, for "class," and place an A there. This A stands for the print class to which you want to output the material. Press ENTER, and the entry for the item on the SDSF H screen will disappear, indicating that it is no longer in a held class. It will now be printed. If you again want to examine it, you may be able to catch it before it completes printing using the SDSF O screen, viewing print on the output queue.

If you wish to purge an item from the held queue without printing it, tab the cursor down the NP column to the appropriate line, and enter a P, for "purge," as shown in Figure 9.7. Press the ENTER

```
SDSF OUTPUT DISPLAY FSBT686A JOB 3920    2 LINE        0  COLUMNS   2  81
COMMAND INPUT ===>                                       SCROLL ===> PAGE
******************************* TOP OF DATA ********************************
                        J E S 2  J O B  L O G  --  S Y S T E M  E X P R  --  N
-------- JOB 3920  IEF097I FSBT686A - USER BT05686 AND GROUP DP2   ASSIGNED
14.50.59 JOB 3920  ICH70001I BT05686  LAST ACCESS AT 14:49:43 ON THURDSAY, SEPTE
14.51.00 JOB 3920  $HASP373 FSBT686A STARTED - INIT  2 - CLASS E - SYS EXPR
14.52.12 JOB 3920  $HASP395 FSBT686A ENDED
------ JES2 JOB STATISTICS ------
08 SEP 88 JOB EXECUTION DATE
        17 CARDS READ
      2875 SYSOUT PRINT RECORDS
         0 SYSOUT PUNCH RECORDS
       362 SYSOUT SPOOL KBYTES
      1.21 MINUTES EXECUTION TIME
     1      //FSBT686A  JOB 1,'DP2-JANOSSY',CLASS=E,MSGCLASS=X,
            //  NOTIFY=BT05686
            ***    CHANGE RACF SECURITY ON DATA SETS
            ***    BT05686.SOURCE.CNTL(RACFCHG)
            ***
     2      //RACFCHG    EXEC PGM=IKJEFT01
     3      //SYSTSPRT   DD SYSOUT=*
     4      //SYSTSIN    DD *
ICH70001I BT05686  LAST ACCESS AT 14:49:43 ON THURSDAY, SEPTEMBER 8, 1988
```

FIGURE 9.6   Viewing output using SDSF

key, and the output will be purged from the held queue without printing. This operation corresponds to the D "delete" function of the TSO 3.8 OUTLIST facility.

The SDSF H screen can process multiple actions at one time. As Figure 9.7 illustrates, two or more output-to-print and purge actions can be entered on the same SDSF held output screen. When the *ENTER* key is pressed, all of the actions are processed at once.

Viewing Print on the Output Queue

Material already queued for printing to print class A, or another such output print class, but not yet reduced by the operating system to paper, can be viewed by selecting the O screen at the SDSF primary option menu. This results in a screen such as that shown in Figure 9.8. This screen is much like that for held output. It has, however, columns at the right containing information on the number of lines printed and the printer to which the output has been

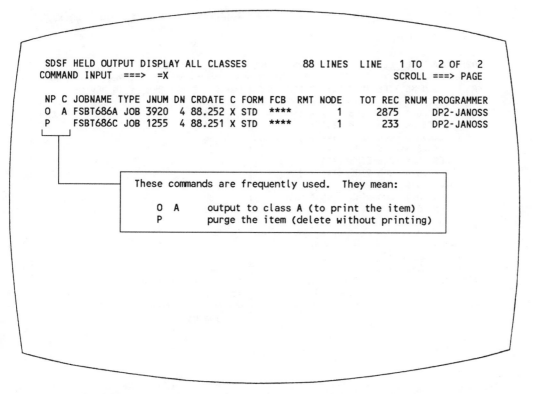

FIGURE 9.7 Using SDSF to requeue held output to print class A

assigned. Lack of an indication in these columns means that the job has not yet started to print; an indication here means that the job is printing. Pressing the *ENTER* key while viewing the SDSF O screen updates the records printed column and shows the progress of printing.

When a job queued for output has been completely printed it is deleted automatically from the output queue. While it is possible to view output awaiting print, the ability to view it is highly time dependent. Output can be deleted from the output queue in the same manner as is done with held output. Move the cursor down the column labeled NP, put a P for "purge" on the line, and press the *ENTER* key.

Split Screen and Output Viewing

TSO/ISPF provides a split screen mode in which the terminal screen is divided into two areas, simulating two logons at once.

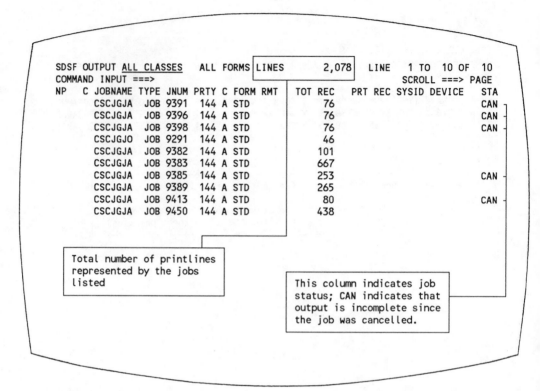

FIGURE 9.8   Using SDSF to view print output in class A, already destined to print but not yet printed

This mode is initiated by placing the cursor near midscreen and pressing the *PF2* key. Once split, the main menu appears on the "new" portion of the screen and can be used to select an operation. You can move the cursor between split screens using the arrow keys or *PF9*, which alternates the cursor between screens while maintaining its position in each. Different functions can be selected in each of the split screens.

You may wish to experiment with split screen mode in connection with the examination of compilation errors and the correction of source code. You cannot simultaneously edit the same partitioned data set member with both portions of the screens. But figure 9.9 illustrates how you can use split screen and SDSF to view the body of the source code listing from a compile as well as the compiler's error messages at the end of the listing bottom. This can speed your identification and resolution of program errors without awaiting printouts.

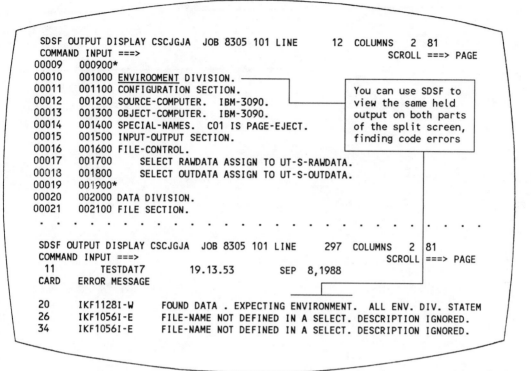

FIGURE 9.9 Using split screen to view top and bottom of same held compile output for online error resolution

To end split screen operation, press the *PF3 END* key in one split screen or the other, and travel up the hierarchy of menus to log off. You can alternatively place =X on the command line and press *ENTER* to log off directly. The remaining screen will once again appear by itself.

═══ 10 ═══

TSO/ISPF Hints and Convenience Features

TSO/ISPF is powerful and so full of features that it can take several months for some of them to become apparent. Here are some especially practical ones that can make a significant difference in ease of use.

FLEXIBLE ENTRY OF A TRANSFER

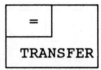

TSO/ISPF allows direct transfer from one functional screen to another using the equal sign = and indication of the desired destination. For example, if you are in TSO 2 EDIT and wish to transfer directly to SDSF to view output, you could put =S on the command line and press the *ENTER* key:

```
COMMAND ===>  =S
```

There is actually no requirement to move the cursor to the command line to make the transfer entry; it can be entered in any field on the screen and will be properly detected, so long as it is not surrounded by apostrophes as part of a data set name. For example, you could indicate a transfer in the ISPF LIBRARY DATA SET name entry field:

```
PROJECT   ===>  BT05686
LIBRARY   ===>  SOURCE
TYPE      ===>  COBOL
MEMBER    ===>  =S
```

This can speed your screen work, especially if your terminal does not provide a convenient *HOME* key to move the cursor to the command line.

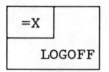

DIRECT LOGOFF WITH =X

While direct transfer between functions with the equal sign = is usually learned quickly, it is easy to overlook the fact that you can also make the logoff selection from the main TSO/ISPF menu the "destination" for a transfer. Placing = X on the command line or on any enterable field on a TSO/ISPF screen will end the TSO/ISPF session directly. Depending on the way your installation has set TSO, this may result in complete logoff, or only return to native mode TSO.

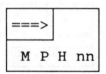

FLEXIBLE SCROLLING WITH COMMAND LINE OVERRIDE

The value contained in the SCROLL field at the upper right corner of the screen governs the amount of forward or backward movement that occurs when the *PF8* forward or *PF7* backward keys are pressed.

Occasions may arise when a different degree of scrolling is desired just once. It is not necessary to alter the value in the SCROLL field to achieve this. Any scrolling value can be entered on the command line to temporarily override the normal scroll value; after one use, TSO/ISPF erases this command line entry. MAX can be entered here and *PF7* pressed to jump to the top of an item being edited; entering MAX at the command line and pressing *PF8* jumps to the bottom of the item. A positive integer number can be entered as well.

For PAGE, HALF, and MAX, it is not necessary to enter the entire word, either in the command line or in the SCROLL field itself. The first letter of each of these words is sufficient.

TSO: PASSTHROUGH COMMAND

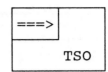

Native mode TSO commands can be entered under ISPF on the command line of any screen simply by prefacing them with the letters "TSO" as illustrated in Figure 10.1.

This capability is quite useful. Some native mode TSO commands that are handy to know about include CANCEL, for batch job cancellation, STATUS, to check on a job without travelling to the 3.8 function, and the SEND command to route brief messages to other personnel.

When a native mode TSO command is invoked from a screen via the TSO passthrough feature, the existing screen is placed on hold and retained. When TSO passthrough has completed, the original screen is automatically restored.

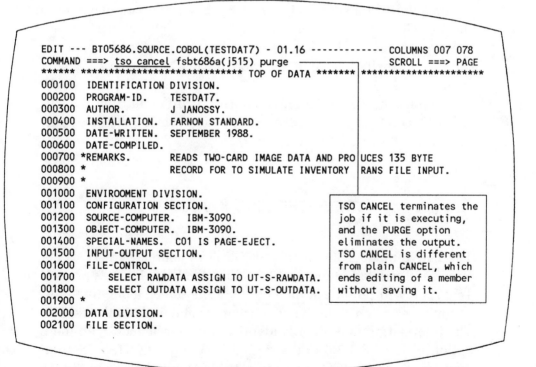

FIGURE 10.1 Native mode TSO "passthrough" command on the COMMAND ===> line

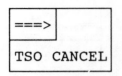

CANCEL: CANCELLING SUBMITTED JOBS

At times you may find it necessary to cancel a batch job already submitted because you discover that it is running too long or producing too much output due to a programming error. The CANCEL command provides the means to do this. If your installation permits programmers to use it, enter it either on the TSO:6 screen—which is nothing more than a blank screen as in native mode TSO—or on the command line of any TSO/ISPF screen. To enter it on the command line, you must preface the command with "TSO" as shown in Figure 10.1.

A job that has not yet started executing can be cancelled, and a job that has started execution can be cancelled. A job that has completed execution obviously cannot be cancelled, but its output can be purged, even if it has started to print. The format of the CANCEL command illustrated in Figure 10.1 shows the command with the PURGE option. If you want to cancel a job but wish to see the system report, job log, and the output produced up to the point of cancellation, omit the word PURGE from the command line.

Note that the TSO CANCEL command is different from the edit CANCEL command that ends an edit without saving the item to its library.

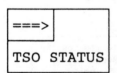

STATUS: CHECKING JOB STATUS

The native mode TSO command STATUS, abbreviated ST, is entered as illustrated in Figure 10.2. When the *ENTER* key is pressed TSO/ISPF will provide at the bottom of the screen a one-line indication for each job of the stated job name that it finds on the system. The information presented is identical to that obtained with the L option of the TSO 3.8 outlist function. Using the STATUS command prefaced by TSO makes it possible to avoid going to the 3.8 screen to check on the status of a job.

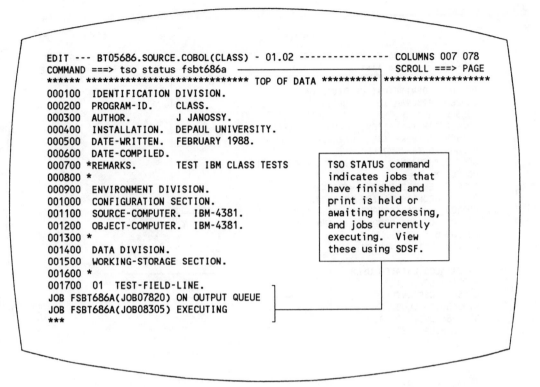

```
EDIT --- BT05686.SOURCE.COBOL(CLASS) - 01.02 --------------- COLUMNS 007 078
COMMAND ===> tso status fsbt686a ────────────────────────    SCROLL ===> PAGE
****** **************************** TOP OF DATA ********** ******************
000100  IDENTIFICATION DIVISION.
000200  PROGRAM-ID.     CLASS.
000300  AUTHOR.         J JANOSSY.
000400  INSTALLATION.   DEPAUL UNIVERSITY.
000500  DATE-WRITTEN.   FEBRUARY 1988.
000600  DATE-COMPILED.
000700 *REMARKS.        TEST IBM CLASS TESTS   ┌─────────────────────┐
000800 *                                       │ TSO STATUS command  │
000900  ENVIRONMENT DIVISION.                  │ indicates jobs that │
001000  CONFIGURATION SECTION.                 │ have finished and   │
001100  SOURCE-COMPUTER.  IBM-4381.            │ print is held or    │
001200  OBJECT-COMPUTER.  IBM-4381.            │ awaiting processing,│
001300 *                                       │ and jobs currently  │
001400  DATA DIVISION.                         │ executing.  View    │
001500  WORKING-STORAGE SECTION.               │ these using SDSF.   │
001600 *                                       └─────────────────────┘
001700  01  TEST-FIELD-LINE.
JOB FSBT686A(JOB07820) ON OUTPUT QUEUE
JOB FSBT686A(JOB08305) EXECUTING
***
```

FIGURE 10.2   Checking processing status of a batch job submitted previously for processing

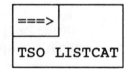

LISTCAT: A LIST OF YOUR TSO/ISPF DATA SETS

The TSO LISTCAT command stands for "list catalog entries" and provides a way to check the system catalog for data sets related to the TSO logon identifier. It is entered on the command line as shown in Figure 10.3 and the *ENTER* key is then pressed. In response, TSO/ISPF provides a listing of the data sets known to MVS named with the TSO identifier as the high order qualifier, or front part. Data sets allocated by TSO for its own use will appear in this list, such as the log and list data sets, and should be ignored.

LISTCAT is adequate to see the names of cataloged data sets associated with your TSO user id, but the TSO/ISPF 3.4 DATA SET LIST utility function is much more powerful. TSO 3.4 allows display of these data set names and provides more information, the

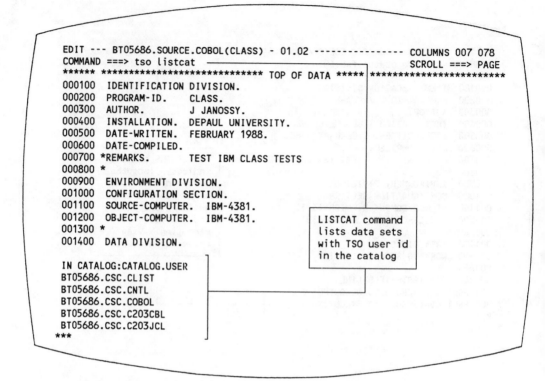

```
EDIT --- BT05686.SOURCE.COBOL(CLASS) - 01.02 --------------- COLUMNS 007 078
COMMAND ===> tso listcat                                      SCROLL ===> PAGE
****** *************************** TOP OF DATA ***** *************************
000100   IDENTIFICATION DIVISION.
000200   PROGRAM-ID.    CLASS.
000300   AUTHOR.        J JANOSSY.
000400   INSTALLATION.  DEPAUL UNIVERSITY.
000500   DATE-WRITTEN.  FEBRUARY 1988.
000600   DATE-COMPILED.
000700  *REMARKS.       TEST IBM CLASS TESTS
000800  *
000900   ENVIRONMENT DIVISION.
001000   CONFIGURATION SECTION.
001100   SOURCE-COMPUTER.  IBM-4381.
001200   OBJECT-COMPUTER.  IBM-4381.           LISTCAT command
001300  *                                      lists data sets
001400   DATA DIVISION.                        with TSO user id
                                               in the catalog
IN CATALOG:CATALOG.USER
BT05686.CSC.CLIST
BT05686.CSC.CNTL
BT05686.CSC.COBOL
BT05686.CSC.C203CBL
BT05686.CSC.C203JCL
***
```

FIGURE 10.3   Using TSO LISTCAT command to generate a list of all data sets for a TSO ID

means to specify other high order name qualifiers and to narrow the list to specific disk devices. In addition, it provides the facility to select any of several functions to be performed upon a data set by pointing to its name with the cursor.

SEND: SENDING A MESSAGE

TSO provides an electronic mail facility, albeit a limited one. It is possible to send a brief message to another TSO user as illustrated in Figure 10.4. Under TSO/ISPF this can be entered on the command line of any screen by prefacing the SEND with the letters TSO; SEND can also be entered without the prefacing "TSO" on the TSO 6 native mode TSO screen.

Messages are limited to 115 characters. When sent via the command line TSO option, the message must be even shorter due to

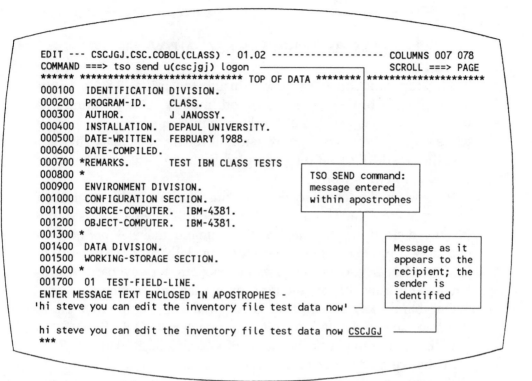

```
EDIT --- CSCJGJ.CSC.COBOL(CLASS) - 01.02 ------------------- COLUMNS 007 078
COMMAND ===> tso send u(cscjgj) logon ─────────────────┐      SCROLL ===> PAGE
****** ****************************** TOP OF DATA ********│********************
000100   IDENTIFICATION DIVISION.                       │
000200   PROGRAM-ID.    CLASS.                           │
000300   AUTHOR.        J JANOSSY.                        │
000400   INSTALLATION.  DEPAUL UNIVERSITY.                │
000500   DATE-WRITTEN.  FEBRUARY 1988.                    │
000600   DATE-COMPILED.                                   │
000700  *REMARKS.       TEST IBM CLASS TESTS          ┌─────────────────────┐
000800  *                                             │ TSO SEND command:   │
000900   ENVIRONMENT DIVISION.                        │ message entered     │
001000   CONFIGURATION SECTION.                       │ within apostrophes  │
001100   SOURCE-COMPUTER.  IBM-4381.                  └─────────────────────┘
001200   OBJECT-COMPUTER.  IBM-4381.
001300  *                                             ┌─────────────────────┐
001400   DATA DIVISION.                               │ Message as it       │
001500   WORKING-STORAGE SECTION.                     │ appears to the      │
001600  *                                             │ recipient; the      │
001700   01   TEST-FIELD-LINE.                         │ sender is           │
ENTER MESSAGE TEXT ENCLOSED IN APOSTROPHES -           │ identified          │
'hi steve you can edit the inventory file test data now' ┘ └─────────────────┘

hi steve you can edit the inventory file test data now CSCJGJ ─────────────────┘
***
```

FIGURE 10.4 Using the SEND command to send a short message to another TSO user (see also Appendix D)

the limited command line area. Use of a CLIST to prompt for and send the message, as illustrated in Appendix D, also makes it possible to send a full-length message. TSO automatically "signs" the logon id of the sender on every message.

A message appears immediately on the screen of the recipient if he or she is logged on. If the recipient is not logged on, the message is stored until he or she does log on. Messages cannot be retrieved or filed, and they appear only once. A message is usually too short to convey much information, but it can prompt someone to use TSO 1 or TSO 2 to access a shared data set into which a full message has been keyed. This is one means of communicating project information between participants in a development environment and is especially useful when the participants are separated geographically.

If no recipient logon id is indicated in the SEND command, the message is sent to the computer console operator.

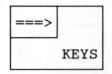

KEYS: REDEFINING PF KEYS ANYWHERE

TSO setup function 0.3 is used during the initial TSO account setup process to view and, if desired, modify PF key settings, as discussed in Chapter 2. But the key definition screen can also be accessed from any other point, without losing your place, by putting the word KEYS on the command line; the letters TSO are *not* placed before this word.

PF keys can be set to any desired command normally entered on the command line. This fact and the TSO/ISPF-wide access to the PF key definitions via the KEYS command make it possible to change settings to customize keys for especially productive editing. While not nearly as powerful as microcomputer keyboard macro-key redefinitions, PF key redefinition is easy and convenient.

One handy key redefinition is illustrated in Figure 10.5. Here, PF12 has been redefined to emit the characters TSO ST BT05686A, which is a way to check the status of jobs named BT05686A. TSO is the native mode indicator, and ST is the abbreviation of the STATUS command. In one action, pressing PF12 will now cause status information to be provided as if TSO ST BT05686A has been entered on the command line and the ENTER key pressed.

Any character string assigned to a PF key is prefaced to the contents of the command line at the time the PF key is pressed. A convenient redefinition of a PF key is to invoke a command procedure, or CLIST, that performs a useful computation. In Appendix D, the command line entry to execute a CLIST out of your own CLIST library is illustrated, as is the way to redefine a PF key to invoke it. A computational CLIST that you invoke often can be made more convenient to use in this manner.

PF keys definitions for the Spool Display and Search Facility product, SDSF, are stored apart from those of TSO/ISPF. SDSF takes defaults similar to those of ISPF, but you may have to use the KEYS command while within SDSF to change the definitions of its PF keys.

PF key definitions established within TSO/ISPF or SDSF apply only to these products. The PF keys have no meaning in native "READY mode" TSO. Similarly, CICS programs have complete control over the handling of program function keys. The definition

```
------------------- PF KEY DEFINITION - ALTERNATE KEYS ------------------------
COMMAND ===>

NOTE: The definitions below apply only to terminals with 24 PF keys.

PF1  ===> HELP
PF2  ===> SPLIT
PF3  ===> END
PF4  ===> PRINT
PF5  ===> RFIND
PF6  ===> RCHANGE
PF7  ===> UP
PF8  ===> DOWN
PF9  ===> SWAP
PF10 ===> LEFT
PF11 ===> RIGHT
PF12 ===> tso st bt05686a

INSTRUCTIONS:
  Press ENTER key to process changes and display primary keys.
  Enter END command to process changes and exit.
```

FIGURE 10.5   Using KEYS facility to redefine PF keys, and setting PF key to TSO STATUS command

of the *PF* keys discussed here and that you establish using setup screen 0.3 or the KEYS command has no bearing on how CICS programs respond to these keys.

Key definitions established under the now obsolete SPF version of TSO/ISPF may be lost when an installation upgrades to ISPF; they must be reestablished manually. This is a minor loss that may affect you if your installation is still running SPF and then converts to ISPF.

EXEC: EXECUTING A CLIST FROM YOUR OWN LIBRARY

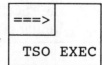

TSO command lists, or CLISTs, provide an interpreted language similar in some respects to BASIC. The CLIST language can be used within TSO to develop interactive routines accessible only in this environment. Computational aids, message distribution mechanisms, and routines that "compose" JCL from prompts answered by the terminal operator are some of the things that can be developed as CLISTs.

CLISTs are usually installed in a special system library so that they may be invoked by their up-to-eight-character name. But the TSO native mode passthrough command can be used in conjunction with the EXEC command to invoke a CLIST from your own CLIST library, without having to first install the CLIST. Appendix D discusses the means to do this, as well as the assignment of the invocation of such a CLIST to a *PF* key. You can thus speed access to CLISTs you develop or use, such as computational routines for disk file blocking and space calculation, VSAM/IDCAMS control statement formation, and other tasks as discussed in Appendix D.

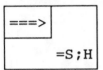

STACKING COMMAND LINE ENTRIES

More than one TSO command can be entered on the command line at one time by separating commands from one another with the command delimiter character specified on the TSO/ISPF 0.1 screen, as illustrated in Figure 10.6. Here, the status of a job is being checked, a TSO listcat obtained, and the status of another job is checked. This is a rather contrived example, however, and this type of command stacking is not commonly useful.

Command stacking can be used to speed the process of logging off when your installation sets TSO/ISPF to regard the selection of X from the main menu as a return to native mode TSO instead of complete logoff. But in this case you must use a different final command delimiter, the field mark symbol at the upper right corner of a real 3270-type terminal keyboard, as illustrated in Figure 10.7. This is necessary because the TSO/ISPF command delimiter symbol is effective only within TSO/ISPF itself; after execution of =X, the TSO/ISPF session has been ended. The system-defined field delimiter of the 3270 terminal family is the field mark.

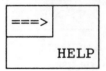 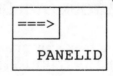

TSO TUTORIAL AND PANELID

A tutorial on TSO/ISPF is accessible via main menu function T or from any screen with the *PF1* key. The tutorial screens can be

```
EDIT --- CSCJGJ.CSC.COBOL(CLASS) - 01.02 ------------------ COLUMNS 007 078
COMMAND ===> tso st cscjgja;tso listcat;tso st cscjgjp        SCROLL ===> PAGE
****** **************************** TOP OF DATA *****************************
000100   IDENTIFICATION DIVISION.
000200   PROGRAM-ID.     CLASS.
000300   AUTHOR.         J JANOSSY.
000400   INSTALLATION.   DEPAUL UNIVERSITY.
000500   DATE-WRITTEN.   JULY 1988.
000600   DATE-COMPILED.
000700   *REMARKS.        DEMONSTRATE IBM NUMERIC/ALPHABETIC CLASS TESTS.
000800   *
000900   ENVIRONMENT DIVISION.
001000   CONFIGURATION SECTION.
001100   SOURCE-COMPUTER.   IBM-4381.
001200   OBJECT-COMPUTER.   IBM-4381.
001300   *
001400   DATA DIVISION.
001500   WORKING-STORAGE SECTION.
001600   *
001700   01   TEST-FIELD-LINE.
001800        12 FILLER                 PIC X(20)   VALUE SPACES.
001900        12 TEST-FIELD-GROUP.
002000           15 TEST-9              PIC 9(5).
002100           15 FILLER             PIC X(2)    VALUE SPACES.
```

FIGURE 10.6 Stacking multiple commands on the command line using a command delimiter

printed for study away from the terminal using the hardcopy print key to the left of the 3270 keyboard, if your terminal is serviced by a controller to which a local printer is attached. Alternatively, images of the screen can be placed into the list data set for batch printing by placing the word PRINT on the command line and pressing the ENTER key, or by assigning the word "print" to a program function key.

The tutorial can be slightly frustrating to follow because it does not provide any identification on screens to tie them into groups or subject areas. But a unique identifier in the upper left corner of every tutorial screen can be made visible by issuing the command PANELID on the command line, as shown in Figure 10.8, and pressing the ENTER key. This toggles the panel identifier on for each screen displayed afterward, which appears with the identifier of the TSO/ISPF panel as shown in Figure 10.9.

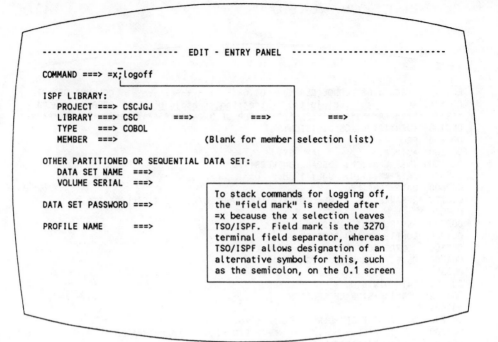

FIGURE 10.7 Stacking commands for logoff from TSO/ISPF on the command line using the field mark delimiter

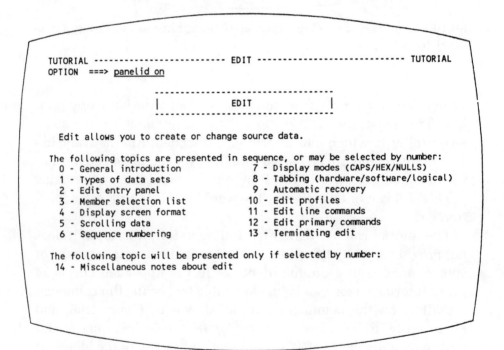

FIGURE 10.8 Setting the panel identifier field on using the PANELID command; PANELID OFF turns it off again

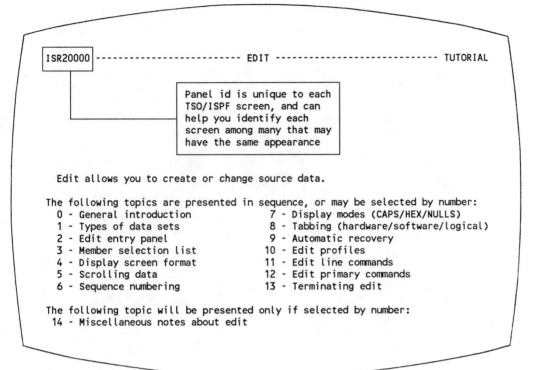

FIGURE 10.9 Result of setting the panel identifier on during use of the help screens or TSO tutorial

The display of the panel identifier can be ended by putting PANELID OFF on the command line and pressing the *ENTER* key; the screen returns to its normal format. The PANELID setting reverts to non-display of the panel identifier after the end of the ISPF session.

=== PART **3** ===

TSO/ISPF GENERAL UTILITY FUNCTIONS

Function 3 can be selected from the TSO/ISPF main menu to access TSO/ISPF utilities. When this is done, the menu on the reverse side of this page is presented.

From this screen several general utility functions are accessible. You can also get to any of them directly by entering the equal sign immediate transfer indication = followed by "3.n" on the command line on any TSO/ISPF screen, and pressing *ENTER*. In this case "n" is the desired function number on the TSO 3 menu screen. For example, to transfer directly to the copy/move utility, place = 3.3 on the command line of any screen and press *ENTER*.

A programmer or end user can perform nearly all actions necessary to manage source code and job control language libraries with the TSO/ISPF utilities. Options exist to copy items, allocate, catalog, uncatalog, or delete members or data sets, and to view the contents of a disk volume table of contents. These functions have supplanted the batch execution of utilities for these purposes, making batch OS utilities such as IEBUPDTE and IEHPROGM almost irrelevant to most personnel.

In this part, separate chapters are dedicated to the TSO 3.1 PDS library member utility, TSO 3.2 data set utilities, TSO 3.3 copy/move utility, and TSO 3.4 data set list utility. Chapter 15 covers the several means of obtaining hardcopy print from TSO/ISPF.

```
------------------------- UTILITY SELECTION MENU -------------------------
OPTION ===>

    3.1  LIBRARY    - Library utility:
                            Print index listing or entire data set
                            Print, rename, delete, or browse members
                            Compress data set
    3.2  DATASET    - Data set utility:
                            Display data set information
                            Allocate, rename, or delete entire data set
                            Catalog or uncatalog data set
    3.3  MOVE/COPY  - Move or copy members or datasets
    3.4  CATALOG    - Catalog management:
                            Display or print catalog entries
                            Initialize or delete user catalog alias
    3.5  RESET      - Reset statistics for members of ISPF library
    3.6  HARDCOPY   - Initiate hardcopy output
    3.7  VTOC       - Display or print VTOC entries for a DASD volume
    3.8  OUTLIST    - Display, delete, or print held job output
```

=== 11 ===

TSO 3.1: PDS Library Member Utility

TSO 3.1 is called the library utility because its options affect individual members of a partitioned data set. Using its options, it is possible to view, print, rename, or delete members. Figure 11.1 illustrates the TSO 3.1 screen. You can proceed directly to the TSO 3.1 screen from anywhere else within TSO/ISPF by placing =3.1 on the command line and pressing the ENTER key.

TSO 3.1: BROWSE, PRINT, RENAME, AND DELETE

The member list option of the TSO 3.1 screen is a convenient and powerful means of manipulating partitioned data set members. It is accessed by entering the name of a TSO library partitioned data set at the ISPF LIBRARY area on the TSO 3.1 screen and leaving both the member name and COMMAND = = => field blank. When the ENTER key is pressed, a list of the members in the partitioned data set is presented, as depicted in Figure 11.2.

Moving the cursor down the left side of the member list, you can enter one of several codes on a line to process the member:

B Selects the member for browsing (viewing) with no ability to edit it

P Prints the member by copying it to the list data set, which is automatically submitted for print when the TSO/ISPF session is ended

```
----------------------------- LIBRARY UTILITY -------------------------------
OPTION  ===>

   C - Compress data set               P - Print member
   X - Print index listing             R - Rename member
   L - Print entire data set           D - Delete member
   blank - Display member list         B - Browse member

ISPF LIBRARY:
   PROJECT ===> BT05686
   LIBRARY ===> SOURCE
   TYPE    ===> CNTL
   MEMBER  ===>                (If option "P", "R", "D", or "B" selected)
   NEWNAME ===>                (If option "R" selected)

OTHER PARTITIONED OR SEQUENTIAL DATA SET:
   DATA SET NAME  ===>
   VOLUME SERIAL  ===>         (If not cataloged)

DATA SET PASSWORD ===>         (If password protected)
```

FIGURE 11.1 TSO 3.1 library utility dealing with partitioned data set members

```
LIBRARY  CSCJGJ.CSC.CNTL --------------------------------------------------
COMMAND ===>                                          SCROLL ===> PAGE
   NAME      RENAME  VER.MOD  CREATED    LAST MODIFIED  SIZE  INIT  MOD   ID
   INTER2            01.00  87/12/04  87/12/04 18:54    12    12    0 CSCJGJ
   JCLBOX            01.00  85/09/29  85/09/29 11:18     5     5    0 CSCJGJ
   JCLINK            01.01  88/03/06  88/03/06 15:36    54    54    1 CSCJGJ
   JCLINKGO          01.00  88/03/06  88/03/06 15:32    66    66    0 CSCJGJ
   JERROR1           01.00  88/01/25  88/01/25 10:49    16    16    0 CSCJGJ
   JGJREORG          01.06  87/10/08  87/10/15 10:31    40    24   39 CSCJGJ
   JOBCARD           01.00  88/03/22  88/03/22 15:53     2     2    0 CSCJGJ
   JUNK              01.00  86/02/15  86/02/15 23:05    13    13    0 CSCJGJ
   LOADCFIL          01.03  88/04/05  88/04/05 13:50    36    37    0 CSCJGJ
   MACHIN            01.08  87/02/24  88/02/09 16:13     8     4    8 CCPN00
   MACHIN2           01.00  88/02/09  88/02/09 16:17     9     9    0 CCPN00
   MACHJOB           01.08  86/10/27  88/02/09 16:06    14     9    9 CCPN00
   MESSAGE           01.00  87/10/04  87/10/04 17:45     8     8    0 CSCJGJ
   MLIST044          01.02  85/09/28  85/09/28 14:45    75     1    0 CSCJGJ
   MYALLO            01.05  86/02/20  88/01/06 16:06    14    20    7 CSCJGJ
   MYCLINK           01.16  86/02/20  88/03/15 13:30    27    39    0 CSCJGJ
   MYMACH            01.02  87/10/30  88/02/09 16:18    13    13    2 CCPN00
   MYOPEN            01.03  86/10/04  87/10/13 21:35    13    12    5 CSCJGJ
   MYPTPCH           01.04  85/09/21  88/02/16 16:23    16    16   16 CCPN00
   MYRACF            01.00  88/03/15  88/03/15 12:55    14    14    0 CCPN00
   NAMES5            01.01  85/11/05  85/11/23 12:18    14    14   14 CSCSMS
```

FIGURE 11.2 TSO 3.1 member list screen for member browse, print, rename, and delete

128

R   Renames a member with the new name you supply
in the RENAME column or field

D   Deletes a member, with no prompt for confirmation
of the delete action

You can initiate the printing of more than one member, rename others, and delete still others on the same member list; just move the cursor to the appropriate lines and make the necessary entries before pressing the *ENTER* key. Figure 11.3(a) illustrates several of these actions; Figure 11.3(b) shows how TSO/ISPF responds by placing a short confirmation message in the RENAME column for each affected member.

When viewing the member list via the 3.1 function, the standard vertical movement *PF* keys work as usual. Pressing the *PF8* key causes the display to move forward the number of lines indicated in the SCROLL = = => field or command line. Pressing the *PF7* key causes the display to move backward this amount in the member list. MAX or M can be placed on the command line prior to pressing either *PF8* or *PF7* to jump to the bottom or top of the member list. The highlighted TSO/ISPF response messages remain in the member list as you move through it.

Browse, print, rename, and delete can also be initiated for a member using the library utility screen itself, by keying in the member name, and a new name if necessary. This manner of selection is expedient if only one member is to be processed. When the *ENTER* key is pressed for such an action, TSO/ISPF responds with a confirmation message at the upper right corner of the screen, as illustrated in Figure 11.4. The hardcopy utility, TSO function 3.6, can also print one member at a time, but initiates the print immediately rather than at the end of the ISPF session.

Indicating the deletion of a member does not prompt for any verification of the intention to delete it. When the D option is selected, the named member is deleted at the next *ENTER* key or *PF* key action, and it cannot be recovered.

A renamed member will not immediately appear in the member list under its new name; it will appear in the list under that name in member list screens generated subsequently. The name of one member cannot be changed to the name of another member.

```
LIBRARY  CSCJGJ.CSC.CNTL -----------------------------------/--------------------
COMMAND ===>                                                 SCROLL ===> PAGE
    NAME     RENAME  VER.MOD  CREATED    LAST MODIFIED   SIZE  INIT   MOD    ID
    INTER2           01.00    87/12/04   87/12/04 18:54   12    12     0  CSCJGJ
    JCLBOX           01.00    85/09/29   85/09/29 11:18    5     5     0  CSCJGJ
  p JCLINK           01.01    88/03/06   88/03/06 15:36   54    54     1  CSCJGJ
    JCLINKGO         01.00    88/03/06   88/03/06 15:32   66    66     0  CSCJGJ
    JERROR1          01.00    88/01/25   88/01/25 10:49   16    16     0  CSCJGJ
  d JGJREORG         01.06    87/10/08   87/10/15 10:31   40    24    39  CSCJGJ
    JOBCARD          01.00    88/03/22   88/03/22 15:53    2     2     0  CSCJGJ
  d JUNK             01.00    86/02/15   86/02/15 23:05   13    13     0  CSCJGJ
    LOADCFIL         01.03    88/C4/05   88/04/05 13:50   36    37     0  CSCJGJ
    MACHIN           01.08    87/02/24   88/02/09 16:13    8     4     8  CCPN00
    MACHIN2          01.00    88/02/09   88/02/09 16:17    9     9     0  CCPN00
    MACHJOB          01.08    86/10/27   88/02/09 16:06   14     9     9  CCPN00
  r MESSAGE  msg001  01.00    87/10/04   87/10/04 17:45    8     8     0  CSCJGJ
    MLIST044         01.02    85/09/28   85/09/28 14:45   75     1     0  CSCJGJ
    MYALLO           01.05    86/02/20   88/01/06 16:06   14    20     7  CSCJGJ
  d MYCLINK          01.16    86/02/20   88/03/15 13:30   27    39     0  CSCJGJ
    MYMACH           01.02    87/10/30   88/02/09 16:18   13    13     2  CCPN00
  d MYOPEN           01.03    86/10/04   87/10/13 21:35   13    12     5  CSCJGJ
    MYPTPCH          01.04    85/09/21   88/02/16 16:23   16    16    16  CCPN00
    MYRACF           01.00    88/03/15   88/03/15 12:55   14    14     0  CCPN00
    NAMES5           01.01    85/11/05   85/11/23 12:18   14    14    14  CSCSMS
```

FIGURE 11.3a Requesting deletion, print, and member rename in combination using the TSO 3.1 member list screen

```
LIBRARY  CSCJGJ.CSC.CNTL -------------------------------------------------------
COMMAND ==                                                   SCROLL ===> PAGE
    NAME    | RENAME  |VER.MOD  CREATED    LAST MODIFIED   SIZE  INIT   MOD    ID
    INTER2  |         |01.00    87/12/04   87/12/04 18:54   12    12     0  CSCJGJ
    JCLBOX  |         |01.00    85/09/29   85/09/29 11:18    5     5     0  CSCJGJ
    JCLINK  |*PRINTED |01.01    88/03/06   88/03/06 15:36   54    54     1  CSCJGJ
    JCLINKGO|         |01.00    88/03/06   88/03/06 15:32   66    66     0  CSCJGJ
    JERROR1 |         |01.00    88/01/25   88/01/25 10:49   16    16     0  CSCJGJ
    JGJREORG|*DELETED |
    JOBCARD |         |01.00    88/03/22   88/03/22 15:53    2     2     0  CSCJGJ
    JUNK    |*DELETED |
    LOADCFIL|         |01.03    88/04/05   88/04/05 13:50   36    37     0  CSCJGJ
    MACHIN  |         |01.08    87/02/24   88/02/09 16:13    8     4     8  CCPN00
    MACHJOB |         |01.08    86/10/27   88/02/09 16:06   14     9     9  CCPN00
    MESSAGE |*RENAMED |
    MLIST044|         |01.02    85/09/28   85/09/28 14:45   75     1     0  CSCJGJ
    MYALLO  |         |01.05    86/02/20   88/01/06 16:06   14    20     7  CSCJGJ
    MYCLINK |*DELETED |
    MYMACH  |         |01.02    87/10/30   88/02/09 16:18   13    13     2  CCPN00
    MYOPEN  |*DELETED |
    MYPTPCH |         |01.04    85/09/21   88/02/16 16:23   16    16    16  CCPN00
                └──────┐
                       │  Result of member print, delete, and rename requests
```

FIGURE 11.3b TSO/ISPF response to request for member deletion, print, and rename

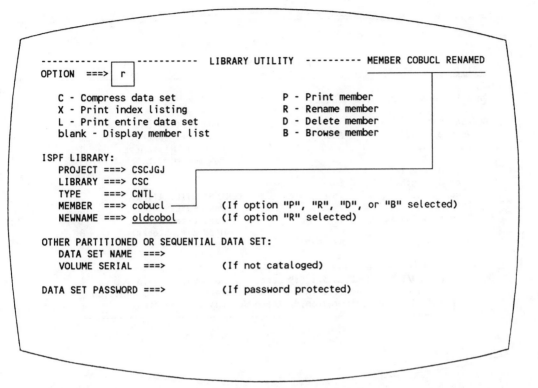

```
----------------        ---------- LIBRARY UTILITY ---------- MEMBER COBUCL RENAMED
OPTION  ===>  r

    C - Compress data set              P - Print member
    X - Print index listing            R - Rename member
    L - Print entire data set          D - Delete member
    blank - Display member list        B - Browse member

ISPF LIBRARY:
    PROJECT ===> CSCJGJ
    LIBRARY ===> CSC
    TYPE    ===> CNTL
    MEMBER  ===> cobucl ──┘   (If option "P", "R", "D", or "B" selected)
    NEWNAME ===> oldcobol     (If option "R" selected)

OTHER PARTITIONED OR SEQUENTIAL DATA SET:
    DATA SET NAME   ===>
    VOLUME SERIAL   ===>      (If not cataloged)

DATA SET PASSWORD ===>        (If password protected)
```

FIGURE 11.4   TSO/ISPF confirmation message in response to a print, rename, or delete action on a single member

MISCELLANEOUS TSO 3.1 OPTIONS

Some library utility options process the entire partitioned data set and cannot be initiated from the member list. These deal with monitoring data set space condition and various "housekeeping" actions.

3.1	I
Data Set Information: *I*	**INFO**

By selecting the I option and naming a partitioned or sequential data set in the indicated fields, a screen of information can be seen that describes the characteristics of the data set, as illustrated in Figure 11.5. The information includes, for a partitioned data set, the number of directory blocks in the PDS, the number of directory blocks used, and the number of members.

Data set information is invaluable in determining when it is prudent to reorganize a partitioned data set. Interpreting the in-

```
------------------------- DATA SET INFORMATION ----------------------------
COMMAND ===>

DATA SET NAME: CSCJGJ.CSC.COBOL

GENERAL DATA:                        CURRENT ALLOCATION:
    Volume serial:     ACSCAC           Allocated TRACKS:      20
    Device type:       3380             Allocated extents:      1
    Organization:      PO               Maximum dir. blocks:   15
    Record format:     FB
    Record length:     80
    Block size:        3840          CURRENT UTILIZATION:
    1st extent TRACKS: 20               Used TRACKS:           18
    Secondary TRACKS:  1                Used extents:           1
                                        Used dir. blocks:       8
    Creation date:     88/09/24         Number of members:     43


    +-------------------------------------------------------------+
    | If TSO/ISPF function 3.1 "I" screen is not available in your |
    | installation, the same information is available as TSO function |
    | 3.2 "data set information."  These screens are identical.   |
    +-------------------------------------------------------------+
```

FIGURE 11.5   TSO 3.1 data set information screen in response to use of I option

formation on the data set information screen, however, requires understanding some disk space concepts related to data set allocation. The data set information screen is described in detail in Chapter 12, dealing with the TSO 3.2 data set utility screen. Data set information is also accessible at TSO 3.2, as well as allocation options, as described on page 146.

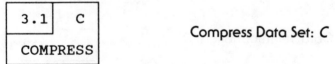

Compress Data Set: C

The C option of TSO 3.1 provides the ability to perform a partitioned data set reorganization online; that is, to compress the members of a PDS to the top of the PDS space. While the C option sounds appealing, online compress is problematic, and some installations do not allow its use. If it is not available to you, you can easily reorganize your partitioned data sets using the job control language provided in Appendix C.

The online compress option poses three problems:

- If compress is in progress and is interrupted, the partitioned data set can be left in an unusable condition.

- Compressing a partitioned data set online can take several minutes on a heavily loaded system, and during the time it is operating the terminal cannot be used for any other work.

- Online compress does not release extra disk space acquired via secondary space allocations as the data set grew, and provides no means to change the space allocation, blocking, or quantity of directory blocks.

Partitioned data set reorganization initiated with a well-designed job stream overcomes all of these limitations and is the recommended method of handling partitioned data set housekeeping, as discussed in Appendix C.

Print a PDS Index (Directory) Listing: *X*

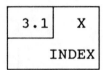

The X selection entered at the command line requires that the name of a partitioned data set be entered on the PROJECT, LIBRARY, and TYPE fields on the library utility screen. When the ENTER key is pressed, TSO/ISPF generates and places into the list data set a formatted report carrying the names of partitioned data set members. This report will be printed when the TSO/ISPF session is ended.

Figure 11.6 depicts a PDS index list, a convenient summary of the characteristics of the PDS and its contents. The report may be helpful in managing the contents of a PDS and identifying members that can be deleted. The column labeled user id reveals the TSO account that originated the member.

Print Entire Library (PDS): *L*

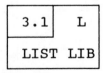

The L option causes TSO/ISPF to generate a report listing the entire contents of a partitioned data set, including every line of every member, placing it into the ISPF list data set. This can be a large volume of print, but one which is not convenient to use. There is usually little need to make this selection.

```
PROJECT: CSCJGJ                                                          DATE: 88/07/09
LIBRARY: CSC                                                             TIME: 13:59
TYPE:    C203CBL                                                         PAGE: 001

GENERAL DATA:                    GENERAL DATA:                   CURRENT UTILIZATION:
  VOLUME SERIAL:  ACSCAB           RECORD FORMAT:     FB           7 TRACKS
  DEVICE TYPE:    3380             RECORD LENGTH:     80           3 EXTENTS
  ORGANIZATION:   PO               BLOCK SIZE:     3,840           2 DIRECTORY BLOCKS
  CREATION DATE: 88/05/26          1ST EXTENT SIZE:    3           6 MEMBERS
                                   SECONDARY QUAN:     2

                                 CURRENT ALLOCATION:
                                   7 TRACKS
                                   3 EXTENTS
                                   5 DIRECTORY BLOCKS

MEMBER     VERS.MOD   CREATION    DATE AND TIME    CURRENT    INITIAL    MODIFIED   USER
NAME       LEVEL      DATE        LAST MODIFIED    NO. LINES  NO. LINES  NO. LINES  ID

ADDCHG13   01.64      88/04/18    88/07/08  16:03    543        114         0       CSCJGJ
CSC001     01.05      88/03/27    88/07/08  16:04     39         25        39       CSCJGJ
PROG1      01.05      88/01/25    88/03/27  22:20    104        101         0       C203A00
PROG2      01.00      88/04/04    88/04/04  09:58    104        104         0       C203A00
PSD187     01.01      88/07/08    88/07/08  18:59    543        543         0       CSCJGJ
PSD200     01.00      88/07/08    88/07/08  18:58     16         16         0       CSCJGJ
```

FIGURE 11.6 Partitioned data set index list generated in response to the TSO 3.1 X option

134

Short Rendition of Data Set Information: *S*

This option, if present on your TSO 3.1 screen, is similar to the option I data set information option. This display, however, is generated only from the system catalog, not from access to the data set itself. It therefore lacks information needed to determine partitioned data set space status and is of little utility.

HINTS

Partitioned Data Set Housekeeping

It is particularly advantageous to use the D option, working from a list of members, immediately prior to reorganizing a partitioned data set. When a member is deleted from a PDS, the space it occupies is not made available for the storage of other items. A PDS reorganization reclaims the space and makes it available.

In combination with the B option from the member list and the D option, you can readily identify members to be deleted and delete them, all within TSO 3.1. Obtain the PDS member list by leaving the command line on the TSO 3.1 screen blank, enter B for a member, and examine it to see if it is a candidate for deletion. Press the *PF3 END* key to return to the member list; enter D on that member and B on the next, causing the first to be deleted and the second to be brought to the screen for browsing, as illustrated in Figure 11.7. You can continue this process, working through the member list, to eliminate members you no longer need. When you are finished with this process, initiate reorganization of the PDS by submitting a job to accomplish it, as described in Appendix C.

Operations on Non-ISPF Data Sets

When a non-ISPF library partitioned data set member is to be renamed, browsed, or printed, the name cannot be entered at the ISPF LIBRARY fields; it is placed into the OTHER PARTITIONED OR SEQUENTIAL DATA SET field. A name placed here will automatically be prefaced with your TSO user id. In order to prevent

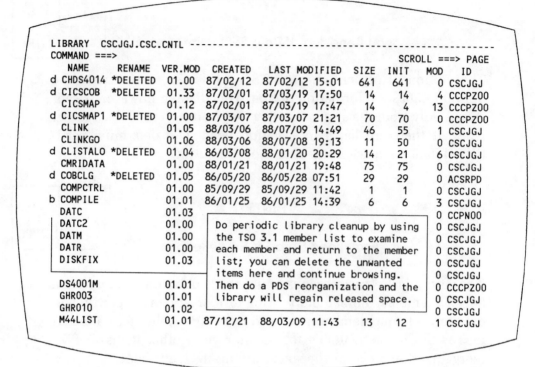

FIGURE 11.7 Performing partitioned data set cleanup online using the TSO 3.1
member list browse and delete options

this, it is necessary to surround the data set name with the IBM
"quote," the apostrophe.

To obtain a member list for a partitioned data set named differently from the PROJECT, LIBRARY, and TYPE format, enter its
name within apostrophes without any member name. For example,
'SYS1.COPYLIB' would be the way to enter the common name of
an installation production copy member library to produce its
member list screen. Any name present at the OTHER data set name
field takes precedence over an ISPF library name in the ISPF LI-
BRARY field.

12

TSO 3.2: Partitioned Data Set Utilities

```
┌──────────┐
│   3.2    │
├──────────┤
│ DATA SET │
└──────────┘
```

The TSO 3.2 function is named the data set utility because options on it deal with partitioned data set libraries as a whole rather than on PDS members. You can get to the TSO 3.2 screen from anywhere else within TSO/ISPF by entering = 3.2 on the command line and pressing the *ENTER* key.

The options provided by the TSO 3.2 include the allocation—definition and space assignment—of a new data set, the renaming of an entire data set, the deletion of an entire partitioned data set or sequential data set, the cataloging or uncataloging of data sets, and the provision of data set creation and space usage information. Figure 12.1 illustrates the TSO 3.2 screen.

ALLOCATE A NEW DATA SET: A

```
┌──────────┬──────────┐
│   3.2    │    A     │
├──────────┴──────────┤
│     ALLOCATE        │
└─────────────────────┘
```

In order to allocate a new partitioned data set to serve as a TSO/ISPF library, the name for it is entered at the ISPF LIBRARY fields, as shown in Figure 12.2. To allocate a data set not named in the TSO/ISPF PROJECT, LIBRARY, and TYPE format, the name is entered in a horizontal format in the OTHER PARTITIONED OR SEQUENTIAL DATA SET NAME field, surrounded by apostrophes, as illustrated in Figure 12.3. An A is placed at the COMMAND ===> field and the *ENTER* key is pressed. In response, TSO/ISPF presents a second screen for the entry of additional information.

Figure 12.4 depicts TSO/ISPF information screen for a new data

```
-------------------------- DATA SET UTILITY --------------------------------
OPTION  ===>

   A - Allocate new data set            C - Catalog data set
   R - Rename entire data set           U - Uncatalog data set
   D - Delete entire data set
   blank - Display data set information

ISPF LIBRARY:
   PROJECT ===>
   LIBRARY ===>
   TYPE    ===>

OTHER PARTITIONED OR SEQUENTIAL DATA SET:
   DATA SET NAME   ===>
   VOLUME SERIAL   ===>           (If not cataloged, required for option "C")

DATA SET PASSWORD ===>           (If password protected)
```

FIGURE 12.1   TSO 3.2 data set utility dealing with whole partitioned data sets

```
-------------------------- DATA SET UTILITY --------------------------------
OPTION  ===> a

   A - Allocate new data set            C - Catalog data set
   R - Rename entire data set           U - Uncatalog data set
   D - Delete entire data set
   blank - Display data set information

ISPF LIBRARY:
   PROJECT ===> CSCJGJ
   LIBRARY ===> CSC
   TYPE    ===> NEWCNTL

OTHER PARTITIONED OR SEQUENTIAL DATA SET:
   DATA SET NAME   ===>
   VOLUME SERIAL   ===>           (If not cataloged, required for option "C")

DATA SET PASSWORD ===>           (If password protected)
```

FIGURE 12.2   Entering the name of a TSO/ISPF partitioned data set library in order to allocate it

```
------------------------------ DATA SET UTILITY ------------------------------
OPTION ===> a

    A - Allocate new data set              C - Catalog data set
    R - Rename entire data set             U - Uncatalog data set
    D - Delete entire data set
    blank - Display data set information
                                        ┌─────────────────────────────┐
                                        │ Entry here overrides normal │
ISPF LIBRARY:                           │ ISPF library name.  Unless  │
    PROJECT ===> CSCJGJ                  │ the name is surrounded with │
    LIBRARY ===> CSC                     │ apostrophes, TSO prefaces it │
    TYPE    ===> CNTL                    │ with the TSO user id         │
                                        │                             │
OTHER PARTITIONED OR SEQUENTIAL DATA SET:│                             │
    DATA SET NAME  ===> 'bt5000.a00.trandata' ──┘
    VOLUME SERIAL  ===>        (If not cataloged, required for option "C")

DATA SET PASSWORD ===>        (If password protected)
```

FIGURE 12.3 Entering the name of a non-TSO/ISPF sequential data set at the OTHER DATA SET NAME fields in order to allocate it

```
------------------------- ALLOCATE NEW DATA SET ------------------------------
COMMAND ===>

DATA SET NAME: BT5000.A00.TRANDATA

    VOLUME SERIAL     ===>         (Blank for authorized default volume)
    SPACE UNITS       ===> TRKS    (BLKS, TRKS, or CYLS)
    PRIMARY QUAN      ===> 10      (In above units)
    SECONDARY QUAN    ===> 2       (In above units)
    DIRECTORY BLOCKS  ===> 4 ──┐   (Zero for sequential data set)
    RECORD FORMAT     ===> FB   │
    RECORD LENGTH     ===> 80   │
    BLOCK SIZE        ===> 3840 │
                                │
              ┌─────────────────┴──────────────────────────────┐
              │ Value entered here dictates whether the new     │
              │ data set will be partitioned or not.  Making    │
              │ this zero indicates a simple sequential data    │
              │ set.  Giving a value other than zero causes     │
              │ allocation of a partitioned data set.  The      │
              │ entries shown are equivalent to this JCL:       │
              │                                                 │
              │ //  DCB=(RECFM=FB,LRECL=80,BLKSIZE=3840),       │
              │ //  SPACE=(TRK,(10,2,4))                        │
              └─────────────────────────────────────────────────┘
```

FIGURE 12.4 TSO 3.2 allocation screen for a new data set

139

set. Ten fields arranged in a column are enterable on this screen; several must be filled in to specify characteristics of the data set that must be stated to the MVS operating system to create it. The values shown in this illustration are typical of those used by a person in a learning environment to allocate a partitioned data set for use as a CNTL job control library. Programmers on the job may be permitted to specify much more space than this to house items relating to multiple large programming assignments.

The ALLOCATE NEW DATA SET screen requires the entry of several fields of information in connection with the establishment of a new data set:

- Either the VOLUME SERIAL field or GENERIC UNIT field must be entered. This combination on the screen is the equivalent of the UNIT specification in MVS job control language, which indicates the device or device type to house the data set. VOLUME SERIAL, if filled in, is the specific volume serial number of a disk. Instead of indicating a VOLUME SERIAL number, a generic unit such as SYSDA (any direct access device) or another symbolic device group name such as DISK or TEST, is usually entered at GENERIC UNIT, allowing MVS to select an available volume.

- SPACE UNITS is the unit of measure for the PRIMARY QUANTITY and SECONDARY QUANTITY field. Blocks, tracks, or cylinders are the three units of measure.

- PRIMARY QUANTITY is the initial disk space allocation amount expressed in the units of space stated in the SPACE UNITS field. A TSO/ISPF source code or JCL partitioned data set library for a newcomer could warrant a primary allocation of 10 or fewer tracks; much more might be allowed for a production programmer.

- SECONDARY QUANTITY specifies the size of each of 15 secondary space allocations that can be accorded to the data set as it grows. A typical secondary space allocation increment for a partitioned data set is 20% of the primary allocation amount. Indicating zero here means that no secondary allocation will be provided; the data set will only be allowed a single primary space allocation. The secondary allocation amount for a person just learning a programming language and using TSO/ISPF might be as small as one track.

Each additional allocation of space occurs as the data set requires it, and will most likely not be contiguous with the space already allocated to it. MVS manages disk space automatically using entries in a disk volume table of contents, or VTOC, a special data set on each disk. An entry in the first part of the first track on each disk indicates the location of the VTOC on it, as specified by an installation when the disk media is acquired.

- DIRECTORY BLOCKS, if specified as greater than zero, indicates that the data set being allocated is a partitioned data set. This is a measure of the quantity of space in the data set allowed for its directory. One directory block for a TSO/ISPF partitioned data set can usually contain information on six members. To be able to house, for example, a maximum of 20 members, four directory blocks would be specified. A newcomer to TSO/ISPF might find this adequate, whereas a production programmer might allocate a source code PDS with several times this quantity of directory blocks.

When a sequential data set is being allocated using the TSO 3.2 function, the DIRECTORY BLOCKS field is entered as zero. *This is the single difference between the entries on the allocation screen for a partitioned data set and for a simple sequential data set.*

The information in the SPACE UNITS, PRIMARY QUANTITY, SECONDARY QUANTITY, and DIRECTORY BLOCKS fields corresponds to coding in the MVS job control language SPACE parameter.

- RECORD FORMAT is indicated as FB, for fixed-length, blocked records. This is the most common record format for source code data sets. However, a record format of VB, for variable blocked, is sometimes appropriate, as with TSO command list (CLIST) data sets, discussed in Appendix D.

- RECORD LENGTH is uniformly 80 characters for source code data sets and the CNTL data sets that house job control language.

A partitioned data set, or sequential data set, can have a record length different from 80, but this length, a carryover from punched card days, is by far the most commonly specified when the 3.2 allocation screen is used.

- BLOCK SIZE indicates the size, in bytes, of a physical I/O block. The choice for this figure has a great impact on disk utilization storage efficiency, and an installation usually publicizes directives concerning the appropriate figure to use for its complement of disk devices. For the 3350 disk, a commonly used value for a TSO/ISPF library is 3,600 bytes, while for the 3380 disk an efficient and customary figure is 3,840 bytes. Chapter 8 of a companion book in this series, *Practical MVS JCL for Today's Programmer* (John Wiley & Sons, 1987) provides complete information on efficient disk block size determination.

- EXPIRATION DATE is normally not filled in for disk data sets since it interferes with their reorganization. If specified, the data set is prevented from being deleted until the expiration date is reached, unless a special parameter is coded with the IDCAMS utility to override the unexpired date.

Allocating a data set does not place any data into it, but carves out the primary space allocation for it and establishes a reference for it in the system catalog.

A TSO library data set must be allocated before it can be accessed. If TSO function 3.1 option A is not available to you, it is possible to allocate a partitioned data set library data set using job control language. The job control language to allocate a partitioned data set suitable for use as a TSO/ISPF library is provided in Chapter 5 as Figure 5.2.

The allocate option can be used in a convenient way to create a new data set based on the characteristics of an existing one. Indicate an existing data set on the 3.2 screen, enter nothing in the command line, and press ENTER. The characteristics of the existing data set will be presented. Press the *PF3 END* key to return to the TSO 3.2 screen, and change the data set name to the new data set to be allocated. Enter A at the command line, and press ENTER. The characteristics of the existing data set, obtained on the data set information display, carry over to the allocation screen. These can now serve as a pattern for the allocation of the new data set, without having to manually enter the values.

The name first specified on the TSO 3.2 screen in the foregoing actions to obtain a pattern for data set allocation need not be an ISPF library data set. The data set name could be entered in a non-ISPF horizontal format within apostrophes at the lower portion of the screen, at the OTHER SEQUENTIAL DATA SET NAME field. An installation library such as SYS2.CLIST, a common command list library, can be used as a pattern. This carryover technique can eliminate errors when data sets will be concatenated and should have identical characteristics.

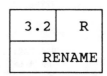

RENAME AN ENTIRE DATA SET: R

Entering the R option on the command line causes the screen illustrated in Figure 12.5 to be presented. The data set name at the top of this screen is carried over from the initial 3.2 screen; the entry of a new name for the data set is entered at the ISPF LIBRARY fields. If the data set being renamed is not a partitioned data set associated with ISPF, the name can be entered in a horizontal job control language format at the OTHER SEQUENTIAL DATA SET NAME field, surrounded by apostrophes.

Renaming an entire data set is not a very commonly performed action. It is sometimes necessary when an installation provides no batch partitioned data set reorganization cataloged procedure. Personnel may rename the original PDS, allocate a new data set with the original name, and use TSO's 3.3 function to copy the renamed original to the newly allocated data set. PDS reorganization is much more efficiently performed using job control language such as that illustrated in Appendix C.

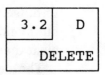

DELETE AN ENTIRE DATA SET: D

The D option of the TSO 3.2 screen makes it possible to delete an entire partitioned data set or sequential data set. This is such a significant action that TSO/ISPF responds to the selection of the

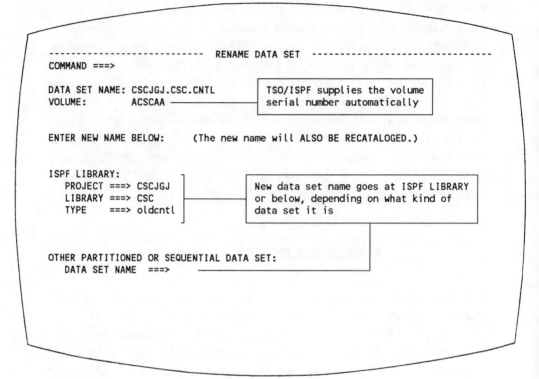

```
------------------------------ RENAME DATA SET ------------------------------
COMMAND ===>

DATA SET NAME: CSCJGJ.CSC.CNTL          TSO/ISPF supplies the volume
VOLUME:        ACSCAA ─────────────┐    serial number automatically


ENTER NEW NAME BELOW:     (The new name will ALSO BE RECATALOGED.)


ISPF LIBRARY:
   PROJECT ===> CSCJGJ   ┐          ┌───────────────────────────────────────┐
   LIBRARY ===> CSC      ├──────────┤ New data set name goes at ISPF LIBRARY │
   TYPE    ===> oldcntl  ┘          │ or below, depending on what kind of    │
                                    │ data set it is                         │


OTHER PARTITIONED OR SEQUENTIAL DATA SET:
   DATA SET NAME   ===>      ────────────────────────────┘
```

FIGURE 12.5   TSO 3.2 rename screen, produced when the R rename option is selected

option with a second screen requesting confirmation of the intention to perform the deletion.

Figure 12.6 depicts the data set deletion confirmation screen. The data set name is carried over from the original 3.2 screen, and the instruction is given to confirm the deletion by pressing the EN-TER key, or cancel the request with the PF3 END key. This choice of keys is a bit unfortunate because human nature inclines toward pressing the ENTER key; it is pressed so often it may be done on impulse. On the other hand, the END key is actually the PF3 key, but by not specifying this explicitly, the confirmation screen is less clear than it could be.

The deletion of a data set frees its space for immediate use by MVS to house another data set. Once deleted, a data set is gone; if a data set is deleted by mistake, it must be restored from a backup. Sequential data sets as well as partitioned data sets can be deleted with the TSO 3.2 deletion option.

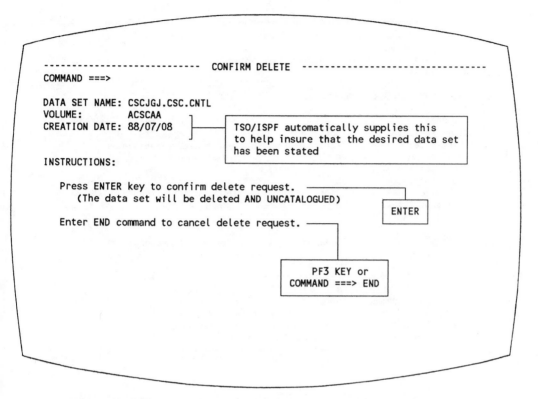

FIGURE 12.6   TSO 3.2 data set deletion confirmation screen, produced when the D deletion option is selected

---

3.2	
	PDS INFO

PDS SPACE USAGE AND REORGANIZATION: b

When the command line on the TSO 3.2 screen is left blank, and a data set name is filled in either at the ISPF LIBRARY or the OTHER DATA SET NAME field below, a screen of data set information is presented. This screen is illustrated in Figure 12.7. If both the ISPF LIBRARY name and the OTHER DATA SET NAME are entered, the OTHER name takes precedence; information for it is presented. It is therefore not necessary to blank out the name that usually carries over in the ISPF LIBRARY fields in order to obtain data set information on a non-ISPF library data set.

The data set information screen indicates the volume serial number of the disk on which the data set resides, the type of device this is by model number, and the other characteristics of the data set

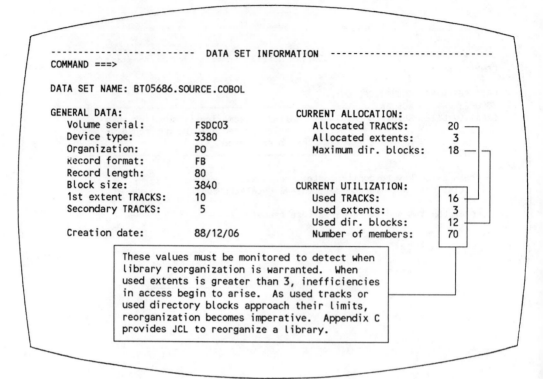

```
-------------------------- DATA SET INFORMATION  ---------------------------
COMMAND ===>

DATA SET NAME: BT05686.SOURCE.COBOL

GENERAL DATA:                              CURRENT ALLOCATION:
    Volume serial:       FSDC03               Allocated TRACKS:      20
    Device type:         3380                 Allocated extents:      3
    Organization:        PO                   Maximum dir. blocks:   18
    Record format:       FB
    Record length:       80
    Block size:          3840              CURRENT UTILIZATION:
    1st extent TRACKS:   10                   Used TRACKS:           16
    Secondary TRACKS:     5                   Used extents:           3
                                              Used dir. blocks:      12
    Creation date:       88/12/06             Number of members:     70
```

These values must be monitored to detect when
library reorganization is warranted. When
used extents is greater than 3, inefficiencies
in access begin to arise. As used tracks or
used directory blocks approach their limits,
reorganization becomes imperative. Appendix C
provides JCL to reorganize a library.

FIGURE 12.7   TSO 3.2 data set space usage information screen, produced when the command line entry is left blank and the ENTER key is pressed

specified at the time of its allocation. On the right side of the information screen, the space consumption of the data set is presented. The ALLOCATED TRACKS figure is a total of the primary and any secondary allocations, while the ALLOCATED EXTENTS indicates how many separate, non-contiguous portions of disk space the data set currently occupies. *This figure includes the primary allocation, and for a partitioned data set it cannot exceed 16, because a PDS cannot span more than one volume.*

The CURRENT UTILIZATION value indicates how many of the allocated tracks, disk extents, and, for partitioned data sets, how many partitioned data set directory blocks are currently in use. This information, and the number of extents, must be monitored in order to detect when a PDS needs reorganization.

"Used tracks" and "used extents" do not indicate "productively used." These figures include the unusable space in a partitioned data set that results from changing and saving a member, or deleting a member.

Knowing when to reorganize a partitioned data set is important. This advice will guide you in monitoring your TSO/ISPF libraries and initiating a reorganization when appropriate:

Reorganize a partitioned data set when the TSO 3.2 data set information screen shows that:

> USED EXTENTS exceeds 10 for a student or
> 3 for a programmer on the job

or

> USED TRACKS approaches ALLOCATED TRACKS when
> no secondary allocation is used

or

> USED DIR BLOCKS approaches MAXIMUM DIR BLOCKS

Any of these conditions indicates that the partitioned data set is becoming inefficient or approaching the point of inability to accept new or edited members.

CATALOG A DATA SET: C

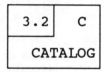

You can catalog a currently uncataloged data set using TSO 3.2 option C. To accomplish this, the data set name must be filled in, typically at the OTHER data set name field. The volume serial number of the disk on which the data set resides must be specified in the VOLUME SERIAL = = = > field.

In response to a request to catalog a data set, the system will examine the volume table of contents (VTOC) of the disk volume specified and try to find the data set in order to obtain certain characteristics of it from its data set label. If the data set cannot be found on the volume specified, TSO/ISPF will provide an error message indicating this fact.

TSO/ISPF data sets are cataloged automatically when allocated using TSO, so that the operating system itself keeps track of what disk media they occupy. The C catalog and U uncatalog functions are occasionally helpful in patching up jobs dealing with non-ISPF data sets, where the job failed and left loose ends. Such a job might have uncataloged a data set that needs to be recataloged to restart the run, or vice versa.

Catalog and uncatalog are not heavily used TSO utility functions, and are limited to disk data sets. These operations can be performed on tape as well as disk data sets with MVS job control language and the IDCAMS utility, as illustrated in Chapter 17 of a companion book in this series, *Practical MVS JCL for Today's Programmer* (John Wiley & Sons, 1987).

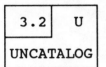

UNCATALOG A DATA SET: *U*

Uncatalog is the reverse of TSO 3.2 option C, catalog. An existing data set that is cataloged can be uncataloged using option U. This function does not require the entry of a volume serial number, but after the data set has been uncataloged, the volume serial number will have to be specified to access it, because the operating system no longer has information about its location. Uncataloging a data set is an action rarely taken.

TSO does not support tape operations, but uncataloging can be performed for tape as well as disk data sets with job control language and the IDCAMS utility. These operations are described in Chapter 17 of a companion book in this series, *Practical MVS JCL for Today's Programmer* (John Wiley & Sons, 1987).

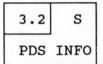

DATA SET INFORMATION (SHORT): *S*

The S option, if present in your TSO/ISPF system, provides a screen similar to that presented when the command line is left blank on the TSO 3.2 data set utility screen. The "short" rendition of data set information, however, does not include the maximum or used directory blocks figure, or the number of members in the data set, and is therefore of no use in monitoring the space condition of a partitioned data set.

13

TSO 3.3: COPY/MOVE Utility

3.3
COPY/MOVE

The TSO 3.3 MOVE/COPY function is aptly named because this is exactly what it lets you do: it can copy a sequential data set from one place to another, or move a partitioned data set member from one partitioned data set to another. It is often used to take a copy of a partitioned data set member from one programmer's library or a production library into the TSO/ISPF partitioned data set library of another person. You can get to the TSO 3.3 function from any other screen within TSO/ISPF by entering =3.3 on the command line and pressing the ENTER key.

Figure 13.1 illustrates the initial 3.3 function screen. The complete screen provides six different options; your installation may limit the codes to as few as two—C copy and M move. All of the options operate similarly, in a two-step manner. Entries are made on the screen shown in Figure 13.1, to indicate the data set from which a copy or move is to be made. Pressing the ENTER key then brings up the second screen, shown in Figure 13.2, on which the destination of the moved or copied item is stated.

The options listed on the left side of the initial 3.3 screen—C and M and P—accomplish a move, copy, or "promotion" without causing the generation of any printed copy of the item acted upon. The options listed at the right side, with codes CP and MP and PP, cause the same actions to occur and a copy of the item to also be placed into the list data set that is submitted for batch print when the ISPF session is ended. The no-print and print versions of the functions themselves are the same. We'll discuss only the no-print options on the left side of the screen.

149

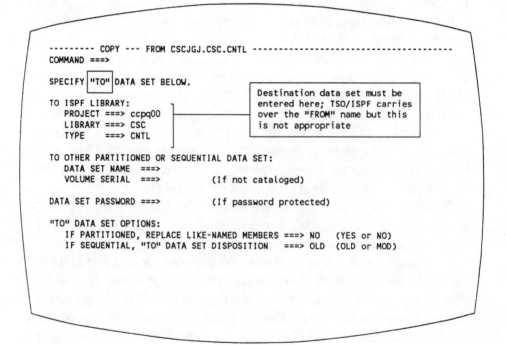

```
---------------------------- MOVE/COPY UTILITY -----------------------------
OPTION  ===>

   CP - Copy data set or member(s) and print        C - Copy without print
   MP - Move data set or member(s) and print        M - Move without print

SPECIFY "FROM" DATA SET BELOW, THEN PRESS ENTER KEY TO SPECIFY "TO" DATA SET

  FROM  ISPF LIBRARY:
                                      ┌─────────────────────────────────────┐
     PROJECT ===> CSCJGJ              │ The library named here or the data set
     LIBRARY ===> CSC                 │ named below is the origin of the items
     TYPE    ===> CNTL                └─────────────────────────────────────┘
     MEMBER  ===>              (Blank for member list, * for all members)

FROM OTHER PARTITIONED OR SEQUENTIAL DATA SET:
   DATA SET NAME  ===> 'BT50000.A00.TESTRECS'
   VOLUME SERIAL  ===>              (If not cataloged)

DATA SET PASSWORD ===>              (If password protected)
```

FIGURE 13.1   TSO 3.3 member or data set MOVE/COPY utility screen

```
--------- COPY --- FROM CSCJGJ.CSC.CNTL -----------------------------------
COMMAND ===>

SPECIFY "TO" DATA SET BELOW.
                                      ┌─────────────────────────────────────┐
TO ISPF LIBRARY:                      │ Destination data set must be
   PROJECT ===> ccpq00                │ entered here; TSO/ISPF carries
   LIBRARY ===> CSC                   │ over the "FROM" name but this
   TYPE    ===> CNTL                  │ is not appropriate
                                      └─────────────────────────────────────┘

TO OTHER PARTITIONED OR SEQUENTIAL DATA SET:
   DATA SET NAME  ===>
   VOLUME SERIAL  ===>              (If not cataloged)

DATA SET PASSWORD ===>              (If password protected)

"TO" DATA SET OPTIONS:
   IF PARTITIONED, REPLACE LIKE-NAMED MEMBERS ===> NO    (YES or NO)
   IF SEQUENTIAL, "TO" DATA SET DISPOSITION   ===> OLD   (OLD or MOD)
```

FIGURE 13.2   TSO/ISPF response in request for a move or copy, screen allowing specification of destination

150

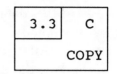

COPY A MEMBER OR DATA SET: C

To copy a partitioned data set member, the PDS name must be entered in the PROJECT, LIBRARY, and TYPE fields. For the MEMBER field, three choices of entries exist:

- A member name can be entered, to copy one member.
- The asterisk * can be entered, to copy all members (rarely useful).
- The field can be left blank, in order to obtain a member list. *If this choice is taken, the member list does not appear until after the second 3.3 entry screen is filled in.*

If the data set from which a member is being copied is a partitioned data set, but not an ISPF library data set, its name can be entered at the bottom of the screen, in the OTHER DATA SET NAME field, surrounded by apostrophes to prevent TSO from prefacing it with your TSO user id. An entry here might take the form:

```
DATA SET NAME ===> 'SYS1.COPYLIB(LFWSTDP1)'
```

to copy a member from an installation copy library. To obtain a member list when the "from" data set is specified in the OTHER DATA SET NAME field, omit a member name and parentheses:

```
DATA SET NAME ===> 'SYS1.COPYLIB'
```

To copy all members from a non-TSO/ISPF data set, you can make the distinctly non-job control language entry in the OTHER DATA SET NAME field:

```
DATA SET NAME ===> 'SYS.COPYLIB(*)'
```

The entry field at the bottom of the screen entitled VOLUME SERIAL must be entered only when the OTHER data set name field is used, and only when the data set from which an item is being copied is not cataloged. DATA SET PASSWORD is used only if

MVS data set password security is in effect for the data set to be copied.

After entering the "from" data set name and pressing the ENTER key, the second 3.3 screen is presented. As a first action, always glance at the bottom of it and see if the "TO" data set option is set in the appropriate manner for your purposes. YES in this field means an incoming item can replace an existing member in a partitioned data set, while NO will prevent this occurrence and give an error message.

If the item being copied is one member of a partitioned data set, and the destination is another PDS, the item copied or moved will retain the same name unless a member name is stated on the second screen. The same or a different member name can be optionally entered on the second screen. If the destination of the item is a non-ISPF partitioned data set, enter the destination name at the OTHER DATA SET NAME field on the second screen. You can leave off the member name if you wish it to be the same as the "from" member name, or enter the PDS name followed by member name in parentheses, the whole entry surrounded by apostrophes.

The bottom of the second move/copy screen contains some additional specifications. The first of these governs the replacement of like-named members and is discussed in the foregoing. The other specifications have various purposes:

- If the destination data set is password protected, its password must be entered in the DATA SET PASSWORD field in order for the copy to proceed.

- An option allows entry of either MOD or OLD. These are job control language disposition parameters and apply only if the destination data set is a simple sequential data. A simple sequential data set can contain one item. This data set must already exist in order to receive a copied or moved item; it can be allocated using the TSO 3.2 A option.

  If the destination data set is a sequential one and MOD is entered here, the copied or moved item will be appended to the end of the existing data set. If OLD is entered here the present contents of the destination sequential data set are replaced by the copied or moved data item.

- An option, not illustrated here, may exist to "pack" the data set being written. This has nothing to do with COMP-3 or "packed decimal" storage, but deals with a compression method by which repeating characters such as spaces are replaced with shorter sequences of codes to save disk space. If packed, a member or data set must be unpacked before it can be compiled or otherwise processed. Packing is not widely used at the source code level where libraries are relatively small in any case. Its main benefit lies in production program source code archives usually maintained by an installation librarian.

After all desired entries are made on the second COPY/MOVE screen, pressing the *ENTER* key starts the copy or move, or, if a source member name was omitted on the first screen, the member list is presented. You can interrupt the move or copy action at any time before pressing the *ENTER* key on the second screen by pressing the *PF3 END* key. *PF3* cannot interrupt a copy or move once the second screen has been filled in and the *ENTER* key pressed.

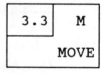

MOVE A MEMBER OR DATA SET: M

The move option is identical to the copy option except that the original item is automatically deleted after it is placed into the destination data set. This meaning of MOVE is not the same as COBOL's use of the word, and more closely approximates the ordinary language meaning. Filling in the initial 3.3 screen and then the second destination screen for a move operation is identical in nature to completing these entries for a copy.

THE MEMBER LIST DURING COPY/MOVE

When the "from" data set is a partitioned data set—specified at either ISPF LIBRARY fields PROJECT, LIBRARY, and TYPE, or at the OTHER DATA SET NAME field—the omission of a member name on the initial 3.3 screen indicates that you want to see and select members from a member list.

Figure 13.3(a) illustrates the move/copy member list, which appears only *after* the completion of the second or copy/move destination screen. Move the cursor down to the line on which the member is listed and enter an S in front of it in order to copy or move it. Any value other than S, for "select," is rejected as an error. It is not possible to copy some members and move others from the same member list, because by the time you reach to the member list you have already indicated whether copy or move actions are underway.

Several members can be copied or moved on one member list screen. When the *ENTER* key, *PF7*, or *PF8* key is pressed, all of the selected members will be processed, and the RENAME field will be filled with *COPIED as shown in Figure 13.3(b). You can then move forward and backward through the member list using the *PF8* and *PF7* keys, continuing to indicate additional members to be copied or moved, and these messages will remain. Using *PF8* to initiate the copies or moves allows working through a member list with minimum screen transmission, helpful when using TSO/ISPF via low-speed dial-up lines. If the need arises, it is possible to terminate processing at the member list without actually making copies or moves by pressing the *PF3 END* key.

If the REPLACE LIKE-NAMED MEMBERS field on the second TSO 3.3 screen is set to NO, and the copy all (*) members specification causes an attempt to write a like-named member to the destination data set, the copy or move will not terminate. Instead, TSO/ISPF will process all of the members in the sending data set before returning control. The message MEMBERS NOT REPLACED will appear at the upper right corner of the screen, indicating that one or more members could not be copied to the destination partitioned data set.

When a member list is used for copying or moving, and some selected members cannot be processed due to a conflict in member names and the setting of the REPLACE LIKE-NAMED MEMBERS field, TSO/ISPF also completes processing of all selected members before returning control. Since the member list is present, TSO/ISPF can indicate individually which members could not be replaced in the destination data set. For these members, it puts a

```
COPY --- FROM CSCJGJ.CSC.CNTL  TO CSCJGJ.CSC.NEWCNTL -------------------------
COMMAND ===>                                              SCROLL ===> PAGE
    NAME    RENAME   VER.MOD  CREATED    LAST MODIFIED  SIZE  INIT  MOD   ID
    ALLOCOB          01.03    88/01/05   88/03/24 13:51   14    14    5 CSCJGJ
  s ALLODAT *COPIED  01.06    88/01/05   88/06/20 19:26   14    14    0 CSCJGJ
    ALLOLOAD         01.01    88/03/08   88/03/08 18:23   14    14    1 CCPN00
    APPL8J           01.05    86/01/31   87/01/22 00:11   28     2    0 CCCPZ00
    BOOKS7           01.02    86/01/12   86/01/25 22:18   38    12    0 CSCSMS
    CHDS4001
    CHDS4012
    CHDS4014         01.00    87/02/12   87/02/12 15:01  641   641    0 CSCJGJ
  s CICSCOB *COPIED  01.33    87/02/01   87/03/19 17:50   14    14    4 CCCPZ00
  s CICSMAP *COPIED  01.12    87/02/01   87/03/19 17:47   14     4   13 CCCPZ00
  s CICSMAP1 *COPIED 01.00    87/03/07   87/03/07 21:21   70    70    0 CCCPZ00
  s CICSMAP2 *COPIED 01.00    87/03/08   87/03/08 06:45  144   144    0 CCCPZ00
    CLASS            01.01    87/12/21   88/03/09 11:43   13    12    1 CSCJGJ
    CLINK            01.05    88/03/06   88/07/09 14:49   46    55    1 CSCJGJ
    CLINKGO          01.06    88/03/06   88/07/08 19:13   11    50    0 CSCJGJ
    CLISTALO         01.04    86/03/08   88/01/20 20:29   14    21    6 CSCJGJ
    CMRIDATA         01.00    88/01/21   88/01/21 19:48   75    75    0 CSCJGJ
    COBCLG           01.05    86/05/20   86/05/28 07:51   29    29    0 ACSRPD
    COMPCTRL         01.00    85/09/29   85/09/29 11:42    1     1    0 CSCJGJ
    COMPILE          01.01    86/01/25   86/01/25 14:39    6     6    3 CSCJGJ
    C203STRT         01.07    88/05/26   88/05/26 10:59   74    26    0 CSCJGJ
```

FIGURE 13.3a Using a library member list to select multiple members for move or copy

```
COPY --- FROM CSCJGJ.CSC.CNTL  TO CSCJGJ.CSC.NEWCNTL -------------------------
COMMAND ===>                                              SCROLL ===> PAGE
    NAME    RENAME   VER.MOD  CREATED    LAST MODIFIED  SIZE  INIT  MOD   ID
    ALLOCOB          01.03    88/01/05   88/03/24 13:51   14    14    5 CSCJGJ
    ALLODAT          01.06    88/01/05   88/06/20 19:26   14    14    0 CSCJGJ
    ALLOLOAD         01.01    88/03/08   88/03/08 18:23   14    14    1 CCPN00
    APPL8J           01.05    86/01/31   87/01/22 00:11   28     2    0 CCCPZ00
    BOOKS7           01.02    86/01/12   86/01/25 22:18   38    12    0 CSCSMS
    CHDS4001
    CHDS4012
    CHDS4014         01.00    87/02/12   87/02/12 15:01  641   641    0 CSCJGJ
  s CICSCOB *NO-REPL 01.33    87/02/01   87/03/19 17:50   14    14    4 CCCPZ00

  ┌──────────────────────────────────────────────────────────────────────┐
  │ *NO-REPL occurs if the member already exists in the destination library│
  │ and this field on the prior screen has been set as indicated:          │
  │                                                                        │
  │   IF PARTITIONED, REPLACE LIKE-NAMED MEMBERS ===> NO   (YES or NO)      │
  └──────────────────────────────────────────────────────────────────────┘

    CLISTALO         01.04    86/03/08   88/01/20 20:29   14    21    6 CSCJGJ
  s CMRIDATA *COPIED 01.00    88/01/21   88/01/21 19:48   75    75    0 CSCJGJ
    COBCLG           01.05    86/05/20   86/05/28 07:51   29    29    0 ACSRPD
    COMPCTRL         01.00    85/09/29   85/09/29 11:42    1     1    0 CSCJGJ
  s COMPILE  *COPIED 01.01    86/01/25   86/01/25 14:39    6     6    3 CSCJGJ
    C203STRT         01.07    88/05/26   88/05/26 10:59   74    26    0 CSCJGJ
```

FIGURE 13.3b TSO/ISPF response to multiple copy request, illustrating result of disallowing like-named member replacement

message of *NO-REPL in the RENAME column, instead of the usual *COPIED or *MOVED.

END OF THE COPY/MOVE OPERATION

If a move or copy operation for only one member has been indicated, or all members were copied using the * specification, the first screen reappears after the completion of processing. Another copy action can be initiated, the *PF3 END* key can be pressed to return to the main TSO menu, or you can transfer directly to another TSO/ISPF screen.

If copies of moves had been initiated using the member list, the member list will return after selected members were processed. In order to return to the initial 3.3 screen, the *PF3 END* key can be pressed. Alternatively, you can transfer directly to another screen from the member list using the = sign and the desired TSO/ISPF function number.

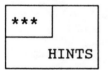

HINTS FOR COPY/MOVE

The 3.3 function is simple to use, and once familiar with it, a person normally uses it readily. However, it is possible to cause a little trouble for yourself if you become too cavalier and hasty in working with it.

If the sending data set is a partitioned data set, and the destination data set is a sequential one and not a PDS, it is appropriate only to copy one member to it. If you use the * specification to copy all members, or a member list selection to copy more than one member, the MOD disposition at the bottom of the second copy/move screen will result in the sequential data set having all of the indicated members placed within it. Since it is not a partitioned data set, however, it will be useless for access purposes, yet the TSO 3.3 COPY function will give no indication of this.

The origin of a useless sequential data set as described above is usually the incorrect allocation of the receiving data set. The only difference between the allocation of a partitioned data set and allocation of a simple sequential data set is the specification of a number of directory blocks. If the TSO 3.2 screen is used for this allocation, and the DIRECTORY BLOCKS field is left blank or with a value of zero, the data set allocated is not a PDS.

3.3	P
PROMOTION	

PROMOTION UTILITY: *P*

"Promotion" denotes elevation of a partitioned data set member to a controlled status. It applies only if an installation uses IBM's Library Management Facility for managing the movement of source code from development to production via a hierarchy of partitioned data set libraries. If your installation uses this method, the procedures for using the promotion utility will be documented locally. Your installation may, on the other hand, use a non-IBM source code management system such as Panvalet or Librarian, in which case the promotion utility is probably of no use to you.

=== 14 ===

TSO 3.4: Data Set List Utility

```
┌──────────┬──────┐
│ 3.4      │      │
├──────────┘      │
│            LIST │
└─────────────────┘
```

TSO 3.4 is a more recent development than many of the other sub-menus. It centralizes access to many of the functions otherwise reachable by browse, edit, and TSO 3.1 functions. It also allows access to disk volume table of contents information, including total disk space utilization.

TSO 3.4 operates as a "selector" screen working from a level higher than other member selection lists. It lets you see a list of all data sets with like high-level qualifiers for their names, across all disk units. You can select from this list to browse, edit, delete, re-name, and do other things with the data sets. You can get to the TSO 3.4 screen by selecting it from the TSO/ISPF main menu or from any other screen by entering =3.4 on the command line and pressing the *ENTER* key.

Figure 14.1 illustrates the initial TSO 3.4 screen. At the top of it are four options. One option so far outshines the others in useful-ness that IBM made it the easiest to enter: the "blank" option. This option, "Display data set list," provides access to lists of data sets. From this list, all of the data set manipulations shown at the bottom of the screen are available.

THE DATA SET LIST

When the OPTION ===> field is left blank on the TSO 3.4 screen in order to obtain a data set list, three means of limiting the scope

```
------------------------ DATA SET LIST UTILITY ----------------------------
OPTION  ===>

   blank - Display data set list *       P  - Print data set list
   V     - Display VTOC information only  PV - Print VTOC information only

Enter one or both of the parameters below:
   DSNAME LEVEL  ===> BT05686
   VOLUME        ===>

SPECIFY THE FOLLOWING, IF DISPLAYING A LIST OF DATA SETS:
   DISPLAY FORMAT OPTION  ===> QUICK   (QUICK, SHORT, LONG)
   CONFIRM DELETE REQUEST ===> YES     (YES or NO)

* The following line commands will be available when the list is displayed

        B - Browse data set           C - Catalog data set
        E - Edit data set             U - Uncatalog data set
        D - Delete entire data set    P - Print entire data set
        R - Rename entire data set    X - Print index listing
        I - Data set information      M - Display member list
        S - Data set information (short)  Z - Compress data set
```

FIGURE 14.1   TSO 3.4 data set utility list screen

scope of the data set list are available, and one of these must be used:

- A high-level data set name qualifier, or "front part," can be specified at the DSNAME LEVEL ===> field, and the VOLUME ===> field can be left blank. In response to pressing the *ENTER* key, all cataloged data sets across the entire system with front portions of their names matching the DSNAME value will be listed on the screen, along with the disk volume serial number on which they reside. Figure 14.2 illustrates the result.

- A disk volume serial number can be specified in the VOLUME ===> field, the DSNAME LEVEL ===> field can be left blank, and the *ENTER* key pressed. All data sets on the specified disk volume, cataloged or uncataloged, will be listed on the screen, in a format similar to that shown in Figure 14.2.

- Both DSNAME LEVEL ===> and VOLUME ===> fields can

```
DSLIST - DATA SETS BEGINNING WITH BT05686 ------------------------ ROW 1 OF 7
COMMAND ===>                                               SCROLL ===> PAGE
  DATA SET NAME                         LAST FUNCTION    VOLUME
-------------------------------------------------------------------------------
  BT05686.A01.SYSDTERM                                   FSDC03
  BT05686.DEVCOPY.COBOL                                  FSDC15
  BT05686.ISPPROF                                        VSLIB2
e BT05686.SOURCE.CLIST                                   FSDC03
  BT05686.SOURCE.CNTL                                    FSDC07
  BT05686.SOURCE.COBOL                                   FSDC03
  BT05686.SOURCE.SYM                                     TEST97
****************************** BOTTOM OF DATA **********************************
```

FIGURE 14.2   TSO/ISPF response when nothing is entered on the command line
of the data set utility screen, and the ENTER key is pressed

be entered, and only data sets matching the name qualifier on
the specified disk volume will be listed.

Programmers and end users find the first means of obtaining a data
set list most useful. By specifying the highest level qualifier TSO
data sets—typically the same as the TSO logon identifier or user
id—and leaving the VOLUME ===> field blank, TSO 3.4 provides a list of data sets on the system and where each resides. This
is possible because the system catalog records the identity of the
disk volume on which each data set is located.

TSO 3.4 CONTROLLING FIELDS

Two one-time controlling fields exist on the TSO 3.4 screen. Once
set, these fields require no further attention. They govern the for-

mat of the data set list and a critical safety feature concerned with the deletion of whole data sets.

The format of the data set list is governed by the DISPLAY FORMAT OPTION ===> field on the initial TSO 3.4 screen. Three choices exist: QUICK, SHORT, and LONG. While any of these formats provide a data set list that can be used to make function selections, as described below, the QUICK option is the best for this purpose. It is called "quick" because it is the fastest for the system to provide. Both SHORT and LONG formats provide more data set information, but they require the system to access not only the catalog but also the disk housing the data set itself, just to produce the list.

All of the functions listed at the bottom of the initial TSO 3.4 screen are accessible from the data set list. As you can see by examining the screen, these functions include nearly all of those a programmer normally uses, with the exception of deleting a member of a partitioned data set.

The deletion of an *entire* data set, partitioned or sequential, is accessible from the data set list. The last controlling field on the TSO 3.4 screen deals with this. The values "YES" or "NO" can be entered at the CONFIRM DELETE REQUEST ===> field; YES means that you desire to be prompted for a confirmation if you indicate that a data set is to be deleted; NO means you don't want this opportunity to reconsider. It is strongly recommended that you set this field to YES and permanently leave it with these contents.

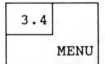

FUNCTION SELECTION FROM THE DATA SET LIST

The data set list depicted in Figure 14.2 is truly a branching off point for any of several desired actions. For example, by moving the cursor down to a data set line, and entering "B," you can "browse" a data set. If it is a PDS, such as a TSO library, you will receive a member list identical to that presented on the TSO 2 EDIT screen when no member name is entered. From that list, you can enter "S" to select a member to be viewed. On the other hand, if the data set selected with a B on the TSO 3.4 data set list is a sequential data set, not a PDS, you will see its contents immediately.

Pressing the *PF3 END* key takes you back to the TSO 3.4 data set list.

You can enter the TSO 2 EDIT function from the data set list. Move the cursor down to the desired data set, enter E on that line, and press *ENTER*. You will arrive at the edit function member list, the very same screen presented via TSO main menu selection 2. TSO 2 EDIT works in exactly the same manner, once you are in it, regardless of whether you invoked it from the main menu or from the TSO 3.4 data set list.

The TSO 3.4 screen presents the data set list function selection codes but can't show them on the data set listing itself. Here are the codes and the other places within TSO/ISPF where these functions are also accessed:

TSO 3.4 Code	Function	Regular Access
B	Browse data set	Main menu function 1
C	Catalog data set	TSO 3.2 option *C*
D	Delete entire data set	TSO 3.2 option *D*
E	Edit data set	Main menu function 2
I	Data set information	TSO 3.2 option "blank"
M	Member list only	—
P	Print entire data set	TSO 3.1 option *L*
R	Rename entire data set	TSO 3.2 option *R*
S	Short data set information	TSO 3.2 option *S*
U	Uncatalog data set	TSO 3.2 option *U*
X	Print data set index listing	TSO 3.1 option *X*
Z	Compress data set	TSO 3.1 option *C*

Many of the TSO 3.4 function codes are mnemonic in nature, but some carry values different from those of the same functions accessed from the TSO 3.1 and 3.2 screens. If you are using TSO 3.4, you might want to put a bookmark at this point to readily glance at this chart as you work.

The data set list screen in its "QUICK" format keeps track of the last action taken with a data set. The column called "LAST FUNCTION" is initially presented with nothing in it. As you make use of various function selections by their letter codes, such as B for browse and E for edit, the LAST FUNCTION column shows the most recent action for each data set. Figure 14.3 depicts this same

```
DSLIST - DATA SETS BEGINNING WITH BT05686 ------------------------- ROW 1 OF 7
COMMAND ===>                                              SCROLL ===> PAGE
DATA SET NAME                          LAST FUNCTION   VOLUME
-----------------------------------------------------------------------
   BT05686.A01.SYSDTERM                                 FSDC03
   BT05686.DEVCOPY.COBOL                 INFO-Q         FSDC15
   BT05686.ISPPROF                                      VSLIB2
   BT05686.SOURCE.CLIST                  EDIT           FSDC03
   BT05686.SOURCE.CNTL                   BROWSE         FSDC07
   BT05686.SOURCE.COBOL                  MEMBLIST       FSDC03
   BT05686.SOURCE.SYM                                   TEST97
***************************** BOTTOM OF DATA ********************************
```

FIGURE 14.3 Data set utility list screen after several functions have been selected from the member list and processed

screen after several different functions have been performed for
various data sets.

TSO 3.4 LESSER-USED OPTIONS

Three options are shown on the initial TSO 3.4 screen in Figure
14.1 in addition to the "blank" data set list:

P *Print data set list:* causes a list of the data sets specified to be
placed into the list data set, for printing when the TSO/ISPF
session ends. The list will be similar to that presented on the
screen and illustrated in our discussion of the "blank" option.

V *Display VTOC information only:* provides information taken
from the volume table of contents of the specified disk. This
shows the number of tracks on a specified disk volume, their

overall usage, and the amount of space left on the disk. This feature and the PV option following are of greater use to systems programmers than applications programmers or information center users.

PV *Print VTOC information:* the same information as displayed on the screen by the V option is placed into the list data set for printing at the time that the ISPF session is ended.

These functions are typically of less use to applications programmers and end users than the selection of functions such as data set names on a disk volume using the TSO 3.4 data set list.

15

Hardcopy Print

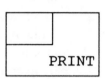

PRINT

A number of ways exist to obtain screen and member listings on paper. Some methods are oriented to very low-volume print created locally, and others to print spanning several pages and output on a high-speed centralized printer.

SCREEN PRINTING

PRINT KEY

The image on a terminal screen may be printed directly if a printer is attached to the same controller as the terminal in use. In this case, the 3270 terminal print key, denoted by a small arrow pointing to a report symbol and located at the lower left side of the keyboard, will initiate print. If a PC with attached printer is used to emulate a 3270 terminal, a screen print can be generated immediately by pressing its PrtSc key in much the same manner.

A "snapshot" image of the screen can be taken at any time and placed into the list data set, *for automatic batch job printing at the end of the TSO/ISPF session*, by entering the word PRINT on the command line and pressing *ENTER*. This action can be speeded by assigning the word PRINT to a *PF* key, such as *PF4*, as illustrated in Chapter 4. If this is done, a snapshot is taken each time *PF4* is pressed.

3.1

PRINT

MEMBER OR DATA SET PRINTING WITH TSO 3.1

The most commonly used printing mechanism for partitioned data sets and members is TSO 3.1, the P option. This copies the item into the list data set, for *automatic batch job printing at the end of the TSO/ISPF session*. Print usually occurs at the high-speed printer attached to the mainframe. If a local printer ID is entered at the 0.2 screen, which carries the instructions for list data set handling, the list data set can be directed to print locally when the TSO/ISPF session is terminated. This requires that the facility has installed the DSPRINT utility, which is required for local printing of the list data set.

Some installations install the optional DSPRINT utility and make it directly accessible, allowing a member to be printed locally at a terminal attached to the same controller as the 3270 terminal by executing DSPRINT in native mode TSO.

TSO 3.6: HARDCOPY UTILITY

It is possible to compose the simple job control language to execute either the IEBGENER or IEBPTPCH utility to copy a member or data set to the printer, as discussed at the end of this chapter. TSO/ISPF, however, provides a utility function named TSO 3.6 that composes this JCL and submits it for execution during a session. This is a simple function that can also initiate local print of a member or data set. This function can be accessed from any point within TSO/ISPF by entering = 3.6 on the command line and pressing the ENTER key.

Figure 15.1 illustrates one type of TSO 3.6 screen; Figure 15.2 illustrates another. Variations in this screen are easy for an installation to make, and the one with which you are presented may not appear exactly as either of these. Most variations of this screen follow the same pattern: they allow entry of a data set name, and some means to specify disposition of the item after the print. If a disposition field appears, you will most likely want to set it to KEEP and have it remain with this setting.

To print an item using TSO 3.6, enter the data set name at the DATA SET NAME field. Since the customary ISPF LIBRARY fields are not provided, any data set or member that is to be printed has to be entered in its normal job control language format but surrounded by apostrophes unless it is appropriate to allow TSO/ISPF to preface it with the TSO user id. For example, for TSO user BT05686 to print member FSBT3708 in his COBOL partitioned data set library, the name could be entered:

```
-------------------------- HARDCOPY UTILITY -------------------------------
OPTION ===> PK

   PK - Print/punch and keep data set          L - Print data set local printer
   PD - Print/punch and delete data set



DATA SET NAME ===>  'BT05686.SOURCE.COBOL(FSBT3708)'
   VOLUME SERIAL       ===>               (If not cataloged)
   DATA SET PASSWORD ===>                 (If password protected)

SYSOUT CLASS      ===> A
LOCAL PRINTER ID ===> DC19DL32

JOB STATEMENT INFORMATION:  (Verify before proceeding)
   ===> //FSBT686A   JOB AKOOTSO,'DP2-JANOSSY',CLASS=E,MSGCLASS=A,
   ===> //  MSGLEVEL=(1,1),NOTIFY=BT05686
   ===> //*
   ===> //*
```

FIGURE 15.1 TSO 3.6 hardcopy print utility screen (business installation)


```
-------------------------- HARDCOPY UTILITY -------------------------------
OPTION ===> J

   J - Generate JCL to print or punch data set



DATA SET NAME ===>
   DISPOSITION       ===> KEEP         (KEEP or DELETE)
   VOLUME SERIAL     ===>              (If not cataloged)
   DATA SET PASSWORD ===>              (If password protected)

SYSOUT CLASS      ===> N
   A - Administrative Center
   L - Lincoln Park
   N - Northwest Center
   O - Oakbrook Center

JOB STATEMENT INFORMATION:  (Verify before proceeding)
   ===> //CSCJGJP   JOB 1,'BIN 7 JANOSSY',MSGCLASS=A,
   ===> //  MSGLEVEL=(1,1),NOTIFY=CSCJGJ
   ===> //*
   ===> //*
```

FIGURE 15.2 TSO 3.6 hardcopy print utility screen (academic installation with print class routing to different computer labs)

```
DATA SET NAME  ===>  SOURCE.COBOL(FSBT3708)
```

or

```
DATA SET NAME  ===>  'BT05686.SOURCE.COBOL(FSBT3708)'
```

Print occurs in TSO 3.6 as the result of a batch job for which job control language is composed and submitted automatically. The program used in the job is actually the MVS utility IEBGENER. The submission occurs when you leave the TSO 3.6 screen, and a message is generated in the extended message area indicating the job number assigned to it, just as for any batch job submission. The JCL composed for the submission includes one step for each item for which you initiate print within the TSO 3.6 screen. The job statement images at the bottom of the TSO 3.6 screen are used to preface the JCL for the job submission. TSO does not perform any validation of the JCL, so if it is entered incorrectly, the print job will fail.

Print can take place at the main installation printer or at a local terminal printer attached to the terminal controller, if one is provided and if the installation has installed the DSPRINT utility. In order for a local printer to be specified for the print, you need to know and enter its communication identifier, or "printer id," on the screen. If the TSO 3.6 screen does not provide a place to insert the printer id, the installation has not made a local print option available.

The job control language at the bottom of the screen can carry a MSGCLASS parameter, but this will affect the routing of the print job messages only, not the actual data set print. The SYSOUT CLASS field on the screen is where you indicate the print class to which you desire the data set print to be directed. It is therefore possible to use TSO 3.6 to print material at remote printers if these are associated with different print classes, unlike the case with TSO 3.1, which is hardcoded to print material at the main system printer local to the computer itself. Figure 15.2 indicates how students at DePaul University can designate at which of many geographically separated computer labs a given print output will be produced, using the appropriate print class.

On the version of the TSO 3.6 screen illustrated in Figure 15.1, the SYSOUT CLASS field need not be specified as a single character. Whatever is entered at this field is used by TSO to form the

SYSOUT specification in the job control language used to submit the print. In an installation where custom form identifiers are in use, a SYSOUT CLASS entry such as:

```
SYSOUT CLASS ===> S,,14RP
```

may be specified via the TSO 3.6 screen to cause custom form stock mounting or a special format of print to be generated.

JOB CONTROL LANGUAGE OR CLISTS FOR PRINTING ITEMS

Figure 15.3 lists the MVS job control language to copy an item from disk to the SYSOUT printer spool. This short job stream is similar to that composed and submitted by the TSO 3.6 HARDCOPY func-

```
EDIT --- CSCJGJ.CSC.CNTL(GENERPRT) - 01.00 ----------------- COLUMNS 001 072
COMMAND ===>                                                 SCROLL ===> PAGE
****** **************************** TOP OF DATA ******************************
000100 //CSCJGJP   JOB 1,'BIN 7 JANOSSY',MSGLEVEL=(1,1),MSGCLASS=A,
000200 //  NOTIFY=CSCJGJ
000300 //*
000400 //*  CSCJGJ.CSC.CNTL(GENERPRT)    J JANOSSY 10-87
000500 //*  JCL TO PRINT WITH IEBGENER
000600 //*
000700 //STEPA     EXEC PGM=IEBGENER
000800 //SYSUT1     DD DSN=CSCJGJ.CSC.COBOL(PROGRAM1),
000900 //  DISP=SHR
001000 //SYSUT2     DD SYSOUT=*
001100 //SYSPRINT   DD SYSOUT=*
001200 //SYSUDUMP   DD DUMMY,DCB=BLKSIZE=121
001300 //SYSIN      DD DUMMY
001400 //
****** **************************** BOTTOM OF DATA ***************************
```

FIGURE 15.3 MVS job control language to copy a disk data set or partitioned data set member to the printer (see Appendix D for a CLIST-edited and submitted version of this JCL)

tion. In order to use this JCL, it should be housed in a CNTL library, and the item to be printed entered at the //SYSUT1 DD statement. //SYSUT2 directs the stream of data to the printer, and the print class or MVS JCL SYSOUT routing specifications dictate its handling.

A handy means of submitting items to print immediately exists in the composition of a TSO command list, or CLIST, that prompts for a few parameters such as data set name, print destination, and internal routing information, and then automatically edits and submits the JCL for a print job. Such a CLIST illustrates capabilities for prompted JCL composition and submission on behalf of end users, and is a focus of discussion in Appendix D, dealing with CLISTs.

3270 Terminal PF Keys, Special Keys, PA Keys

The IBM 3270 terminal family provides special function keys not found on ordinary ASCII or microcomputer keyboards. Two categories of special functions keys exist: program function (PF) keys, which can be given command meanings, and program access (PA) keys, which do not transmit screen data to the computer but do signal it for special attention.

Program function keys simply "emit" the word commands discussed here as if the words had been entered on the COMMAND ===> line. The intended action can be obtained by keying in this word on the command line if your terminal does not provide dedicated *PF* keys.

PROGRAM FUNCTION KEYS

The 12 program function keys associated with IBM 3270 terminals are given default meanings under TSO/ISPF. Some models of terminals provide 24 keys, in which case these defaults are assigned two pairs of keys, for example, *PF1* and *PF13* are the same, *PF2* and *PF14* are the same, and so forth. The assignment of functions to *PF* keys can be changed using TSO function 0.3, or from within any screen by placing the word KEYS on the command line and pressing *ENTER*.

The arrangement of the function keys on the common 12-function-key IBM model 3270 terminal family is shown in Chapter 1 in Figure 1.1. Some newer models of the 3270 family group func-

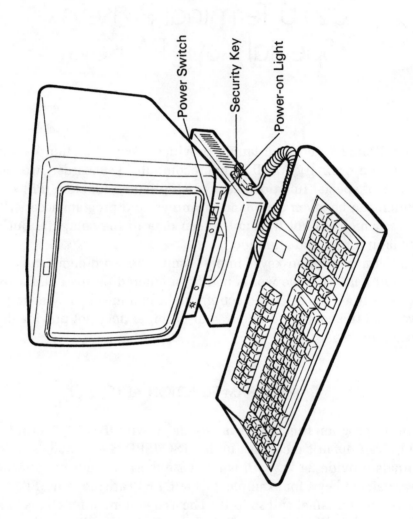

Power Switch

Security Key

Power-on Light

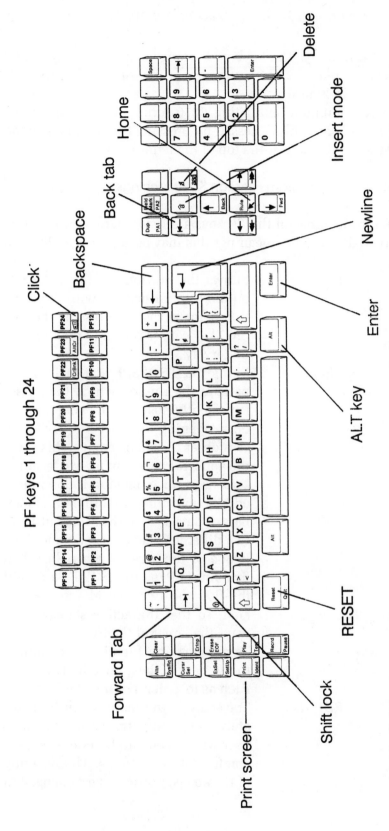

FIGURE A.1 IBM 3191 terminal and programming keyboard. (Reprinted with permission from *IBM 3191 Display Station User's Guide*, Copyright 1987 by International Business Machines Corporation.)

tion keys differently. The keyboard arrangement of the newer IBM 3191 terminal places 24 function keys at the top of the entry area, as illustrated in Figure A.1.

On microcomputers emulating 3270 terminals, program function keys are commonly accessed by pressing the *ESCape* key followed by a number key at the top of the letter keys.

Program Function Key Meanings

The default meanings of the *PF* keys are listed here. At the end of the chart are listed other meanings that may be assigned to *PF* keys.

PF1	*HELP*	Shows the portions of the TSO/ISPF online tutorial dealing with the function being accessed. Pressing the *PF3 END* key causes return to the function underway.
PF2	*SPLIT*	Splits the TSO/ISPF screen into two parts at the line on which the cursor is presently positioned, using a row of dots, opening up a second TSO/ISPF session at the main menu. This gives the appearance of having two terminal screens at once, making it possible to edit or examine two different members or data sets, or the same outlist in two different places, at the same time. If one of the screens is smaller than five lines, *PF9*, the *SWAP* key, will flip-flop the two logical screens created, so that the active screen is always the larger of the two.
PF3	*END*	Terminates any function and returns to the next highest level in TSO/ISPF, such as to a menu or member list.
PF4	*RETURN*	Traverses to the main menu immediately. This is slightly helpful to a new user when access to functions is most comfortable via menus. The meaning of the key is, however, best changed to

		PRINT at some point. A picture of the screen can then be placed into the list data set for printing by pressing the PF4 key. This capability is handy for taking a copy of a TSO/ISPF tutorial screen, PDS member list, or small item of job control language or source code.
PF5	RFIND	REPEAT FIND is the function of this key. During edit it is possible to seek a specific character string or word in a member with the command line FIND command. The PF5 key lets the same find action be repeated without reentry of the phrase in the command line.
PF6	RCHANGE	REPEAT CHANGE can be performed with this key. During edit it is possible to specify replacement of a character or character string with another value using the command line CHANGE command. PF6 allows the action to be repeated without having to reenter anything on the command line. Every instance of the change can then be seen as it occurs. The CHANGE ALL command, entered on the TSO/ISPF command line, makes all changes at once without manual intervention.
PF7	UP	When pressed, PF7 moves the 21-line window of the screen up in the data set or, in other words, scrolls it backward. The amount of scrolling action is specified in the SCROLL ===> field as PAGE, HALF, MAX or CSR for "cursor position," or an integer representing the number of lines.
PF8	DOWN	When pressed, PF8 moves the 21-line window of the screen down in the data set or, in other words, scrolls it forward. The amount of scrolling

		action is specified in the SCROLL ===> field as PAGE, HALF, MAX or CSR for "cursor position," or an integer representing the number of lines.
PF9	SWAP	SWAP is useful only when the split screen mode initiated with PF2 is in effect. It allows switching from one of the screens to the other, restoring the cursor to its former position. If one of the screens is smaller than five lines, the PF9 SWAP key will flip-flop the two logical screens so that the active screen is always the larger of the two.
PF10	LEFT	When pressed, PF10 moves the 80-column window of the screen left to show columns left of the screen. When TSO/ISPF displays items in a data set or member it indicates in the upper right corner of the screen the columns of the records being shown. Pressing this key when columns 1 through 72 are being shown has no effect since there is nothing leftward. Pressing PF10 after PF11 has been used allows moving back to the "other side" of the records. The amount of leftward movement is governed by the value in the SCROLL ===> field, and can be a number of columns, or HALF, PAGE, or MAX.
PF11	RIGHT	When pressed, PF11 moves the 80-column window of the screen right to show columns right of the screen. When TSO/ISPF displays items in a data set or member, it indicates in the upper right corner of the screen the columns of the records being shown. Pressing this key when columns 1 through 72 or 7 through 78 are being

shown moves the screen rightward if there are undisplayed columns there. If the far right side of the data is already being displayed, pressing this key has no effect. The amount of rightward movement is governed by the value in the SCROLL ===> field, and can be a number of columns, or HALF, PAGE, or MAX.

PF12   *CURSOR*   Tabs to the first enterable field on line 2 of the display, but the same effect is gotten faster by pressing the *HOME* key, the *ALT/left tab* above *NEWLINE*. Under TSO/SPF, the version in use before TSO/ISPF was made available, it was common to assign *PF12* to *RETURN* and it, not *ENTER*, had to be pressed to make the "=" transfer function operate. On IBM keyboards the "=" sign resides on the *PF12* key, which is the combination *ALT/=*. Under TSO/ISPF you can assign this key a meaning that you prefer since the "=" immediate transfer is handled by the ENTER key. Assigning *PF12* the invocation of a computational CLIST can be especially handy, as discussed in Chapter 10 and Appendix D.

Additional Function Key Commands

Default function key meanings can be replaced with these additional commands at the option of a programmer. These commands can also be invoked by entering them on the command line.

PRINT—Takes a copy of the lines on the screen and places it into the list data set for printing when the TSO/ISPF session is ended. If the terminal is a model that can display more than 80 characters, and a line longer than 121 characters is on the screen, the TSO/ISPF 0.5 PARMS function must be used to change the characteristics of the list data set to accommodate it. Figure A.2 illustrates the 0.5 screen, showing specification of a fixed, blocked record format, 130-byte records, and a screen line length of 132 bytes. The screen line length can range from 80 to 160 bytes, and if it is longer than that of the list data set record length, the line output to print is truncated. The entries on the 0.5 screen take effect immediately if the list data set has not yet been allocated due to use, or for the next ISPF session if this data set has already been associated with the current session.

PRINT-HI—Causes copying of the screen contents to the list data set, but printing characters shown in high intensity on the screen with overstrike to give them a bold appearance on the hard-copy. This enhanced form of print is not available on all types of local terminal printing devices, which may be the destination of list data set print.

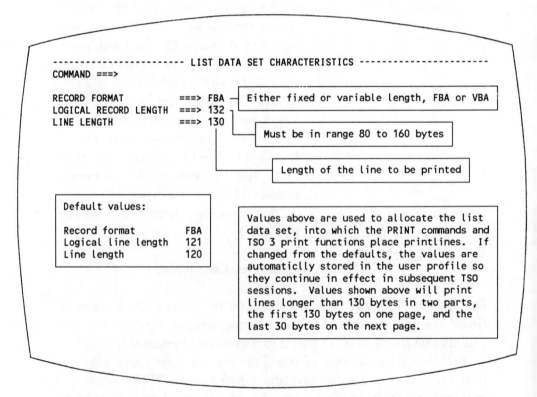

```
-------------------- LIST DATA SET CHARACTERISTICS --------------------
COMMAND ===>

RECORD FORMAT           ===> FBA  ─ Either fixed or variable length, FBA or VBA
LOGICAL RECORD LENGTH   ===> 132
LINE LENGTH             ===> 130
                                    Must be in range 80 to 160 bytes

                                    Length of the line to be printed


  Default values:
                                 Values above are used to allocate the list
  Record format        FBA       data set, into which the PRINT commands and
  Logical line length  121       TSO 3 print functions place printlines.  If
  Line length          120       changed from the defaults, the values are
                                 automaticlly stored in the user profile so
                                 they continue in effect in subsequent TSO
                                 sessions.  Values shown above will print
                                 lines longer than 130 bytes in two parts,
                                 the first 130 bytes on one page, and the
                                 last 30 bytes on the next page.
```

FIGURE A.2 TSO 0.5 PARMS setup screen, providing the means to change the characteristics of the list data set created during the TSO/ISPF session, to print screen images wider than 132 characters

PRINTL—Causes copying of the logical screen contents to the list data set, as with *PRINT*. The logical screen refers to the screen "behind" the viewed image when split screen operation is underway.

PRINTLHI—Causes copying of the logical screen contents to the list data set with high intensity characters printed with double strike, as with *PRINT-HI*. The logical screen refers to the screen "behind" the viewed image when split screen operation is underway. This enhanced form of print is not available on all types of local terminal printing devices, which may be the destination of list data set print.

SPLITV—The IBM 3290 gas plasma terminal provides a viewing area equal to four ordinary terminal screens. This large screen can be split vertically as well as horizontally to create four logical screens capable of displaying four different TSO/ISPF operations at the same time. *SPLITV* operates the same for vertical splitting as *SPLIT* does for horizontal splitting.

Use of the *TSO*, *KEYS*, and *PANELID* function key commands is described and illustrated in Chapter 10.

PROGRAM ACCESS KEYS

Unlike the case with program function keys, the meaning of the program access keys cannot be changed.

PA1	*ATTENTION*	*PA1* should not be pressed within TSO/ISPF, except to interrupt execution of a CLIST. It causes current processing to be terminated and may cause a partially cleared screen. *PA1* can be pressed during a logon sequence to step backward in the logon for reentry of the last prompted input, but TSO messages concerning that entry are terse and often difficult to interpret correctly.
PA2	*RESHOW*	Causes redisplay of the last full screen image. This can be pressed if the screen has unintentionally been

CLEAR

cleared by pressing the *CLEAR* key or *ERASE INPUT* key.

Clears the terminal and controller of screen data. This key should not be pressed within TSO/ISPF. If it is pressed, press *PF3* to get to the main menu, and then reenter the function underway. Unless this is done, only part of the screen image will be replaced by the next regular TSO/ISPF panel, since entire screen images are not transmitted for every action.

Emulating IBM Terminals with ASCII Terminals and Microcomputers

In some environments with widely dispersed workstations, and in many educational institutions, ASCII terminals such as the Digital Equipment Corporation VT-100 or compatibles are used in place of 3270s. In order for this to be possible, a protocol converter is placed between the terminals and the mainframe. The IBM 7171 ASCII Device Attachment Unit is sometimes employed in this capacity; the HyDra-II protocol converter manufactured by JDS Microprocessing is another popular unit.

When an ASCII device is used as a TSO terminal, it is necessary to use a combination of keys to emulate many of the 3270 special function keys. The combinations used vary, depending on the manner in which the protocol converter is programmed. The following table indicates the terminal key combinations by which many of the special keys of the 3270 are emulated by the IBM 7171 and the Hydra-II.

If you are using a VT-100 terminal or like device the key combinations listed in Figure B.1 will work. If you are using a microcomputer as a terminal and your terminal emulation program can mimic a VT-100, most of these key combinations will work, but you should read the special note at the end of this listing concerning CLEAR and INSERT MODE key emulation.

The applicable reference manual for the IBM 7171 is *IBM 7171 Reference Manual and Programming Guide*, GA24-4020, available from IBM publication distribution offices. The *HyDra-II User's Guide* is available from JDS Microprocessing, Inc., 22611 Lambert Street, El Toro, California 92630.

3270 KEY/FUNCTION	IBM 7171 / VT-100	HYDRA / VT-100
ENTER	Return	Return
NEWLINE	Line feed	Line feed
CLEAR	Numeric pad ENTER	Ctrl/C
DELETE	Del	Del
HOME (ALT/left tab)	Backspace	Ctrl/V
Erase EOF	Esc/DEL	Ctrl/F
Set insert mode	Numeric pad period	Ctrl/G
Reset	(see below)	Ctrl/R
Left arrow	Left arrow	Ctrl/H
Down arrow	Down arrow	Ctrl/J
Up arrow	Up arrow	Ctrl/K
Right arrow	Right arrow	Ctrl/L
Right tab	Esc/right arrow	Right tab
Left tab	Esc/left arrow	Backspace
PA1	Esc/comma	Esc/Q
PA2	Esc/period	Esc/W
PA3	Esc/slash	Esc/E
PF1 - Help	Esc/1	Esc/1
PF2 - Split	Esc/2	Esc/2
PF3 - End	Esc/3	Esc/3
PF4 - Return	Esc/4	Esc/4
PF5 - Repeat find	Esc/5	Esc/5
PF6 - Repeat change	Esc/6	Esc/6
PF7 - Scroll back	Esc/7	Esc/7
PF8 - Scroll ahead	Esc/8	Esc/8
PF9 - Swap split screens	Esc/9	Esc/9
PF10 - Window left	Esc/0	Esc/0
PF11 - Window right	Esc/-	Esc/Esc/1
PF12 - Cursor	Esc/=	Esc/Esc/2
Redisplay	Ctrl/V	Ctrl/Q
Erase input	--	Ctrl/E
Test request	--	Esc/R
Column right tab	Right tab	Ctrl/I
Column left tab	Esc/right tab	Ctrl/B
INDENT	Esc/up arrow	--
Undent	Esc/down arrow	--
Print	--	--
Dup	--	--
Device Cancel (DEV CNCL)	--	--
Field mark	--	--
Cursor select	--	--

FIGURE B.1 Key combinations to simulate 3270 PF keys and special keys using the IBM 7171 ASCII/EBCDIC protocol converter or JDS Microsystems HyDra series of protocol converters

The following sequences are particular to the IBM 7171 and are not passed through by it to the mainframe. These key sequences communicate only between the terminal and the IBM 7171 and clear transmission problems between the devices:

```
Master reset               Ctrl/G
Character error reset       Ctrl/R
Unlock keyboard            Ctrl/T
Purge buffer               Ctrl/X
"Pacing" start             Ctrl/S    (ASCII "pause transmission")
"Pacing" stop              Ctrl/Q    (ASCII "resume transmission")
```

The following sequences are particular to the Hydra-II and are not passed through by it to the mainframe. These key sequences communicate only between the terminal and the Hydra-II:

```
Insert a blank without Erase EOF                  Ctrl/A
Disconnect from Hydra                             Ctrl/@
ASCII "pause transmission"                        Ctrl/S
ASCII "resume transmission"                       Ctrl/Q
```

SPECIAL NOTE

CLEAR and INSERT MODE toggle keys on microcomputers used to emulate terminals with the IBM 7171 protocol converter:

If using a microcomputer to emulate a VT-100 you will not have a "numeric key pad ENTER" key, which is usually assigned the function of emulating the CLEAR key. You will need use a CLEAR key signal if you build and test CICS online programs, and to log off from CICS.

To generate CLEAR on a microcomputer emulating a VT-100, press these keys in sequence:

```
CLEAR KEY:       Escape, capital letter O, capital M
```

To generate the signal translated to the INSERT MODE key, use this key combination:

```
INSERT KEY:      Escape, capital letter O, lower case N
```

With the IBM 7171 and the HyDra-II, the protocol converter handles the "insert mode" on behalf of the terminal, and it's not necessary to be concerned with pressing an "Erase EOF" key at the end of a line in order to insert characters into the line.

FIGURE B.1 (continued)

185

APPENDIX C

Partitioned Data Set
Reorganization JCL

(This appendix item first appeared as Appendix B in *Practical MVS JCL for Today's Programmer*, published in 1987 by John Wiley & Sons. It appears here with the permission of the publisher as a matter of convenience to programmers and end users.)

The job control language provided in Figure C.1 performs partitioned data set reorganization in a batch manner and allows respecification of partitioned data set space and secondary allocations, directory size, and blocking. It requires no control card use, provides safeguards against data set loss by interruption or failure, and as a cataloged procedure can be invoked by anyone with a simple one-line EXEC statement. The job stream does not require the party submitting it to know the disk volume on which the PDS resides, but the PDS is always written back automatically to this same disk volume, thus precluding unintended migration of the PDS to other volumes.

This job control language can be entered from the listing, but it is one of several items also available on diskette for uploading to a mainframe via a suitably equipped PC. See Appendix E for information on how to obtain a copy of the nominal-cost diskette.

BACKGROUND

TSO libraries are partitioned data sets; every individual program or set of job control language is a partitioned data set member. A

```
****** *************************** TOP OF DATA ****************************
000100 //PDSREORG PROC  PDS='***',
000200 //  RECFORM='FB',
000300 //    QREC='80',
000400 //    QBLK='3840',        'USE 3600 FOR 3350 DISK, 3840 FOR 3380 DISK
000500 //   ALLOC='TRK',
000600 //   QPRIM='4',
000700 //    QSEC='2',
000800 //  QDIRBLK='10'
000900 //*
001000 //*    PROC TO REALLOCATE AND REORGANIZE A PARTITIONED DATA SET
001100 //*    ORIG 10-15-85 J JANOSSY    LAST CHANGE 10-27-85  J JANOSSY
001200 //***********************************************************************
001300 //*  COPYRIGHT 1987 JAMES G. JANOSSY -- PERMISSION GRANTED TO COPY *
001400 //*         AND USE FOR PERSONAL OR INSTRUCTIONAL PURPOSES         *
001500 //*                                                               *
001600 //*    THIS IS A FIGURE ORIGINALLY PUBLISHED IN A BOOK ENTITLED   *
001700 //*         PRACTICAL MVS JCL FOR TODAY'S PROGRAMMERS             *
001800 //*      (JOHN WILEY AND SONS, INC., 1987, ISBM 0-471-83648-6)    *
001900 //***********************************************************************
002000 //*
002100 //***********************************************************************
002200 //*                                                               *
002300 //*    FIND ORIGINAL PDS TO BE REORGANIZED                      A *
002400 //*                                                               *
002500 //***********************************************************************
002600 //STEPA    EXEC PGM=IEFBR14
002700 //FIND1    DD DSN=&PDS,
002800 // DISP=(OLD,KEEP)
002900 //*
003000 //***********************************************************************
003100 //*                                                               *
003200 //*    COPY PDS TO ANOTHER  SAME NAME BUT .NEWCOPY APPENDED       *
003300 //*    NOTE: THERE IS NO IEFBR14 OF THE .NEWCOPY DATA SET         *
003400 //*    AHEAD OF THIS BECAUSE .NEWCOPY IF PRESENT WHEN THIS      B *
003500 //*    STARTS INDICATES A PROBLEM WITH A PRIOR REORG THAT         *
003600 //*    SHOULD BE CORRECTED WITH RECOVERY ACTIONS                  *
003700 //*                                                               *
003800 //***********************************************************************
003900 //STEPB    EXEC PGM=IEBCOPY,COND=(0,LT)
004000 //SYSPRINT    DD DUMMY,DCB=BLKSIZE=121
004100 //SYSUDUMP    DD SYSOUT=A
004200 //SYSUT1    DD DSN=&PDS,
004300 // DISP=(OLD,KEEP)
004400 //SYSUT2    DD DSN=&PDS..NEWCOPY,
004500 // UNIT=SYSDA,
004600 // DISP=(NEW,CATLG,DELETE),
004700 // DCB=(RECFM=&RECFORM,LRECL=&QREC,BLKSIZE=&QBLK),
004800 // SPACE=(&ALLOC,(&QPRIM,&QSEC,&QDIRBLK)),
004900 // VOL=REF=*.STEPA.FIND1
005000 //SYSUT3    DD UNIT=SYSDA,SPACE=(CYL,(1,1))
005100 //SYSUT4    DD UNIT=SYSDA,SPACE=(CYL,(1,1))
005200 //SYSIN    DD DUMMY
005300 //*
005400 //***********************************************************************
005500 //*                                                               *
005600 //*    DELETE ORIGINAL PDS SINCE COPY WAS MADE OK               C *
005700 //*                                                               *
005800 //***********************************************************************
```

FIGURE C.1 Job control language to reorganize a partitioned data set with options to change blocking, space allocation, and quantity of directory blocks

188

```
005900 //STEPC     EXEC PGM=IEFBR14,COND=(0,LT)
006000 //DEL1         DD DSN=&PDS,
006100 // DISP=(MOD,DELETE),
006200 // SPACE=(TRK,0)
006300 //*
006400 //**********************************************************************
006500 //*                                                                  *
006600 //*    COPY .NEWCOPY BACK TO ORIGINAL PDS NAME                  D    *
006700 //*                                                                  *
006800 //**********************************************************************
006900 //STEPD     EXEC PGM=IEBCOPY,COND=(0,LT)
007000 //SYSPRINT   DD SYSOUT=*
007100 //SYSUDUMP   DD SYSOUT=A
007200 //SYSUT1     DD DSN=&PDS..NEWCOPY,
007300 // DISP=(OLD,KEEP)
007400 //SYSUT2     DD DSN=&PDS,
007500 // UNIT=SYSDA,
007600 // DISP=(NEW,CATLG,DELETE),
007700 // DCB=(RECFM=&RECFORM,LRECL=&QREC,BLKSIZE=&QBLK),
007800 // SPACE=(&ALLOC,(&QPRIM,&QSEC,&QDIRBLK)),
007900 // VOL=REF=*.STEPA.FIND1
008000 //SYSUT3     DD UNIT=SYSDA,SPACE=(CYL,(1,1))
008100 //SYSUT4     DD UNIT=SYSDA,SPACE=(CYL,(1,1))
008200 //SYSIN      DD DUMMY
008300 //*
008400 //**********************************************************************
008500 //*                                                                  *
008600 //*    IF ALL OK, DELETE THE .NEWCOPY                           E    *
008700 //*                                                                  *
008800 //**********************************************************************
008900 //STEPE     EXEC PGM=IEFBR14,COND=(0,LT)
009000 //DEL1         DD DSN=&PDS..NEWCOPY,
009100 // DISP=(MOD,DELETE),
009200 // SPACE=(TRK,0)
****** ************************** BOTTOM OF DATA **************************
```

FIGURE C.1 (continued)

programmer usually has at least two PDS's: one with the last part of the name COBOL, PLI, ASM, or FORT, for source code statements, and one with a final name portion of CNTL to house JCL statements.

When a given program or job control language member is updated by TSO and subsequently saved at the end of the edit session, it is written back into its partitioned data set library in toto. It is not written back into the space it had occupied; that copy of the information remains but is dead and no longer accessible. The updated member is automatically written to unused space at the end of the present PDS members by using, if necessary, secondary allocation of disk space if defined as a characteristic of the PDS when established. When a member is deleted, the space it occupies is not reusable by any other member; it, too, becomes dead space.

A partitioned data set will eventually become filled with dead space and members. Reclaiming the dead space occupied by superseded members is often called compressing a PDS because, at least conceptually, it appears afterward that the members have been squeezed upward to eliminate the dead space and leave all unused space available at the tail end of the PDS. Although the online TSO compression function may appear to be appealing, it is time-consuming, especially for large data sets, and it demands that the terminal that invokes it remain inactive during the time it is operating. Online compress also carries the potential of corrupting a data set if an interruption occurs during the operation. TSO online compress does not release secondary space allocations that the PDS may have acquired as it grew. A batch compress, performed with job control language, overcomes these problems.

USING THE PDS REORGANIZATION PROC

The job control language for the reorganization proc is listed in Figure C.1. This should be entered as a member of a CNTL partitioned data set. The JCL uses only the standard IBM utilities IEFBR14 and IEBCOPY, which are present as MVS operating system software.

To invoke this as an instream procedure, place your normal job statement at the front of the job control language, a // PEND statement after the last line of the JCL, and follow with the invocation of the procedure that names the partitioned data set to be reorganized:

```
//RUNIT  EXEC PDSREORG,PDS='BT05686.SOURCE.COBOL'
//
```

To invoke the reorganization as a cataloged procedure, enter it into a partitioned data set, have it transferred into SYS1.PROCLIB or the designated proc library in your installation, and invoke it with only a JOB statement and the EXEC statement.

The procedure was written with symbolic parameters for the partitioned data set characteristics that are likely to differ between common library types and data sets. Typical default values are provided for all but the PDS name symbolic parameters in the procedure itself. An installation can make these defaults appropriate to local customs and conventions; personnel can then invoke the procedure specifying only the PDS name. COND tests built into the job control language skip processing if an abnormal condition is encountered.

EXPLANATION OF THE PROC

//STEPA of this job control language accomplishes no data set manipulation action at all; it uses the IEFBR14 null program as an excuse to have MVS act on the //FIND1 DD statement. This step causes MVS to look for the data set in the system catalog, find the volume on which it resides, and ensure that exclusive use of the data set is possible. Because of this step, subsequent steps can use a referback to //FIND1 to supply the volume serial number of the disk on which the reorganized partitioned data set is to be placed. The party running the job therefore does not have to know or specify this volume serial number.

The job uses IEBCOPY to copy the partitioned data set to another data set, named similarly to the original but with .NEWCOPY appended to the data set name. A data set by this name should not exist on the disk if prior runs of the reorganization ended successfully; therefore we intentionally provide no "housekeeping" IEFBR14 to delete a data set of the .NEWCOPY name. The .NEW-COPY data set will be written with the same space specification that is intended to apply to the final reorganized data set; if this space allocation cannot be made, the job will stop without doing anything to the original PDS.

Once the .NEWCOPY has been successfully created the original partitioned data set is deleted at //STEPC. In //STEPD the .NEW-COPY is copied back to a PDS of the original name. The same symbolic parameters for data set space are employed here as in the first copy. Finally, if everything goes as planned, the .NEWCOPY data set is deleted.

IEBCOPY accepts input at //SYSUT1 and directs its output to //SYSUT2. No control cards are required for this method of operation, and the //SYSIN DD statement is assigned to DUMMY status. The entire procedure may therefore be packaged as a self-contained proc. The //SYSPRINT output of the initial IEBCOPY is assigned to dummy status to avoid duplication of member listings. The //SYS-PRINT listing from the second IEBCOPY is assigned to print and is a useful inventory of the members in the data set.

REBLOCKING A PDS CHANGING THE SPACE OR DIRECTORY ALLOCATION

If a change in partitioned data set blocking, space allocation, or directory size is desired, it can be done at the time of reorganization by specifying the items in the EXEC statement, overriding the default values. For example, to invoke the procedure to change blocking to 3,600 bytes, a more efficient value than 3,840 bytes for the IBM 3350 disk, PDSREORG can be invoked in this way:

```
//RUNIT   EXEC PDSREORG,PDS='BT05686.SOURCE.COBOL',
//  QBLK=3600
//
```

If the primary and secondary space allocations are to be changed, but the default blocking is to prevail, the invocation can be done as:

```
//RUNIT   EXEC PDSREORG,PDS='BT05686.SOURCE.COBOL',
//  QPRIM=90,
//  QSEC=50
//
```

Similarly, the number of directory blocks can be changed in the course of the reorganization:

```
//RUNIT   EXEC PDSREORG,PDS='BT05686.SOURCE.COBOL',
//  QDIRBLK=60
//
```

or all of the defaults can be overridden at one time.

To use the procedure to reorganize a load module library, it can be executed with:

```
//RUNIT   EXEC PDSREORG,PDS='BT05686.TEST.LOADMODS',
//  RECFORM=U,
```

```
// QREC=0,
// QBLK=23476   'FOR IBM 3380
//
```

The value for QBLK in this case should be track size; 23,476 allows two blocks to fit on the 47,476-byte tracks of the IBM 3380. For the IBM 3350 disk drive a value of 19,069 can be used, and for the IBM 3330-II, 13,030. The values for primary and secondary allocation and directory blocks can also be specified to match or modify the nature of the existing load module library.

WHAT TO DO IF THE REORGANIZATION RUN FAILS

The reorganization procedure will fail if space is not available to house the .NEWCOPY copy of the data set. In this case, try the run again. This type of abend causes no change in the name or status of the original data set.

If the run fails after //STEPB, the .NEWCOPY of the partitioned data set will exist. Depending on whether the run failed during or after //STEPC, the original PDS may or may not exist, or it may exist but be incomplete as a result of interruption in //STEPD. To recover from the failure, rename the original PDS to some unique name by using the TSO 3.2 function, manually allocate a new PDS with the desired characteristics under the original name, and use TSO 3.3 or a job control language invocation of IEBCOPY to copy the .NEW-COPY data set back to the newly allocated original. Verify that the new data set of the original name is intact. Then use TSO function 3.2 to delete the renamed and .NEWCOPY versions of it.

TSO Command Lists (CLISTs)

TSO command lists, commonly called CLISTs, as in "see-lists," are in many ways a curiosity. They provide the means to perform customized online actions within TSO and some other useful functions. But they do not take the place of job control language (JCL), and while interactive, they are not a means of creating online dialogs suitable for production usage. Unlike the command files of the microcomputer and VAX environments, TSO command lists must be executed under TSO, and they do not deal directly with the operating system of the computer.

CLIST BACKGROUND

CLISTs provide the means to package raw native mode TSO commands in a form that can be invoked by name. This capability provided a way to streamline often-taken actions within the early native mode TSO environment. The importance of CLISTs to applications programmers diminished when the original line editing, panel-less format of TSO was enhanced with ISPF. Systems programming personnel do make use of the CLIST language, however, because it is the means by which customized panels and dialogs are implemented "behind the scenes" within the TSO/ISPF environment.

To use TSO CLISTs, one must know TSO native mode commands and their syntax. In the contemporary MVS environment, the packaging of these commands in CLISTs provides the means of locally implementing these specialized conveniences:

- streamlined access within TSO and TSO/ISPF to utilities of benefit to programmers and end users, including procedures to select source code from production archives, replace source code in archives, inquire into a tape management system, and perform disk space management chores;
- computational routines that aid in calculating efficient disk blocking and space usage, VSAM data set design and IDCAMS control statement coding, and TSO message sending;
- prompted composition and submission of job control language on behalf of end users. This capability involves a CLIST to prompt for values and validate them, and then invoke native mode TSO/ISPF FIND and CHANGE commands against a base of reference JCL to edit it with the values input. This hides the JCL and automates the editing and submission of it for a run. The traditional way to accomplish this relies on cataloged procedures and symbolic parameters.

After allocating a partitioned data set to house CLIST source code, it is possible to explore some practical applications of CLISTs to the applications-programming environment.

ALLOCATING A CLIST LIBRARY

A CLIST partitioned data set library contains variable-length, blocked records that may be up to 255 bytes in length. In order to experiment with CLISTs, use the TSO 3.2 allocate option to create a partitioned data set with the characteristics illustrated in Figure D.1. Name it in such a way that the last part of the name is CLIST, the standard identifier for this type of partitioned data set library. If you cannot access the TSO 3.2 allocate function, you can allocate a CLIST library using MVS job control language such as this:

```
// (your own local JOB statement)
//STEPA   EXEC PGM=IEFBR14
//ALLO    DD DSN=BT05686.SOURCE.CLIST,
// UNIT=SYSDA,
// DISP=(NEW,CATLG,DELETE),
// DCB=(RECFM=VB,LRECL=255,BLKSIZE=6233),
// SPACE=(TRK,(10,(5,7))
//
```

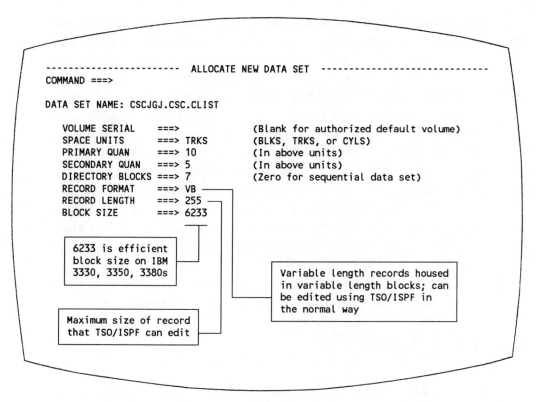

FIGURE D.1 TSO 3.2 screen filled out to allocate a TSO CLIST library

For further information concerning job control language, see a companion book in this series, *Practical MVS JCL for Today's Programmer* (John Wiley & Sons, 1987).

CLIST SYNTAX

To enter CLISTs into your CLIST library, use the TSO 2 EDIT function. TSO/ISPF provides exactly the same editing facilities for variable-length records as for fixed-record-length source code and job control language. The first eight positions of each line of CLIST code can contain an eight-digit line number. If you have the profile for the edit session set for standard numbers, these numbers will be applied automatically, and TSO/ISPF will position text entry to begin in position 9 of the records. CLIST source code can be unnumbered as well.

Since CLIST lines are not constrained to be 80-byte card images, you may have to window rightward with the PF11 key during edit if a given line is to be wider than the screen. The column indicators at the upper right corner of the edit screen show the record positions on which you are positioned at any time.

The symbols /* and */ begin and end CLIST source code comments. Variable names can be up to 32 letters and numbers in length; the first of these must be an ampersand & and the second must be a letter. Computations are limited to integer math only, must state the SET verb on the left side of the equal sign, and follow the same use of symbols as do most programming languages. Addition is denoted by the plus sign +, subtraction by the minus sign −, multiplication by the asterisk *, and division by the slash /. The assignment operator is the single equal sign =. Exponentiation is denoted by two asterisks **.

Within the CLIST syntax the remainder of a division can be obtained by coding two slashes //. As a result of these statements:

```
SET &NEWVAL1 = 20 / 12
SET &NEWVAL2 = 20 // 12
```

the variable &NEWVAL1 assumes a value of 1, while &NEWVAL2 takes on the value of 8. The use of the remainder operator // does not require the prior use of the division operator.

A number of "control variables" exist. These are variables assigned values by the system either from operating system information or due to previous CLIST actions. Figure D.2 lists the most useful control variables, some of which are employed in the CLIST examples that follow. These examples show typical CLIST coding, which resembles a crude form of the BASIC programming language.

A SIMPLE CLIST FOR TAPE BLOCK SIZE
CALCULATION

TAPEINFO is a CLIST listed in Figure D.3. It prompts for the length of records to be written to a tape data set, and returns with the largest block size that will fit into the maximum block-length limitation of 32,760 bytes. It also composes and presents the actual JCL DCB parameter needed.

TAPEINFO exhibits some of the most obvious elements of CLIST

VARIABLES: Named with ampersand and up to 31 alphanumeric characters; first must be alphabetic.
No distinction is made in naming numeric and alphanumeric variables.
Numeric range is limited to integers in the range -2,147,483,648 to +2,147,483,647.

CODING: Lines are continued with the symbols - or +.
A label can serve as a target for a GOTO transfer of control instruction.
Label is defined by coding a name followed by a colon and the line must contain
    an instruction or be continued with a - symbol.
Line numbers are optional but if used consume the first eight position of the line.
DO WHILE and END establish iterative loops.

DETERMINING THE CLASS OF AN ENTERED ITEM:

&DATATYPE(&USERINPUT)

&DATATYPE invokes a built-in function that tests the nature of the item within the
parenetheses. If it is entirely numeric, the symbolic variable &DATATYPE assumes a
value of 'NUM'. If the item is not numeric, &DATATYPE takes on a value of 'CHAR'.

Example: if &USERINPUT is 12345, &DATATYPE(&USERINPUT) leaves &DATATYPE as NUM

STRING OPERATIONS:

&SUBSTR(x, y, character-string)

x identifies a starting position in character-string
y identifies the ending position in character-string
&SUBSTR assumes the value of the portion of character-string delimited by x and y

Example: if &MESSAGE is HELLOHOWAREYOU,
        &SUBSTR(6,8,&MESSAGE) makes &SUBSTR assume the value HOW

OPERATORS

Arithmetic	+	Addition
	-	Subtraction
	*	Multiplication
	/	Division
	**	Exponentiation
	//	Remainder
Comparative	EQ or =	Equal
	NE	Not equal
	LT or <	Less than
	GT or >	Greater than
	LE or <=	Less than or equal
	GE or >=	Greater than or equal
	NG	Not greater than
	NL	Not less than
Logical	&& or AND	Logical AND
	|| or OR	Logical OR

COMMON SYSTEM-DEFINED SYMBOLIC VARIABLES

&SYSUID   The current TSO user's id

&SYSTIME   Current system time, in the format HH:MM:SS

&SYSDATE   Current system date in the format MM/DD/YY (slashes foul TSO editing)

FIGURE D.2 CLIST language control variables providing the means to access
user id, system date and system time

syntax. WRITENR is the command for "write with no return"; the phrase following will be written on the terminal, and the cursor will remain on the same line. In the first statement, the semicolon near the end is actually part of the information to be displayed upon the screen, not an element of syntax. The lack of quotation marks or other character string framing symbols in syntax of the CLIST language is an unfortunate detraction from clarity. The plus sign at the end of the first line indicates that the line is continued; a minus sign can also be used to signify continuation of a line.

READ acquires data from the keyboard and assigns it to the variable named. No distinction is made in naming character or numeric input, and no declaration of variable type is available. Instead, data is accepted as entered, but if non-numeric data enters at a variable used in computation, the CLIST fails in execution.

TAPEINFO prompts for entry of a single item of data, the length of the records to be written to a fixed, blocked tape data set. It computes the maximum number of such records that will fit into the maximum block size of 32,760 bytes permitted by MVS, and suggests this value as the block size for most efficient tape data storage.

To experiment with the TAPEINFO CLIST, create a CLIST library as described in the foregoing, then use TSO 2 EDIT to enter the CLIST source code. To test the CLIST, leave the edit screen by which it was created, so that it is saved to disk. Then place a command similar to that shown in Figure D.4 on the command line, and press the ENTER key. The CLIST will begin execution and will prompt for entry of a record length. Enter 250 and press ENTER; the result should be a message indicating that the best blocking factor is 131, and MVS JCL coded for a block size of 32,750 should be presented on the screen.

A CLIST THAT COMPOSES DISK SPACE JCL

In the modern business data-processing environment, installations use the IBM 3380, the 3350, and the 3330 disk units, each of which have different track size characteristics. The most efficient blocking factor for records of a given length is different for each model of disk. Computing an appropriate block size, and then composing the specific JCL statements to allocate a new data set to house the records, is a chore readily automated with a computational CLIST.

```
EDIT --- CSCJGJ.CSC.CLIST(TAPEINFO) - 01.01 -------------- COLUMNS 009 080
COMMAND ===>                                                SCROLL ===> PAGE
****** **************************** TOP OF DATA ****************************
000100 WRITENR *** TAPEINFO CLIST AT &SYSTIME ON &SYSDATE; +
000200    RECORD LENGTH?
000300 READ &RECLEN
000400 SET &BLKCNT = 32760 / &RECLEN
000500 SET &BLKSIZ = &BLKCNT * &RECLEN
000600 WRITE *** BEST BLOCKING IS &BLKCNT RECORDS PER BLOCK; JCL IS:
000700 WRITE      // DCB=(RECFM=FB,LRECL=&RECLEN,BLKSIZE=&BLKSIZ)
****** **************************** BOTTOM OF DATA *************************
```

FIGURE D.3 TAPEINFO, a computational CLIST that computes the most efficient block size for fixed-length-record tape data sets

```
EDIT --- CSCJGJ.CSC.CNTL(CLINKGO) - 01.06 ---------------- COLUMNS 001 072
COMMAND ===> tso exec csc.clist(print)                      SCROLL ===> PAGE
****** **************************** TOP OF DATA ****************************
000001 //CSCJGJA  JOB 1,'BIN 7 JANOSSY',MSGCLASS=X,MSGLEVEL=(1,1),
000002 // NOTIFY=CSCJGJ
000003 //**********************************************************************
000004 //*                                                                   *
000005 //*    CLINKGO     COMPILE, LINK, AND RUN WITH CCP PROC CLINKGO        *
000006 //*                                                                   *
000007 //**********************************************************************
000008 //STEPA   EXEC  PROC=CLINKGO,
000009 //      PDS='CSCJGJ.CSC.COBOL',
000010 //   MEMBER='TESTDAT'
000011 //
****** **************************** BOTTOM OF DATA *************************
```

FIGURE D.4 Executing a CLIST from your own library using the native mode TSO "passthrough" and EXEC commands; use the name TAPEINFO in parentheses to execute the CLIST shown in Figure D.3

DISKJCL is provided in Figure D.5. This is a comprehensive CLIST that uses a single-line prompt for disk type, record length, and an estimate of the quantity of records to be housed in the new disk data set. DISKJCL computes the most efficient block size and composes the DCB and SPACE statements required to define it using a primary space allocation large enough to house the estimated number of records, and allowing an amount equal to 20% of the primary space amount for each secondary space allocation.

DISKJCL is most convenient to invoke using the "TSO" passthrough feature on the command line when actually composing JCL. Its interactions are limited to the few "extended message" overlay lines at the bottom of the screen, so it will not result in a "***" bottom of screen prompt until it finishes execution.

The DISKJCL CLIST illustrates the use of labels for CLIST logic modules, which appear on the left side of lines and are followed immediately with a colon. In order to make the labels more visible, they can appear alone on lines, but the line must then be continued as is done here with the hyphen. This CLIST also illustrates the use of the DO/END construct, which enhances clarity.

DISKINFO, listed in Figure D.6, is an expanded version of DISKJCL, which in addition computes the efficiency of the block size on the type of disk unit specified. In the case of the "compromise" block size of 6,233 bytes, which is effective for all three types of disk units, DISKINFO provides a comparison of efficiency on all three units. DISKINFO prompts for the input values of disk model, record length, and estimated number of records in the data set individually, and provides an explanatory menu. Invoking DISKINFO from the command line with the TSO passthrough feature will require pressing the ENTER key in mid-operation, because its screen messages are more numerous.

A CLIST FOR MESSAGE SENDING

TSO allows sending a very short message to another TSO user id or the system console operator. The message is limited to 115 bytes, and can be sent in native mode TSO or on the command line with the TSO passthrough facility. The format of the SEND command is discussed in Chapter 10:

```
****** **************************** TOP OF DATA ******************************
000100 /* CLIST 'DISKJCL'                        J JANOSSY   2-24-86 */
000200     SET &SECFRAC = 5        /* THIS IS 20% FOR SECONDARY ALLOCATION  */
000300 MENU: -
000400 WRITENR ENTER DISK OR "ANY", LRECL, #RECS, EG., 3350 80 1000 ===>
000500 SELECT: -
000600     READ &OPT, &RECLEN, &RECNO
000700     IF &OPT EQ 3330 THEN DO
000800        SET &DISK = 3330
000900        SET &BLK  = 13030
001000        SET &TCAP = 13030
001100        GOTO GETLEN
001200        END
001300     IF &OPT EQ 3350 THEN DO
001400        SET &DISK = 3350
001500        SET &BLK  = 19069
001600        SET &TCAP = 19069
001700        GOTO GETLEN
001800        END
001900     IF &OPT EQ 3380 THEN DO
002000        SET &DISK = 3380
002100        SET &BLK  = 23476    /* CAN'T USE 47,476 SINCE 32,760 I/O LIMIT */
002200                             /* SO WE SETTLE FOR TWO BLOCKS/TRK MAX     */
002300        SET &TCAP = 47476
002400        GOTO GETLEN
002500        END
002600     IF &OPT EQ ANY THEN DO
002700        SET &DISK = COMPROMISE
002800        SET &BLK  = 6233
002900        GOTO GETLEN
003000        END
003100 OPTBAD: DO
003200     WRITE *** INVALID ENTRY, MUST BE 3330, 3350, 3380, OR WORD "ANY"
003300     GOTO MENU
003400     END
003500 GETLEN: -
003600     IF &RECLEN GT &BLK THEN DO
003700        WRITE >>> RECORD LENGTH EXCEEDS &BLK, CHECK VALUES, START OVER
003800        EXIT
003900        END
004000 COMPUTE: -
004100     SET &RECPBLK = &BLK / &RECLEN
004200     SET &BLKSIZ = &RECPBLK * &RECLEN
004300     SET &BLKNEED = ( &RECNO / &RECPBLK ) + 1
004400     SET &SECNEED = ( &BLKNEED / &SECFRAC ) + 1
004500     WRITE      // DCB=(RECFM=FB,LRECL=&RECLEN,BLKSIZE=&BLKSIZ),
004600     WRITE      // SPACE=(&BLKSIZ,(&BLKNEED,&SECNEED),RLSE)
004700     END  /*END OF CLIST*/
****** **************************** BOTTOM OF DATA ***************************
```

FIGURE D.5   DISKJCL, a computational CLIST that computes the most efficient block size for fixed-length-record disk data sets

```
000100 /* CLIST 'DISKINFO'                          J JANOSSY   8-24-86 */
000200    SET &SECFRAC = 5          /* THIS IS 20% FOR SECONDARY ALLOCATION   */
000300    WRITE *** DISKINFO CLIST FOR DATA SET SPACE AT &SYSTIME +
000400       ON &SYSDATE
000500 MENU: -
000600    WRITE              1 - IBM 3330
000700    WRITE              2 - IBM 3350
000800    WRITE              3 - IBM 3380
000900    WRITE              4 - COMPROMISE BLOCKING, OK FOR 3330/50/80
001000    WRITENR      COMPUTATION OPTION?
001100 SELECT: -
001200    READ &OPT
001300    IF &OPT EQ 1 THEN DO
001400       SET &DISK = 3330
001500       SET &BLK  = 13030
001600       SET &TCAP = 13030
001700       GOTO OPTOK
001800       END
001900    IF &OPT EQ 2 THEN DO
002000       SET &DISK = 3350
002100       SET &BLK  = 19069
002200       SET &TCAP = 19069
002300       GOTO OPTOK
002400       END
002500    IF &OPT EQ 3 THEN DO
002600       SET &DISK = 3380
002700       SET &BLK  = 23476      /* CAN'T USE 47,476 SINCE 32,767 I/O LIMIT */
002800                              /* SO WE SETTLE FOR TWO BLOCKS/TRK MAX     */
002900       SET &TCAP = 47476
003000       GOTO OPTOK
003100       END
003200    IF &OPT EQ 4 THEN DO
003300       SET &DISK = COMPROMISE
003400       SET &BLK  = 6233
003500       GOTO OPTOK
003600       END
003700 OPTBAD: DO
003800    WRITE *** INVALID SELECTION
003900    WRITE
004000    GOTO MENU
004100    END
004200 OPTOK: DO
004300    IF &DISK = COMPROMISE THEN -
004400       WRITENR *** COMPROMISE TARGET OF &BLK USED, REC LEN? (NO COMMAS)
004500    ELSE -
004600       WRITENR *** TRACK SIZE TARGET OF &BLK USED, REC LEN? (NO COMMAS)
004700    END
004800 GETLEN: -
004900    READ &RECLEN
005000    IF &RECLEN GT &BLK THEN DO
005100       WRITE >>> RECORD LENGTH EXCEEDS &BLK
005200       WRITE    RECHECK YOUR FIGURES AND START OVER
005300       WRITE    NOTE: TRACK OVERFLOW IS NOT DESIRABLE
005400       EXIT
005500       END
005600 COMPUTE: -
005700    SET &RECPBLK = &BLK / &RECLEN
```

FIGURE D.6 DISKINFO, a computational CLIST that computes the most efficient block size for fixed-length-record disk data sets and also provides information on disk storage space efficiency

204

```
005800     SET &BLKSIZ = &RECPBLK * &RECLEN
005900     WRITE       BLOCK SIZE IS &BLKSIZ, WITH &RECPBLK RECORDS PER BLOCK
006000 JCLHELP: -
006100     WRITENR *** ESTIMATED RECORDS IN DATA SET? (NO COMMAS)
006200     READ &RECNO
006300     SET &BLKNEED = ( &RECNO / &RECPBLK ) + 1
006400     SET &SECNEED = ( &BLKNEED / &SECFRAC ) + 1
006500     WRITE       DATA SET SHOULD BE ALLOCATED WITH AT LEAST &BLKNEED BLOCKS
006600     WRITE *** WORKABLE JCL FOR THIS IS:
006700     WRITE       // DCB=(RECFM=FB,LRECL=&RECLEN,BLKSIZE=&BLKSIZ),
006800     WRITE       // SPACE=(&BLKSIZ,(&BLKNEED,&SECNEED),RLSE)
006900 STATS: -
007000     IF &DISK = 3330 OR &DISK = COMPROMISE THEN DO
007100        SET &BLKPTRK = 0
007200        IF &BLKSIZ LE 13030 THEN SET &BLKPTRK = &BLKPTRK + 1
007300        IF &BLKSIZ LE  6447 THEN SET &BLKPTRK = &BLKPTRK + 1
007400        IF &BLKSIZ LE  4253 THEN SET &BLKPTRK = &BLKPTRK + 1
007500        IF &BLKSIZ LE  3156 THEN SET &BLKPTRK = &BLKPTRK + 1
007600        IF &BLKSIZ LE  2498 THEN SET &BLKPTRK = &BLKPTRK + 1  /* NEVER */
007700        SET &BPT3330 = &BLKPTRK
007800        END
007900     IF &DISK = 3350 OR &DISK = COMPROMISE THEN DO
008000        SET &BLKPTRK = 0
008100        IF &BLKSIZ LE 19069 THEN SET &BLKPTRK = &BLKPTRK + 1
008200        IF &BLKSIZ LE  9442 THEN SET &BLKPTRK = &BLKPTRK + 1
008300        IF &BLKSIZ LE  6233 THEN SET &BLKPTRK = &BLKPTRK + 1
008400        IF &BLKSIZ LE  4628 THEN SET &BLKPTRK = &BLKPTRK + 1
008500        IF &BLKSIZ LE  3665 THEN SET &BLKPTRK = &BLKPTRK + 1
008600        IF &BLKSIZ LE  3024 THEN SET &BLKPTRK = &BLKPTRK + 1  /* NEVER */
008700        SET &BPT3350 = &BLKPTRK
008800        END
008900     IF &DISK = 3380 OR &DISK = COMPROMISE THEN DO
009000        SET &BLKPTRK = 0
009100        IF &BLKSIZ LE 23476 THEN SET &BLKPTRK = &BLKPTRK + 2  /* 2/TRK */
009200        IF &BLKSIZ LE 15476 THEN SET &BLKPTRK = &BLKPTRK + 1
009300        IF &BLKSIZ LE 11476 THEN SET &BLKPTRK = &BLKPTRK + 1
009400        IF &BLKSIZ LE  9076 THEN SET &BLKPTRK = &BLKPTRK + 1
009500        IF &BLKSIZ LE  7476 THEN SET &BLKPTRK = &BLKPTRK + 1
009600        IF &BLKSIZ LE  6356 THEN SET &BLKPTRK = &BLKPTRK + 1
009700        IF &BLKSIZ LE  5492 THEN SET &BLKPTRK = &BLKPTRK + 1
009800        IF &BLKSIZ LE  4820 THEN SET &BLKPTRK = &BLKPTRK + 1
009900        IF &BLKSIZ LE  4276 THEN SET &BLKPTRK = &BLKPTRK + 1
010000        IF &BLKSIZ LE  3860 THEN SET &BLKPTRK = &BLKPTRK + 1
010100        IF &BLKSIZ LE  3476 THEN SET &BLKPTRK = &BLKPTRK + 1
010200        IF &BLKSIZ LE  3188 THEN SET &BLKPTRK = &BLKPTRK + 1
010300        IF &BLKSIZ LE  2932 THEN SET &BLKPTRK = &BLKPTRK + 1  /* NEVER */
010400        SET &BPT3380 = &BLKPTRK
010500        END
010600 /* NOTE: 1 ADDED IN SOME CALCS TO COMPENSATE FOR INTEGER ROUNDING */
010700     IF &DISK = COMPROMISE THEN DO
010800        SET &EFF3330 = ( &BPT3330 * &BLKSIZ * 100 ) / 13030
010900        SET &TRT3330 = ( &BLKNEED / &BPT3330 ) + 1
011000 /* */
011100        SET &EFF3350 = ( &BPT3350 * &BLKSIZ * 100 ) / 19069
011200        SET &TRT3350 = ( &BLKNEED / &BPT3350 ) + 1
011300 /* */
011400        SET &EFF3380 = ( &BPT3380 * &BLKSIZ * 100 ) / 46476
011500        SET &TRT3380 = ( &BLKNEED / &BPT3380 ) + 1
011600 /* */
011700        WRITE       EFFICIENCY STATISTICS FOR &RECNO RECORDS +
011800           USING &BLKSIZ BLOCKSIZE:
```

FIGURE D.6 (continued)

```
011900      WRITE     3330: &EFF3330%      3350: &EFF3350%      3380: &EFF3380%
012000      WRITE     TRKS: &TRT3330       TRKS: &TRT3350       TRKS: &TRT3380
012100      END
012200    ELSE DO
012300      SET &EFF = ( &BLKPTRK * &BLKSIZ * 100 ) / &TCAP
012400      SET &TRTOT = ( &BLKNEED / &BLKPTRK ) + 1
012500      WRITE     THIS IS &EFF% EFFICIENT DISK UTILIZATION AND
012600      WRITE     A TOTAL OF &TRTOT TRACKS WILL BE REQUIRED
012700      END
012800    END  /*END OF CLIST*/
012900
****** **************************** BOTTOM OF DATA ****************************
```

FIGURE D.6 (*continued*)

```
COMMAND  ===>  TSO SEND 'HELLO' USER(BT05677) LOGON
```

If the message text is omitted, TSO/ISPF accepts the command and prompts for entry of the message at the bottom of the screen.

If a CLIST is arranged to prompt for the entry of a message, it can use the entry to form the SEND command and execute it. This makes it possible to stay within the panel environment of TSO/ISPF but overcome the size limitation of the command line in composing a message, and to easily send the same message to multiple parties.

Figure D.7 lists a simple CLIST that facilitates sending messages. When invoked as in Figure D.8 or D.9 from any other TSO/ISPF screen, it uses the message overlay area at the bottom of the screen to request the entry of the message recipient, and then the entry of the message within apostrophes. The prompt carries the warning that the message entered must not contain any commas, because commas are regarded by the CLIST READ verb as delimiters for different input variables. After the message is entered, the MSG echoes it, as in Figure D.10. Figure D.11 illustrates how the message appears on the recipient's screen either at logon time or immediately if they are active at the time it is sent.

A CLIST TO BROADCAST MESSAGES

It makes it possible to send the same message to multiple TSO user ids, as a crude form of "broadcast" mail, using a CLIST. Figure D.12 illustrates a "brute force" CLIST to send the same message to all members of a training class. But while this CLIST works, it lacks

```
EDIT --- CSCJGJ.CSC.CLIST(MSG) ----------------------------- COLUMNS 009 080
COMMAND ===>                                                 SCROLL ===> PAGE
****** **************************** TOP OF DATA ****************************
000100 /*CLIST 'MSG' J. JANOSSY 7/7/88 */
000200    WRITE >>> TSO MAIL, MAX 2 LINE MESSAGE ONLY, WRAPAROUND OK
000300    WRITENR SEND MSG TO WHAT TSO ID? (ENTER)
000400    READ &TO
000500    WRITENR ENTER MSG WITHIN APOSTROPHES, PRESS "ENTER" TO SEND
000600    READ &MSG
000700    SEND '&MSG' USER(&TO) LOGON
000800    SEND 'MSG ECHO>>> &MSG' USER(&SYSUID) LOGON
****** **************************** BOTTOM OF DATA ****************************
```

FIGURE D.7   MSG, a simple CLIST for sending messages to another TSO user

```
                                    ┌─────────────────────────────┐
                                    │ No TSO user id or apostrophes │
                                    └─────────────────────────────┘
EDIT --- CSCJGJ.CSC.CNTL(HOUND) - 01.00 ------|------------- COLUMNS 001 072
COMMAND ===> tso exec csc.clist(msg) ─────────┘            SCROLL ===> PAGE
****** **************************** TOP OF DATA ****************************
000100      The sun was already sinking when I reached the summit of the hill,
000200 and the long slopes beneath me were all golden-green on one side and
000300 gray shadow on the other.  A haze lay low upon the farthest skyline,
000400 out of which jutted the fantastic shapes of Belliver and Vixen Tor.
000500 Over the wide expanse there was no sound and no movement.  One great
000600 gray bird, a gull or curlew, soared aloft in the blue heaven.  He and
000700 I seemed to be the only living things between the huge arch of the sky
000800 and the desert beneath it.  The barren scene, the sense of loneliness,
000900 and the mystery and urgency of my task all struck a chill into my
001000 heart.  The boy was nowhere to be seen.  But down beneath me in a
001100 cleft of the hills there was a circle of the old stone huts, and in
001200 the middle of them there was one which retained sufficient roof to act
001300 as a screen against the weather.  My heart leaped within me as I saw
001400 it.  This must be the burrow where the stranger lurked.  At last my
001500 foot was on the threshold of his hiding-place -- his secret was within
001600 my grasp.
****** **************************** BOTTOM OF DATA ****************************
```

FIGURE D.8   Executing MSG from an unrelated screen in TSO/ISPF, allowing the system to preface the source data set with the TSO user id (the CLIST must be in the library of the party executing it)

```
                              ┌─────────────────────────────────────────────┐
                              │ Full data set name surrounded by apostrophes │
                              └─────────────────────────────────────────────┘
EDIT --- CSCJGJ.CSC.CNTL(HOUND) - 01.00 ----------------┐----- COLUMNS 001 072
COMMAND ===> tso exec 'bt05686.source.clist(msg)' ──────┘      SCROLL ===> PAGE
****** ***************************** TOP OF DATA ******************************
000100     The sun was already sinking when I reached the summit of the hill,
000200 and the long slopes beneath me were all golden-green on one side and
000300 gray shadow on the other. A haze lay low upon the farthest skyline,
000400 out of which jutted the fantastic shapes of Belliver and Vixen Tor.
000500 Over the wide expanse there was no sound and no movement. One great
000600 gray bird, a gull or curlew, soared aloft in the blue heaven. He and
000700 I seemed to be the only living things between the huge arch of the sky
000800 and the desert beneath it. The barren scene, the sense of loneliness,
000900 and the mystery and urgency of my task all struck a chill into my
001000 heart. The boy was nowhere to be seen. But down beneath me in a
001100 cleft of the hills there was a circle of the old stone huts, and in
001200 the middle of them there was one which retained sufficient roof to act
001300 as a screen against the weather. My heart leaped within me as I saw
001400 it. This must be the burrow where the stranger lurked. At last my
001500 foot was on the threshold of his hiding-place -- his secret was within
001600 my grasp.
****** *************************** BOTTOM OF DATA *****************************
```

FIGURE D.9 Executing MSG from an unrelated screen in TSO/ISPF, specifying the CLIST source data set explicitly (it need not be in the library of the party executing it)

```
EDIT --- CSCJGJ.CSC.CNTL(HOUND) - 01.00 -------------------- COLUMNS 001 072
COMMAND ===> tso exec csc.clist(msg)                         SCROLL ===> PAGE
****** ***************************** TOP OF DATA ******************************
000100     The sun was already sinking when I reached the summit of the hill,
000200 and the long slopes beneath me were all golden-green on one side and
000300 gray shadow on the other. A haze lay low upon the farthest skyline,
000400 out of which jutted the fantastic shapes of Belliver and Vixen Tor.
000500 Over the wide expanse there was no sound and no movement. One great
000600 gray bird, a gull or curlew, soared aloft in the blue heaven. He and
000700 I seemed to be the only living things between the huge arch of the sky
000800 and the desert beneath it. The barren scene, the sense of lonliness,
000900 and the mystery and urgency of my task all struck a chill into my
001000 heart. The boy was nowhere to be seen. But down beneath me in a
001100 cleft of the hills there was a circle of the old stone huts, and in
001200 the middle of them there was one which retained sufficient roof to act
001300 as a screen against the weather. My heart leaped within me as I saw
001400 it. This must be the burrow where the stranger lurked. At last my

>>> TSO MAIL, MAX 2 LINE MESSAGE ONLY, WRAPAROUND OK
SEND MSG TO WHAT TSO ID? (ENTER) cscjgj
ENTER MSG WITHIN APOSTROPHES, PRESS "ENTER" TO SEND 'this is a test of the msg
sending clist'

MSG ECHO>>> THIS IS A TEST OF THE MSG SENDING CLIST CSCJGJ
***
```

FIGURE D.10 The MSG message sending CLIST echoes the message to be sent with the WRITE verb

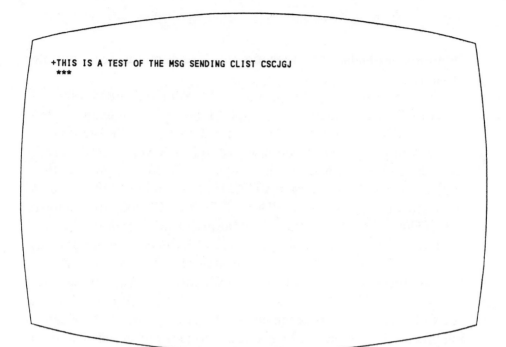

```
+THIS IS A TEST OF THE MSG SENDING CLIST CSCJGJ
 ***
```

FIGURE D.11 The message recipient's logon screen, illustrating how a message sent by the MSG CLIST will be received

```
EDIT --- CSCJGJ.CSC.CLIST(DISMSG) ----------------------------- COLUMNS 009 080
COMMAND ===>                                                    SCROLL ===> PAGE
****** *************************** TOP OF DATA *******************************
000100 /*CLIST 'DISMSG' JANOSSY 7/9/88 */
000200    WRITE >>> DISTRIBUTION MSG TO CCPQ 2 LINES ONLY
000300    WRITENR ENTER MSG WITHIN APOSTROPHES, PRESS "ENTER" TO SEND
000400    READ &MSG
000500    SEND '&MSG' USER(CCPQ01) LOGON
000600    SEND '&MSG' USER(CCPQ02) LOGON
000700    SEND '&MSG' USER(CCPQ03) LOGON
000800    SEND '&MSG' USER(CCPQ04) LOGON
000900    SEND '&MSG' USER(CCPQ05) LOGON
001000    SEND '&MSG' USER(CCPQ06) LOGON
001100    SEND '&MSG' USER(CCPQ07) LOGON
001200    SEND '&MSG' USER(CCPQ08) LOGON
001300    SEND '&MSG' USER(CCPQ09) LOGON
001400    SEND '&MSG' USER(CCPQ10) LOGON
001500    SEND '&MSG' USER(CCPQ11) LOGON
001600    SEND '&MSG' USER(CCPQ12) LOGON
001700    SEND '&MSG' USER(CCPQ13) LOGON
001800    SEND '&MSG' USER(CCPQ14) LOGON
001900    SEND '&MSG' USER(CCPQ15) LOGON
002000    SEND '&MSG' USER(CCPQ16) LOGON
002100    SEND '&MSG' USER(CCPQ17) LOGON
```

FIGURE D.12 DISMSG, a "brute force" message sending CLIST that prompts for a message and then broadcasts it to multiple TSO users

flexibility and also provides no indication of message-sending progress.

Figure D.13 illustrates a more refined version of a broadcast message CLIST, which makes use of CLIST looping logic elements. Line 500 initializes a variable named &ACCT to 1, and the DO/WHILE loop of lines 700 through 1100 uses it to form a series of nine TSO user ids. Line 800 illustrates the simple CLIST string concatenation syntax, in which the literals "CCPQ0" are joined with the variable to create strings such as CCPQ01, CCPQ02, CCPQ03, and so forth to CCPQ09. The loop in lines 1200 through 1600 continues the generation of TSO user ids from 10 through 12; the only reason for this second loop is to allow the concatenation to use the literals "CCPQ" instead of "CCPQ0" to properly form these TSO user ids.

When the CLIST of Figure D.13 is invoked, it prompts for the entry of the message to be broadcast. It then confirms that the sending process is starting, and a status message is presented each time a message is dispatched. Figure D.14 illustrates the sender's screen as the message distribution concludes.

EDITING BASE JCL AND SUBMITTING A JOB VIA A CLIST

The editing of base JCL using data obtained by screen prompts, and the submission of the JCL for execution, is perhaps the most interesting and potentially productive application of CLISTs. We'll use here a simple but complete example of this process.

Figure D.15 lists job control language stored as a member named PRINTJCL. This serves as generalized base JCL for the simple process of copying a member of a TSO/ISPF library to the printer. This one-step job stream executes the IEBGENER utility program, which copies a data set input at its //SYSUT1 DD statement to the //SYSUT2 DD statement.

The base JCL contains "place holders" at job name, MSGCLASS, input data set high level qualifier, type, and member name, and also in a comment line. The use of a dollar sign $ as a leading character in these place holders is simply a convention, not a requirement. As it stands, this JCL is not valid for submission, but by editing it to replace the place holders with specific values, it can become valid.

Figure D.16 depicts a short CLIST named PRINT that, when invoked, provides a message line citing print destinations available

```
EDIT --- CSCJGJ.CSC.CLIST(DISMSG2) ------------------------- COLUMNS 009 080
COMMAND ===>                                                 SCROLL ===> PAGE
****** *************************** TOP OF DATA ********************************
000100 /*CLIST 'DISMSG2' JANOSSY 7/15/88 */
000200    WRITE >>> DISTRIBUTION MSG TO CCPQ 2 LINES ONLY
000300    WRITENR ENTER MSG WITHIN APOSTROPHES, PRESS "ENTER" TO SEND
000400    READ &MSG
000500    SET &ACCT = 1
000600    WRITE STARTING TO SEND MSGS
000700  ┌ DO WHILE &ACCT <= 9
000800  │   SEND '&MSG' USER(CCPQ0&ACCT) LOGON
000900  │   WRITE HAVE SENT &ACCT MESSAGES NOW
001000  │   SET &ACCT = &ACCT + 1
001100  └ END
001200    DO WHILE &ACCT <= 30
001300      SEND '&MSG' USER(CCPQ&ACCT) LOGON
001400      WRITE HAVE SENT &ACCT MESSAGES NOW
001500      SET &ACCT = &ACCT + 1
001600    END
001700    WRITE ALL MESSAGES HAVE BEEN SENT, BROADCAST MAIL FINISHED
****** *************************** BOTTOM OF DATA ****************************
```

> This construct is a loop in CLIST syntax

FIGURE D.13 DISMSG2, a more flexible broadcast message CLIST that illustrates the looping capability of the CLIST language

```
-------------------------- EDIT - ENTRY PANEL -----------------------------
COMMAND ===> tso exec csc.clist(dismsg2)

ISPF LIBRARY:
    PROJECT ===> CSCJGJ
    LIBRARY ===> CSC        ===>            ===>           ===>
    TYPE    ===> CLIST
    MEMBER  ===>                   (Blank for member selection list)

OTHER PARTITIONED OR SEQUENTIAL DATA SET:
    DATA SET NAME  ===>
    VOLUME SERIAL  ===>            (If not cataloged)

>>> DISTRIBUTION MSG TO CCPQ 2 LINES ONLY
ENTER MSG WITHIN APOSTROPHES, PRESS "ENTER" TO SEND 'keep up the good work'
STARTING TO SEND MSGS
HAVE SENT 1 MESSAGES NOW
HAVE SENT 2 MESSAGES NOW
HAVE SENT 3 MESSAGES NOW
    -
    -
HAVE SENT 29 MESSAGES NOW
HAVE SENT 30 MESSAGES NOW
ALL MESSAGES HAVE BEEN SENT, BROADCAST MAIL FINISHED
***
```

FIGURE D.14 Message sending progress indications provided to the sender by the DISMSG2 message sending CLIST

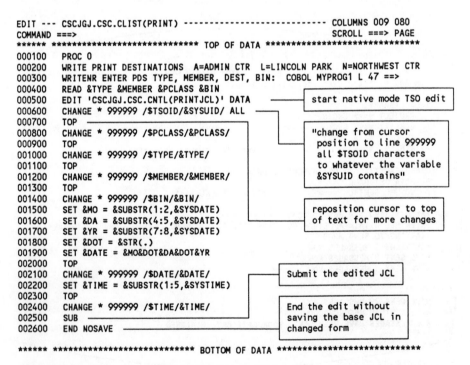

```
EDIT --- CSCJGJ.CSC.CNTL(PRINTJCL) - 01.12 ----------------- COLUMNS 001 072
COMMAND ===>                                                 SCROLL ===> PAGE
****** **************************** TOP OF DATA ******************************
000100 //$TSOIDP    JOB 01,'BIN $BIN',MSGLEVEL=(1,1),MSGCLASS=$PCLASS,
000200 //  NOTIFY=$TSOID
000300 //*
000400 //*   CSCJGJ.CSC.CNTL(PRINTJCL)      J JANOSSY 7-88
000500 //*   BASE JCL TO BE EDITED BY CLIST 'PRINT'
000600 //*
000700 //*             ********************************
000800 //*   THIS PRINT WAS INITIATED ON  *  $DATE AT $TIME BY $TSOID  *
000900 //*             ********************************
001000 //*
001100 //STEPA     EXEC PGM=IEBGENER
001200 //SYSUT1      DD DSN=$TSOID.CSC.$TYPE($MEMBER),
001300 //  DISP=SHR
001400 //SYSUT2      DD SYSOUT=*                       ┌──────────────────────┐
001500 //SYSPRINT    DD SYSOUT=*                       │ Items named with $ are│
001600 //SYSUDUMP    DD DUMMY,DCB=BLKSIZE=121          │ symbolic and are      │
001700 //SYSIN       DD DUMMY                          │ replaced by entered   │
001800 //                                              │ values by the         │
                                                       │ CLIST editing this JCL│
                                                       └──────────────────────┘
****** *************************** BOTTOM OF DATA ***************************
```

FIGURE D.15 PRINTJCL, base JCL to be edited by a CLIST as part of a copy-to-print function

```
EDIT --- CSCJGJ.CSC.CLIST(PRINT) --------------------------- COLUMNS 009 080
COMMAND ===>                                                 SCROLL ===> PAGE
****** **************************** TOP OF DATA ******************************
000100   PROC 0
000200   WRITE PRINT DESTINATIONS  A=ADMIN CTR  L=LINCOLN PARK  N=NORTHWEST CTR
000300   WRITENR ENTER PDS TYPE, MEMBER, DEST, BIN: COBOL MYPROG1 L 47 ==>
000400   READ &TYPE &MEMBER &PCLASS &BIN
000500   EDIT 'CSCJGJ.CSC.CNTL(PRINTJCL)' DATA ─────┐ ┌─ start native mode TSO edit
000600   CHANGE * 999999 /$TSOID/&SYSUID/ ALL ──────┘
000700   TOP ───────────────┐                       ┌───────────────────────┐
000800   CHANGE * 999999 /$PCLASS/&PCLASS/          │ "change from cursor    │
000900   TOP            └──────────────────────────┘│  position to line 999999│
001000   CHANGE * 999999 /$TYPE/&TYPE/               │  all $TSOID characters │
001100   TOP                                         │  to whatever the variable│
001200   CHANGE * 999999 /$MEMBER/&MEMBER/           │  &SYSUID contains"     │
001300   TOP                                         └───────────────────────┘
001400   CHANGE * 999999 /$BIN/&BIN/
001500   SET &MO = &SUBSTR(1:2,&SYSDATE)            ┌───────────────────────┐
001600   SET &DA = &SUBSTR(4:5,&SYSDATE) ───────────│ reposition cursor to top│
001700   SET &YR = &SUBSTR(7:8,&SYSDATE)            │ of text for more changes│
001800   SET &DOT = &STR(.)                         └───────────────────────┘
001900   SET &DATE = &MO&DOT&DA&DOT&YR
002000   TOP
002100   CHANGE * 999999 /$DATE/&DATE/              ┌───────────────────────┐
002200   SET &TIME = &SUBSTR(1:5,&SYSTIME)          │ Submit the edited JCL  │
002300   TOP                                        └───────────────────────┘
002400   CHANGE * 999999 /$TIME/&TIME/              ┌───────────────────────┐
002500   SUB ───────────────────────────────────────│ End the edit without   │
002600   END NOSAVE ─────────────────────────────────│ saving the base JCL in │
                                                     │ changed form           │
                                                     └───────────────────────┘
****** *************************** BOTTOM OF DATA ***************************
```

FIGURE D.16 PRINT editing CLIST that prompts for the name of the item to be printed and the desired print destination, then automatically edits PRINTJCL with these values and submits it for execution in a particular installation, and prompts for the entry of four items all in one line. The prompt seeks the data set type (such as COBOL or CNTL), the name of the member to be printed, the destination, which in this case is actually a print class, and a bin number to be used to house printed output awaiting pickup. These might be entered in this way by a person at a terminal:

```
===>  COBOL NUMCHECK A 47
```

to indicate that COBOL data set member NUMCHECK is to print at destination A and be placed into bin number 47.

The PRINT CLIST contains a native mode TSO command, EDIT, at line 500 to begin editing of the base JCL. *This edit will proceed without being visible on the terminal screen.* Line 600 issues a mass CHANGE command to replace any occurrence of the place holder $TSOID with the control variable &SYSUID, the id of the TSO user who is invoking the CLIST. Line 700 then repositions the edit to the beginning of the base JCL being edited.

Line 800 in the PRINT CLIST issues a mass change for the $PCLASS place holder, and subsequent lines again reposition to the beginning of the item and replace other place holders with data received from the prompted input. Lines 1500 through 1800 use the CLIST SUBSTR operator to pick apart the date string obtainable from the control variable &SYSDATE, and then concatenate a new rendition of it without slashes in &DATE. SUBSTR returns a string taken from the start-position, for a length indicated by end-position from the source-string:

```
&NEWVAL = &SUBSTR( start-position, end-position,
source-string )
```

The slashes within the original rendition of &SYSDATE, if not changed to some other character, would conflict with the syntax of the native mode TSO CHANGE command that performs the editing desired. Line 1900 performs the concatenation of date fragments into &DATE, accomplished simply by coding CLIST variables immediately after one another. Additional native mode TSO editing commands follow.

At line 2500, the edited JCL is submitted for execution. Line 2600 then ends the edit, with NOSAVE omitting the saving of it.

Saving the edited JCL would be disastrous since it would become unusable as base JCL, having lost the place holder values needed for editing and replacement.

Figure D.17 depicts the result when the PRINT CLIST is invoked. The command line entry of the TSO passthrough command can be assigned to a function key using the KEYS accessible from any TSO screen, as described in Chapter 10, or the command can be entered in its entirety on the command line. The prompt appears at the bottom of the screen in the message overlay area; Figure D.17 illustrates the entry of the prompted data. The CLIST performs the edit entirely behind the scene, and the only thing apparent to the TSO terminal operator is the normal job submission message.

Figure D.18 depicts the use of SDSF to view the submitted job on the system output queue. The editing performed by the CLIST has resulted in fully valid JCL, and the framed box of comments

```
EDIT --- CSCJGJ.CSC.CNTL ---------------------------------------------------
COMMAND ===> tso exec csc.clist(print)                    SCROLL ===> PAGE
   NAME          VER.MOD  CREATED    LAST MODIFIED  SIZE  INIT   MOD   ID
   DATC          01.03   85/11/20  88/03/01 19:05    20    20     0 CCPN00
   DATC2         01.00   85/11/22  85/11/22 00:20    20    20     0 CSCJGJ
   DATM          01.00   85/11/20  85/11/20 13:22    10    10     0 CSCJGJ
   DATR          01.00   85/11/20  85/11/20 13:15     8     8     0 CSCJGJ
   DISKFIX       01.03   85/10/14  87/08/01 10:39    25     4     0 CSCJGJ
   DSATEST1      01.01   85/10/27  85/10/31 21:51   121   121     0 CSCJGJ
   DS4001M       01.01   87/02/12  87/02/12 18:39    73    72     0 CCCPZ00
   DS4012M       01.01   87/02/12  87/02/12 18:55   129   129     0 CCCPZ00
   DS4014M       01.01   87/02/12  87/02/12 18:56   143   143     0 CCCPZ00
   ERRMSG        01.00   85/10/23  85/10/23 21:21    14    14     0 CSCJGJ
   FIGURE22      01.03   88/04/05  88/04/05 14:23    58    47     0 CSCJGJ
   FRUITOOT      01.00   88/03/15  88/03/15 13:07    53    53     0 CSCJGJ
   GENERPDS      01.09   85/10/31  85/11/19 12:53    25    13    18 CSCJGJ
   GHERKIN       01.00   88/03/15  88/03/15 12:51    15    15     0 CCPN00
   HOUND         01.00   88/07/09  88/07/09 12:56    16    16     0 CSCJGJ

PRINT DESTINATIONS  A=ADMIN CTR  L=LINCOLN PARK  N=NORTHWEST CTR  O=OAKBROOK
ENTER PDS TYPE, MEMBER, DEST, BIN:  COBOL MYPROG1 L 47 ==> cntl fruitoot x 7
JOB CSCJGJP(JOB09838) SUBMITTED
***                              CLIST edits base JCL with the values
                                 entered, then submits the edited JCL
```

FIGURE D.17 Executing the PRINT CLIST from an unrelated point within TSO ISPF; the CLIST prompts are presented in the message overlay area at the bottom of the screen

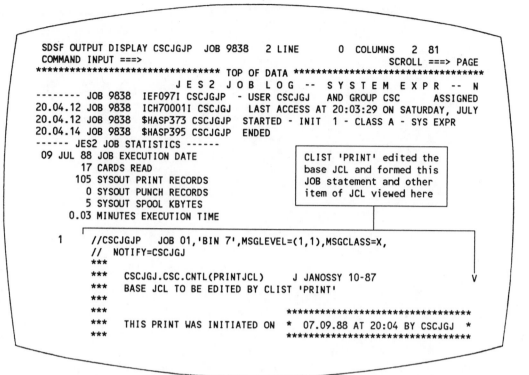

```
SDSF OUTPUT DISPLAY CSCJGJP   JOB 9838   2 LINE        0  COLUMNS   2  81
COMMAND INPUT ===>                                         SCROLL ===> PAGE
****************************** TOP OF DATA ********************************
                      J E S 2   J O B   L O G  --  S Y S T E M  E X P R  --  N
-------- JOB 9838  IEF097I CSCJGJP  - USER CSCJGJ   AND GROUP CSC    ASSIGNED
20.04.12 JOB 9838  ICH70001I CSCJGJ   LAST ACCESS AT 20:03:29 ON SATURDAY, JULY
20.04.12 JOB 9838  $HASP373 CSCJGJP  STARTED - INIT  1 - CLASS A - SYS EXPR
20.04.14 JOB 9838  $HASP395 CSCJGJP  ENDED
------ JES2 JOB STATISTICS ------
09 JUL 88 JOB EXECUTION DATE                 ┌──────────────────────────┐
        17 CARDS READ                        │ CLIST 'PRINT' edited the │
       105 SYSOUT PRINT RECORDS              │ base JCL and formed this │
         0 SYSOUT PUNCH RECORDS              │ JOB statement and other  │
         5 SYSOUT SPOOL KBYTES               │ item of JCL viewed here  │
      0.03 MINUTES EXECUTION TIME            └──────────────────────────┘

    1    //CSCJGJP   JOB 01,'BIN 7',MSGLEVEL=(1,1),MSGCLASS=X,
         //  NOTIFY=CSCJGJ
         ***
         ***   CSCJGJ.CSC.CNTL(PRINTJCL)     J JANOSSY 10-87              V
         ***   BASE JCL TO BE EDITED BY CLIST 'PRINT'
         ***
         ***                                 **********************************
         ***   THIS PRINT WAS INITIATED ON  *  07.09.88 AT 20:04 BY CSCJGJ  *
         ***                                 **********************************
```

FIGURE D.18   The output of the print job on the output queue using SDSF, illustrating the PRINTJCL as automatically edited and submitted by the PRINT CLIST

provides a convenience in having the print automatically date- and time-stamped with the moment it was originated. The place holder $TSOID appears in three places in the base PRINTJCL, and all three occurrences have been replaced by the actual TSO user id in the submitted JCL.

The PRINTJCL and its editing CLIST are simple, but illustrate how CLISTs can be arranged to prompt for and garner many items of information needed to compose a complex job stream and finalize it. CLISTs used in this way can prompt end users for the entry of runtime parameters and then, behind the scenes, customize base JCL for a job and submit it. This capability has relevance to certain information center activities and can lead to especially productive and amicable working relationships between the information center and its non-technical end users.

Obtaining PDS Reorganization JCL and CLISTs on Diskette for Uploading

The job control language depicted in Appendix C and the TSO command lists in Appendix D can be entered manually into a computer system, but these items are also available on diskette for uploading to a mainframe via a suitably equipped PC. The diskette can be obtained by sending a check or money order for $6.00 ($US) to cover the cost of media, reproduction, handling, and mailing to:

Practical Distribution Diskettes
P.O. Box 46078
Chicago, Illinois 60646

Please request diskette #317, which is available in 5¼" MS-DOS 360K format.

TSO/ISPF Command Explanation and Syntax Reference

This is a consolidated reference of TSO/ISPF edit-line and primary editing commands. Both are presented here in one alphabetized listing.

Edit-line commands are entered in the line number area of the lines being edited. They are noted here with trailing zeroes or 000000 underneath to simulate the edit line.

Primary editing commands are entered on the COMMAND ===> line at the top of the screen during edit and other TSO/ISPF actions. They are listed here with the arrow ===> after which they are entered.

A 0000

Denotes the line *after* which copied in or moved text is to appear. Entering a number after the A indicates that multiple copies of the copied or moved line are to be inserted after this point.

===> AUTOLIST [*ON*|OFF]   (Part of the editing profile)

If set on, AUTOLIST places a listing of the edited item in the list data set for printing at the end of the ISPF session. The copy is taken when the edit is ended. Once set on, AUTOLIST remains on for all subsequent editing sessions of the partitioned data set, until set off.

===> AUTONUM [*ON*|OFF]   (Part of the editing profile)

If set on causes a RENUM to be performed automatically whenever a SAVE is done explicitly or at the end of editing. When set on, AUTONUM remains on as a part of the editing profile for the partitioned data set.

===> AUTOSAVE [ON|OFF]   (Part of the editing profile)
              [OFF [PROMPT]]
              [OFF [NOPROMPT]]

If set on, causes the edited item to be saved to disk when the edit is ended. When set off, the PROMPT specification causes a prompt by TSO/ISPF asking whether the edited item is to be saved if it has been changed; NOPROMPT omits this safety feature when AUTOSAVE is off. As part of the editing profile for the partitioned data set, this setting is retained for future editing sessions on it.

B 0000

Denotes the line *before* which copied in or moved text is to appear. Entering a number after the B indicates that multiple copies of the copied or moved line are to be inserted after this point.

===> BOUNDS   [left–column right–column]
     BNDS
     BND

Sets the left and right column boundaries in which the cursor will be active. Using this command places the settings into the edit profile in effect. As part of the editing profile for the partitioned data set, this setting is retained for future editing sessions on it.

BOUNDS
000000

Displays a column boundary line showing where the boundaries of the active screen are currently set. The editing boundaries may be changed by placing a < at the desired left boundary column and a > at the desired right boundary column. The boundary line is removed from the display by placing a D edit line command in its line number area or with RESET on the COMMAND ===> line. TSO/ISPF defaults the editing boundaries to positions 1 and 71 for ASM data sets, 7 and 72 for COBOL data sets, and 1 and record length for other fixed-record-length data sets. Numbered variable-length records receive a boundary default position of 9 and maximum record length, while unnumbered variable-length data sets receive a default of 1 and maximum record length.

===> BUILTIN

Highly specialized, this command allows use of the ISPF/PDF edit facility even when the TSO/ISPF user has created an editing macro of the same name as a command.

C 0000

Identifies a line to be *copied*. CC and CC are used to identify the starting and ending lines of a group of lines to be copied. Multiple lines can also be copied by entering a line count after the C in the line number area of a line.

===> CANCEL
     CAN

Ends the edit session without saving any changes made during it, even if AUTOSAVE is on.

===> CANCEL job-name [job-id] [,PURGE]   (native mode TSO
     CAN   command)

Allows cancellation of a submitted batch job, even if it has already started to execute. Specification of PURGE not only causes job cancellation but deletion of the MVS system reporting and any output the job has generated.

===> CAPS [ON|OFF]   (Part of the editing profile)

If set on, causes lowercase letters entered at the terminal to be "folded" to uppercase letters. Neither VSCOBOL or MVS JCL accept lowercase letters as part of operable statements. As part of the editing profile for the partitioned data set, this setting is retained for future editing sessions on it.

```
===> CHANGE strgl strg2 [range] [NEXT ] [CHARS ] [X ] [col-1] [col-2]]
     CHG                            [ALL  ] [PREFIX] [NX]
     C                              [FIRST] [SUFFIX]
                                    [LAST ] [WORD  ]
                                    [PREV ]
```

Replaces a character string strg1 with the string specified as strg2. The screen display is shifted so that the cursor lies at the end of the first string changed. The optional specifications serve to broaden or limit the amount of text affected by the change; range is [from-line-number   to-line-number]. To secure complete processing of the entire item being edited, position the cursor to the top of the item and specify the ALL option as illustrated in Chapter 8.

COLS
000000

Displays a column ruler line imbedded within the text. The line can be eliminated using RESET on the COMMAND ===> line. The column ruler line does not become part of the text and is removed automatically by TSO/ISPF when editing of the member is ended.

===> COPY [member-name] [A "after" indicator in text]
                        [B "before" indicator in text]

Copies data from one place to another. Used when editing an existing member, this allows copying in another member from the same partitioned data set after or before the line annotated with A or B in the line number area. If specified at the start of editing of a new member, no A or B indication is necessary. If member name is omitted when editing an existing member, a second screen is presented allowing specification of the source for the copy, which may then be a different partitioned data set or sequential data set.

===> CREATE [member-name] [from-line-number to-line-number]

Blocks of lines in an item being edited can be marked with CC/CC or MM/MM and CREATE executed to copy or move them out to a specified member in the same partitioned data set. Instead of marking lines to be processed, they can alternatively be indicated with a line-number range after the command. If member-name is omitted, a second screen is presented allowing specification of any existing data set name to receive the lines. Note: CREATE generates only a new partitioned data set member. REPLACE can generate a new member to replace an existing member of the same name, or rewrite the contents of an existing sequential data set.

```
===> DEFINE name [CM MACRO|  ⎤
                  PGM MACRO|  ⎥
                  ALIAS name| ⎥         one required
                  NOP|        ⎥
                  RESET]      ⎦
```

Specifies either a program or CLIST macro, assigns an alias to the name of a built-in command or macro, or disables the definition of a name as a macro.

D 0000

Identifies a line to be *deleted*. DD and DD are used to identify the starting and ending lines of a group of lines to be deleted. A group of lines can also be deleted by placing a line number count after the command in the line-number area of the line being edited.

```
===> DELETE [ALL X|ALL NX] [from-line-number to-line-number]
     DEL
```

Deletes one or more lines from an item being edited. The optional specifications limit the deletion either by a range of line numbers or to excluded or non-excluded lines only.

```
===> EDIT member
```

Invokes the editing of another member or item while within the edit of a member.

```
===> EXCLUDE string-1 [range]  [NEXT ]  [CHARS ]  [X ]  [col1-col2]
     EX                        [ALL  ]  [PREFIX]  [NX]
     X                         [FIRST]  [SUFFIX]
                               [LAST ]  [WORD  ]
                               [PREV ]
```

Hides from view lines within an item being edited. The optional specifications provide a variety of ways to focus the exclusion of groups of lines; range is [from-line-number   to-line-number]. Excluded lines are again made visible by use of the SHOW edit-line command, or all excluded lines can be made visible using the RESET command on the command line.

```
===> FIND string [range]  [NEXT ]  [CHARS ]  [X ]  [col1 [col2]]
                          [ALL  ]  [PREFIX]  [NX]
                          [FIRST]  [SUFFIX]
                          [LAST ]  [WORD  ]
                          [PREV ]
```

Finds and positions the cursor at the specified character string. The optional specifications each serve to limit the lines of text affected by the change; range is [from-line-number to-line-number]. To secure complete processing of the entire item being edited, position the cursor at the top of the item and specify the ALL option as illustrated in Chapter 8.

F 0000

Causes the *first* line of a group of excluded lines to be made visible. Multiple leading lines in a group of excluded lines can be made visible by entering a line count after the F.

===> HEX [ON] [*VERT*]   (Part of the editing profile)
         [*OFF*] [DATA]

Presents the item being edited in hexadecimal as well as character format. VERT|DATA controls whether the two-position hexadecimal code is presented vertically or horizontally. The hexadecimal values are editable and take precedence over the character representation. See Chapter 8 for examples of using HEX ON to create otherwise inaccessible byte values.

I 0000

Inserts a line after the one marked. Multiple lines can be inserted by specifying a number after the I.

===> IMACRO [name]   (Part of the editing profile)
            [NONE]

Places the name of a macro into the edit profile so that the macro is executed at the beginning of each edit session for the type of partitioned data set.

L 0000

Causes the *last* line of a group of excluded lines to be made visible. Multiple trailing lines of a group of excluded lines can be made visible by entering a line count after the L on the line indicating excluded lines.

===> LEVEL number
     LEV

Sets the modification level of the item being edited. Modification level is one of the member statistics maintained when STATS ON is coded in the edit profile.

```
===> LOCATE line-number|label
     LOC
     L
```

Positions the cursor to the line carrying the specified line number, leading field, or label, when editing or browsing an item or when viewing a partitioned data set member list.

```
M 0000
```

Identifies a line to be *moved*. MM and MM are used to identify the starting and ending lines of a group of lines to be copied. Multiple lines can also be copied by indicating a line count after the M. The B "before" or A "after" indicator must be placed in the line-number area of a line outside the marked group designating the destination of the moved lines.

```
MASK
000000
```

Displays the insert mask, which allows preentry of data on inserted lines. When the mask line is displayed, it can be changed by moving the cursor within it and entering characters. The mask line is a template for lines created with the I "insert" line command, and usually carries all spaces. The mask line is also used to generate the lines added with TE text entry mode and TS text split. The mask line can be made invisible by putting RESET on the command line. Create it by inserting a line with the word MASK in the line number area in the profile.

```
===> MODEL [model-name [.qualifier...]]] [AFTER  label] [NOTE ]
                                         [BEFORE label] [NONOTE]
```

Places data from a skeleton partitioned data set library into the item being edited at the point marked with A or B. Models are suggested for IBM for use in developing the CLIST logic that drives custom-built panels and interactive dialogs such as those that make up TSO/ISPF itself. This aspect of TSO/ISPF usage is usually limited to systems programmers and has little or no role in the work of applications programmers.

```
===> MOVE [member-name]   [BEFORE label|AFTER label]
```

Moves data from one place to another. Used within edit of an existing member, this allows moving in another member from the same partitioned data set after or before the line annotated with A or B in the edit-line command area. If specified at the start of edit for a new member, no A or B indication is necessary. If member name is omitted when editing an existing member, a second screen is presented allowing specification of the source for the move outside of the same partitioned data set.

===> NOTE [ON|OFF]   (Part of the editing profile)
Used in conjunction with the MODEL command, NOTE causes tutorial notes to be included with the model item.

===> NULLS [ON|OFF] [ALL]   (Part of the editing profile)
Controls the nature of the trailing characters on a line of text. In the IBM mainframe environment, lines of source code or JCL actually represent punched cards, and each line is 80 characters in length. The content of the trailing portion of each line is transmitted if it is blanks, but not transmitted if it is nulls, the LOW-VALUES bit pattern of hexadecimal 00. Use of NULLS ON requires spacing to the right of the line to be done with the space bar, not the arrow keys, or the contents of the line will "squish left" in processing.

===> NUMBER [ON|OFF] [STD] [COBOL] [DISPLAY]
If set on, generates sequence numbers for any new lines created via copy, insert, or repeat. Setting NUMBER OFF causes omission of line numbers for these lines. NUMBER is part of the editing profile.

0 0000   (Letter "oh" in the first position)
Identifies a line to be *overlaid* by copied or moved-in data. This "target" specification differs from A "after" or B "before" in that the existing line is destroyed rather than moved down or up. Multiple lines can be overlaid by specifying a line count after the letter O. The O edit line command is actually a combination of a move or copy in, and a single or group line delete.

===> PACK [ON|OFF]   (Part of the editing profile)
If set on conserves disk space by storing an item in a coded form in which repeating characters are replaced with semaphores. Program source code stored in packed form must be unpacked before compilation, and job control language stored in this manner must be unpacked before submission for execution.

===> PROFILE [name] [number]
     PROF
     PRO

Displays the current settings of the edit mode parameters. Changes made to profile settings while the profile is displayed are seen immediately, but it is not necessary to be viewing the profile in order to change parameters. Switching to a different profile during edit is possible by changing the profile name field in the profile display. Placing RESET on the command line and pressing ENTER removes the profile display.

===> PROFILE [LOCK|UNLOCK]   (Part of the editing profile)
     PROF
     PRO

Locks or unlocks the profile in effect, either preventing or allowing further changes to it.

R 0000

Repeats the line, inserting a copy of it immediately following. Multiple repetitions can be inserted by specifying a number after the command. A group of lines can be repeated by placing RR at the first line in the group and RR at the last such line. Multiple copies of a group of lines can be repeated by placing a number after the RR on the first line of the group.

===> RECOVERY [ON|OFF]

Enables a recovery feature that journals changes to the item as they are made, and initiates an automatic recovery if the edit is terminated with a system interruption, terminal disconnection, or TSO/ISPF timeout due to terminal inactivity. Recovery actions, when necessary, are made known to the terminal operator at the next attempt to edit the data set. RECOVERY ON causes additional data sets to be maintained by TSO/ISPF, generating extra overhead, and is usually set on only when significant potential for system interruption exists.

===> RENUM [STD] [COBOL] [DISPLAY]

Turns on the line numbering mode and renumbers the COBOL, STD, or both sets of lines, depending on whether they presently exist. The type of numbers to be applied to a currently unnumbered item are specified with the optional phrases. DISPLAY causes COBOL items to be presented with the leading line number fields visible and editable.

===> REPLACE [member-name] [from-line-number to-line-number]

Blocks of lines in an item being edited can be marked with CC/ CC or MM/MM and REPLACE executed to copy or move them out to a specified member in the same partitioned data set. Instead of marking lines to be processed they can alternatively be indicated with a line number range after the command. If member-name is omitted, a second screen is presented allowing specification of any existing data set name to receive the lines. Note: REPLACE can replace an existing member of the same name, or rewrite the contents of an existing sequential data set.

===> RESET [LABEL] [COM] [ERR] [CHG] [SPECIAL] [EX] [range]

Eliminates from the display any TSO/ISPF message lines, COLS column rulers, indications from CHANGE commands, removes pending line copy or move commands, and causes all excluded lines to be made visible. The optional specifications all serve to limit the scope of the reset. Range is [from-line-number to-line-number].

===> RMACRO [name]
            [NONE]

The name of the recovery macro specified in the command is saved in the edit profile. The recovery macro is invoked after the recovery of a data set which was interrupted during edit.

===> SAVE

Writes the item being edited back to disk, and continues the edit session. Note that each explicit SAVE causes further depletion of the available space in a partitioned data set; a high level of SAVEs will create the need to reorganize TSO/ISPF partitioned data sets on a frequent basis.

S 0000

"Shows" or makes visible the excluded line on which it is indicated. Multiple excluded lines can be made visible by indicating a line count after the S on the line indicating excluded lines.

===> SORT major minor

Within the TSO 3.4 data set list function, allows sorting the data set list on NAME, VOLUME, SIZE, EDATE (expiration date), RDATE (last referenced date), CDATE (creation date), or USED, the percentage of data set space used.

===> SORT [range] [X] [sort–fieldl ... sort–field5]
                   [NX]

Within TSO 2 edit, sorts the lines within the item being edited. The sort is performed using only the data falling within the current boundaries of the edit. With no operands coded, the lines are ordered based on their full content in ascending EBCDIC collation sequence. The optional specifications allow limiting the sort to a line range where range is [from-line-number to-line-number]. X limits the sort to excluded lines, while NX limits it to non-excluded lines. Up to five sort fields may be designated, in the form [A|D start-column end-column], and if end-column is omitted, it defaults to the right edit boundary.

===> STATS [ON|OFF]   (Part of the editing profile)

Statistics are carried for the item in the partitioned data set directory when STATS is set ON. The statistics concerning last change date, size, version, and so forth are updated when the member is created, saved, or replaced. STATS OFF causes no statistics to be carried for the item.

===> SUBMIT [from–line–number to–line–number]

Copies the item to the internal reader, to place it into the JES input queue as a set of job control language for execution. It is appropriate to use this command only when editing a CNTL or other job control language item. The optional line number range is of little practical use since each job stream is typically stored as a single member of a partitioned data set.

===> TABS [ON|OFF] [tab–character] [ALL]   (Editing profile)

Enables or disables hardware or logical tabs at the positions defined in the tab line. Tab-character defines the character to be regarded as the delimiter between fields entered continuously but shifted to tab positions logically when the ENTER key is pressed. If the optional ALL specification is omitted, hardware tabs are created only at positions in each line that fall under asterisk-defined tabs and are blank. ALL causes hardware tabs to

be created at all asterisk-defined positions in every line of the
display, even if this means obscuring data on some lines with
3270 attribute bytes that constitute hardware tabs. TABS is part
of the editing profile.

```
TABS
TAB
000000
```

Displays the tab line, allowing its use to define software, logical
or hardware cursor tab stop positions.

Software tabs are designated by an underscore or hyphen in
the tab line, and take effect immediately upon definition. The
cursor is moved to the next software tab position when the EN-
TER key is pressed. Software tabs are not affected by the ===>
TABS ON or ===> TABS OFF command line entries. Create a
TABS line by inserting a line with this word in the line number
area in the profile.

Logical and hardware tabs are defined in the tabs line using
the asterisk. Logical tabs rely on the tab-character specified in
the TABS command. With the tab line containing an asterisk at
position 5, 15, 25, and 35, and the command TAB ON % invoked,
the entry of this line:

```
%THIS%WILL%BE%TABBED
```

results in this handling of the line when the ENTER key is
pressed:

```
5      15    25 35
|       |     |  |
THIS  WILL  BE  TABBED
```

Hardware tabs are created by the insertion of attribute bytes into
the screen lines at the positions indicated in the tab line with asterisks. This is done when the TABS command is issued *without*
the tab-character indication. TSO/ISPF send the attribute bytes to
the 3270 and "programs" it locally for tab positions that are
reached by pressing the tab key on the keyboard. Hardware tab at-
tributes consume a display field each on the screen, and these positions become unenterable while the hardware tabs are in effect.

Data in the tab attribute positions is obscured while the tables are in effect, but is restored to visibility when tabs are set off. The tab key reaches the position immediately after that defined by the asterisk in the tab line.

TE 000

Switches to "text entry" mode, eliminating cursor location in the line number area on the remainder of the screen. Normal mode is restored using RESET on the COMMAND ===> line. Text entry can be started and multiple blank lines following obtained all at once by indicating a line count after the TE.

TF 000

"Reflows" text from the cursor position to the end of the paragraph. Useful only if TSO/ISPF has been used to enter narrative text, not source code or job control language. Text flow from the left boundary through only an indicated column can be accomplished by indicating a number after the TF, representing the right column boundary for the text flow.

TS 000

Splits text at the cursor position, starting a new line at this point to facilitate the entry of more text. Generally useful only if TSO/ISPF has been used to enter narrative text, not source code or job control language. Text split can be done and multiple blank lines following the split obtained all at once by indicating a line count after the TS.

===> UNNUM

Changes all COBOL and STD sequence numbers to spaces, and turns off NUMBER mode. UNNUM before a RENUM is the method to strip STD numbers from source code and create COBOL line numbers instead.

===> VERSION number
      VERS
      VER

Sets the version number of the item being edited, one of the statistics carried for an item when the profile STATS ON setting is in effect. Version number is automatically incremented by 1 each time a member is edited and saved.

X 0000

Excludes lines from the screen, hiding them. This may also be used as an optional specification on the FIND or CHANGE commands to limit the extent of their operation. A group of lines can be excluded by marking the first line and the last line with XX. A group of lines can also be excluded by placing the number of lines after the X in the line number area of the line being edited.

< 0000

Shifts data contents of the line leftward two columns. Data is reformatted according to rules that govern the treatment of spaces and characters: spaces are not removed between apostrophes, and characters are never deleted or truncated. An error message is generated if the shift would violate the text treatment rules. Multiple column shift can be indicated by placing a number after the command. A block of lines can be shifted left in this manner by specifying <<nn at the first line in the block and << at the last line in the block.

> 0000

Shifts data contents of the line rightward two columns. Data is reformatted according to rules that govern the treatment of spaces and characters: spaces are not removed between apostrophes, and characters are never deleted or truncated. An error message is generated if the shift would violate the text treatment rules. Multiple column shift can be indicated by placing a number after the command. A block of lines can be shifted right in this manner by specifying >>nn at the first line in the block and >> at the last line in the block.

(0000

Shifts the line leftward two columns. The shift is a literal shift of the number of columns indicated; if this results in text being truncated or lost, no warning message is issued. Multiple column shift can be indicated by placing a number after the command. A block of lines can be shifted left in this manner by specifying ((nn at the first line in the block and ((at the last line in the block.

) 0000

Shift the line rightward two columns. The shift is a literal shift of the number of columns indicated; if this results in text being truncated or lost, no warning message is issued. Multiple column shift can be indicated by placing a number after the command. A block of lines can be shifted right in this manner by specifying))nn at the first line in the block and)) at the last line in the block.

. xxxxx
000000

Creates a label named ".xxxxx" that can be used to position the cursor or specify ranges of lines during browse and edit, and for certain other commands. The "xxxxx" can be one to five alphabetic characters but must not start with the letter Z. A single label can be eliminated by blanking it out in the edit line area. All labels can be removed with the RESET command on the command line, carrying the optional specification LABELS.

TSO/ISPF Horror Stories With Happy Endings

Certain situations can arise that may cause you to panic as you use TSO/ISPF. An item being edited may appear in jeopardy of loss because the partitioned data set that houses it is depleted of space, a job you have submitted is discovered to be grossly in error and needs to be terminated so as not to produce large volumes of output, or your edit session has been terminated due to an interruption in your communication line or on the system. Collected here is advice to aid you in overcoming these problems with a minimum of lost time or work.

The author is indebted to Dawne Tortorella, director of Academic Computing Services at DePaul University, who suggested the inclusion of this appendix drawing from the experiences of many personnel new to the TSO/ISPF environment. Contributions made by instructors of the DePaul University Computer Career Program, including its director, Steve Samuels, and David Calascibetta, Joel Bernstein, Cyndee Llewellyn, Dennis Ford, Steve Page, Dermott Kane, and Krysia Jacobs also broadened this appendix.

Problem: Can't log on due to password rejection

The RACF security system is particularly terse in its prompts and messages. If your password expires and RACF prompts you to "re-enter password," you must respond with a new password, not the old expired one. For more information on RACF password usage and procedures, check Chapter 2.

Problem: Session is interrupted and you must reconnect to TSO/ISPF

It is possible to reconnect with a TSO session if you have been disconnected due to a dial-up telephone line disruption, failure of your terminal, or inadvertent terminal shutoff. You must log on again, but specify the word "RECONNECT" after your TSO user id or account number, as explained in Chapter 2.

Problem: Can't save an edited member because PDS needs to be compressed (error code E37)

This problem will arise if you do not monitor the space status of the partitioned data sets that are your TSO/ISPF libraries, as discussed in Chapter 12. If you have invested time and effort in editing an item, only to be confronted with this error message when attempting to end the edit, you can still save the item and not lose it, but this requires a bit of effort. It involves saving the item to a different partitioned data set, reorganizing the PDS that is out of space, and copying the item back to this data set. Follow these steps:

1. Place CC in the line-number area of the first line of the item.
2. Place CC in the line-number area of the last line of the item.
3. Put the cursor on the command line, enter the word CREATE, and press the ENTER key.
4. A screen will appear allowing you to indicate the name of a data set to which the item being edited will be copied. Since job control language and source code are both housed as 80-byte punched-card-image records, specify either your CNTL library or your source code library, whichever you have *not* been editing. Press ENTER. The item will be copied to the specified data set, and the edit screen will reappear.
5. Place CANCEL on the command line, to end the edit without attempting to save the edited item in the partitioned data set that is out of space.
6. Using the TSO 3.1 browse screen, do cleanups of the PDS that is out of space by examining and deleting unneeded members. Delete the item you were editing, since it is not now the most current version of the item.
7. Perform a reorganization of the partitioned data set, using JCL

such as is found in Appendix C. If your need for additional PDS space is justified, specify additional space and additional directory blocks using the symbolic parameters provided by this procedure.

8. Using TSO 3.3, copy the item you were editing from your CNTL or source code library to the correct library.

9. Delete the item you were editing from the inappropriate library where you had saved it to avoid losing it.

From this point on, make sure you periodically check the space status of each of your partitioned data sets, as discussed in Chapter 12 under "PDS Space Usage and Reorganization," page 145.

Problem: PDS directory out of directory blocks (error code B14)

A partitioned data set may have space remaining but be unable to accommodate another new member because the entire PDS directory is full. This will produce a condition similar to the E37 error code discussed above, but reported with code B14. You can save the effort invested in the new member by following the same steps outlined for an out-of-space PDS. When reorganizing the PDS as a part of those steps, specify a larger quantity of directory blocks.

Problem: COBOL source code entered in wrong columns in a CNTL data set

COBOL source code begins in column 7, whereas job control language begins in column 1. If you inadvertently begin creating COBOL source code in your CNTL library, it will be too far left by six positions. You can use the block text shift right command)) with the value 6 to shift the lines rightward into the appropriate columns. Mark the first line of the item with))6 in the line number area, and the last line with)) in the line number area, and press the ENTER key. Then move the member to your COBOL partitioned data set library.

Problem: JCL entered into wrong columns in a COBOL data set

Job control language begins in column 1, whereas COBOL source code begins in column 7. If you inadvertently begin creating JCL in your COBOL library, it will be too far right by six positions. You can use the block text shift left command ((with the value 6 to shift the lines leftward into the appropriate columns. Mark the first line of the item with ((6 in the line number area, and the last line with ((in the line number area, and press the ENTER key. Then move the member to your CNTL partitioned data set library.

Problem: Session interrupted and TSO 2 EDIT presents a recovery screen

If you have the RECOVERY parameter set ON in the edit profile for the type of partitioned data set you are editing, TSO/ISPF automatically journals edit actions and creates an independent means of reestablishing the currency of the data set even if the system fails or you are logged off due to inactivity. The next time you begin to edit an item in the partitioned data set, you will be presented with a screen as shown in Figure G.1. In order to resume editing with minimal loss of editing actions, simply press the ENTER key. Check the most recent edit action, which should be the only one affected by the interruption.

Problem: Session ended with error code 522

A system completion code of 522 indicates that the TSO/ISPF session has been terminated due to inactivity. An installation can establish a time limit for terminal inactivity, such as three minutes, and if no ENTER key, PF key, or PA key is pressed for this length of time, the terminal is assumed to be unattended. Moving the cursor on the screen using the arrow or tab keys, and pressing the letter and number keys, does not send information from the terminal to the computer and is not detected by TSO/ISPF as activity. You must periodically press ENTER or use a PF key in order to avoid being logged off by TSO/ISPF in this manner.

Problem: Error code 80A received when attempting to edit

System completion code 80A indicates that a program does not have sufficient memory to operate. In connection with TSO/ISPF, receiving an 80A means that your TSO session has not been allocated enough work space. You can obtain more space for a TSO session at the time you logon, using the optional SIZE parameter as illustrated in Figure G.2. Your installation may have established a size limit that causes the specification to be rejected, as illustrated in Figure G.3. If this is the case you must arrange with the

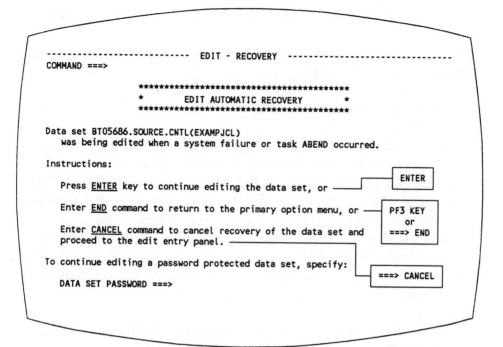

```
-------------------------------- EDIT - RECOVERY --------------------------------
COMMAND ===>

              *****************************************
              *          EDIT AUTOMATIC RECOVERY      *
              *****************************************

Data set BTO5686.SOURCE.CNTL(EXAMPJCL)
   was being edited when a system failure or task ABEND occurred.

Instructions:
                                                          ┌─────────┐
   Press ENTER key to continue editing the data set, or ──┤ ENTER   │
                                                          └─────────┘

   Enter END command to return to the primary option menu, or ──┌─────────┐
                                                                 │ PF3 KEY │
                                                                 │   or    │
   Enter CANCEL command to cancel recovery of the data set and   │ ===> END│
   proceed to the edit entry panel. ─────────────────────────────└─────────┘

To continue editing a password protected data set, specify:
                                                          ┌──────────────┐
   DATA SET PASSWORD ===>                                 │ ===> CANCEL  │
                                                          └──────────────┘
```

FIGURE G.1 Edit recovery screen from the RECOVERY ON setting, presented when beginning to edit a member in a partitioned data set that was being edited at the time of a system failure or logoff due to inactivity

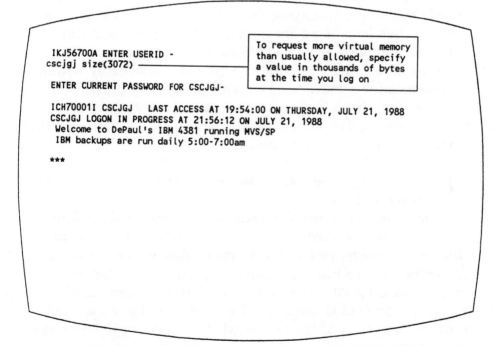

```
   IKJ56700A ENTER USERID -              ┌─────────────────────────────────┐
cscjgj size(3072) ──────────────────────┤ To request more virtual memory   │
                                         │ than usually allowed, specify    │
ENTER CURRENT PASSWORD FOR CSCJGJ-       │ a value in thousands of bytes    │
                                         │ at the time you log on           │
                                         └─────────────────────────────────┘
ICH70001I CSCJGJ   LAST ACCESS AT 19:54:00 ON THURSDAY, JULY 21, 1988
CSCJGJ LOGON IN PROGRESS AT 21:56:12 ON JULY 21, 1988
 Welcome to DePaul's IBM 4381 running MVS/SP
 IBM backups are run daily 5:00-7:00am

***
```

FIGURE G.2 Use of the SIZE parameter at logon to increase the amount of work space allowed for the TSO/ISPF session

systems programmer at your facility to justify and obtain the ability to use a larger TSO work space.

Problem: Need to cancel a submitted job and kill its print output

You may discover that a job you have submitted is either running too long or erroneously producing large volumes of printed output. You can cancel its execution using the native mode TSO CANCEL command with the PURGE option, as illustrated in Chapter 10. You can also use the SDSF I screen, viewing the system job input queue, to purge a job awaiting execution. This involves simply moving the cursor down the screen to the line listing the job, placing a C for "cancel" or a P for "purge" on it, and pressing ENTER, as illustrated in Figure G.4.

Problem: Partitioned data set corrupted with wrong length records

If you inadvertently write data with an inappropriate record length or block size to a partitioned data set using JCL and a job submission, the recorded characteristics of the data set will be altered by the operating system to those of the new member. Your error in this case is specifying record length and block size for the newly written item; these are specified when a sequential data set is written, but not when an additional member is added to an existing partitioned data set. You can cure the problem by writing another member to the data set with JCL and a job submission, this time specifying the original record length and block size of the partitioned data set. The item written incorrectly to the data set will not be accessible in a usable form.

Problem: You would like to share access to a data set with another TSO user

If your installation uses the RACF security system, it is possible for you to release security on your partitioned data set libraries to allow selected other parties to read and/or update them. Figure G.5 illustrates the MVS JCL to accomplish this, which invokes the utility program IKJEFT01. The data set name is cited after the phrase PERMIT, and the id is that of the TSO user or group of users to be permitted access. ACCESS defines whether READ or UPDATE access is to be permitted.

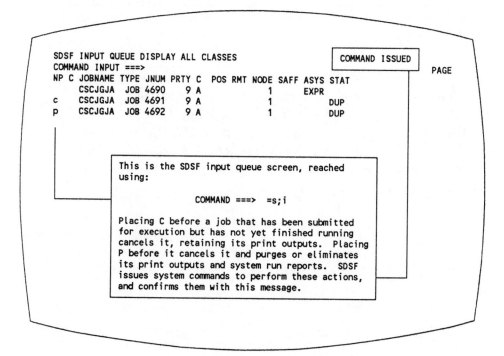

```
        IKJ56700A ENTER USERID -                          This is the way to request
        ccpq00 size(3072)                                 TSO work space to access
        ENTER CURRENT PASSWORD FOR CCPQ00-                large data sets or members.
                                                          The figure is in thousands
                                                          of bytes of virtual memory.

        ICH70001I CCPQ00   LAST ACCESS AT 13:56:50 ON THURSDAY, JULY 21, 1988

        REGION SIZE 03072 EXCEEDS LIMIT SIZE 01024
        REENTER -                                         But an installation limit
        2048                                              may preclude allocation
                                                          of the requested space,
        REGION SIZE 02048 EXCEEDS LIMIT SIZE 01024        as indicated here
        REENTER -
        1024

        CCPQ00 LOGON IN PROGRESS AT 21:57:21 ON JULY 21, 1988
         Welcome to DePaul's IBM 4381 running MVS/SP
         IBM backups are run daily 5:00-7:00am

        ***
```

FIGURE G.3   TSO response to use of the logon SIZE parameter if the installation has established a lower SIZE limit for TSO users

```
        SDSF INPUT QUEUE DISPLAY ALL CLASSES                   COMMAND ISSUED
        COMMAND INPUT ===>                                                       PAGE
        NP C JOBNAME TYPE JNUM PRTY C  POS RMT NODE SAFF ASYS STAT
             CSCJGJA  JOB 4690   9 A         1         EXPR
          c  CSCJGJA  JOB 4691   9 A         1              DUP
          p  CSCJGJA  JOB 4692   9 A         1              DUP



                    This is the SDSF input queue screen, reached
                    using:

                                COMMAND ===>  =s;i

                    Placing C before a job that has been submitted
                    for execution but has not yet finished running
                    cancels it, retaining its print outputs.  Placing
                    P before it cancels it and purges or eliminates
                    its print outputs and system run reports.  SDSF
                    issues system commands to perform these actions,
                    and confirms them with this message.
```

FIGURE G.4   Purging a submitted job from the input queue using the SDSF I screen

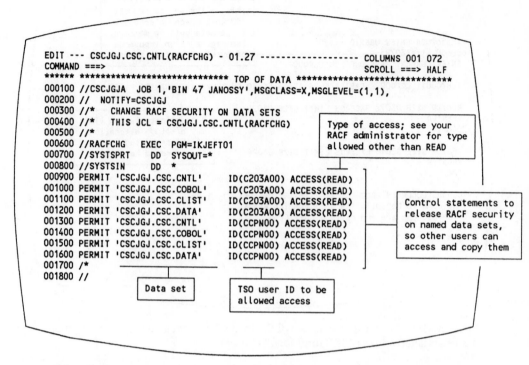

```
EDIT --- CSCJGJ.CSC.CNTL(RACFCHG) - 01.27 ------------------ COLUMNS 001 072
COMMAND ===>                                              SCROLL ===> HALF
****** **************************** TOP OF DATA *******************************
000100 //CSCJGJA  JOB 1,'BIN 47 JANOSSY',MSGCLASS=X,MSGLEVEL=(1,1),
000200 //  NOTIFY=CSCJGJ
000300 //*   CHANGE RACF SECURITY ON DATA SETS
000400 //*    THIS JCL = CSCJGJ.CSC.CNTL(RACFCHG)
000500 //*
000600 //RACFCHG   EXEC  PGM=IKJEFT01
000700 //SYSTSPRT    DD  SYSOUT=*
000800 //SYSTSIN     DD  *
000900 PERMIT 'CSCJGJ.CSC.CNTL'    ID(C203A00) ACCESS(READ)
001000 PERMIT 'CSCJGJ.CSC.COBOL'   ID(C203A00) ACCESS(READ)
001100 PERMIT 'CSCJGJ.CSC.CLIST'   ID(C203A00) ACCESS(READ)
001200 PERMIT 'CSCJGJ.CSC.DATA'    ID(C203A00) ACCESS(READ)
001300 PERMIT 'CSCJGJ.CSC.CNTL'    ID(CCPN00) ACCESS(READ)
001400 PERMIT 'CSCJGJ.CSC.COBOL'   ID(CCPN00) ACCESS(READ)
001500 PERMIT 'CSCJGJ.CSC.CLIST'   ID(CCPN00) ACCESS(READ)
001600 PERMIT 'CSCJGJ.CSC.DATA'    ID(CCPN00) ACCESS(READ)
001700 /*
001800 //
```

Type of access; see your RACF administrator for type allowed other than READ

Control statements to release RACF security on named data sets, so other users can access and copy them

Data set

TSO user ID to be allowed access

FIGURE G.5 MVS job control language to execute IKJEFT01 to release RACF security on TSO data sets, so that TSO users other than the data set owner can access them

Note: RACF security information is housed within the partitioned data set catalog entry. When you reorganize a PDS by copying it, deleting it, and renaming or copying it back to a data set of the original name, its RACF security reverts to the default for a new data set. You will have to run the RACF release after every such PDS reorganization in order to provide uninterrupted access to the data set to other TSO users.

TSO Statistics, TSO 3.5 "RESET," and PDS Directory Internals

TSO/ISPF libraries take the form of partitioned data sets, as discussed in Chapter 5. The directory of a partitioned data set, located by the system at the beginning of the physical disk space allocated to the data set, contains a pointer called the "TTR" for each member in the PDS data space. These pointers are used by system software to locate each member when it is accessed.

Each member record in the directory can optionally contain "user" information including the date the member was created and when it was last modified, its present and original size in records, and the TSO user id of its originator. When a member list of a TSO library is viewed, as in Figure H.1, the user information fields of each member's directory record are presented on the screen.

TSO/ISPF FUNCTION 3.5: ALTERING MEMBER STATISTICS

The TSO/ISPF 3.5 function allows "resetting" of fields in the directory record for all or selected members of a TSO library. When accessed from the TSO/ISPF main menu or function 3 submenu, a screen similar to that shown in Figure H.2 is presented. These selections are available from the TSO 3.5 screen:

R   create or change member information, called "statistics," renumbering source code or JCL lines in any members carrying valid line numbers

```
EDIT --- CSCJGJ.CSC.C203CBL ------------------------------------------------------
COMMAND ===>                                              SCROLL ===> PAGE
    NAME          VER.MOD  CREATED    LAST MODIFIED   SIZE  INIT  MOD   ID
  AGNES4          01.64   88/04/18  88/07/08 16:03    543   114    0 CSCJGJ
  CSC001          01.05   88/03/27  88/07/08 16:04     39    25   39 CSCJGJ
  PROG1           01.05   88/01/25  88/03/27 22:20    104   101    0 C203A00
  PROG2           01.00   88/04/04  88/04/04 09:58    104   104    0 C203A00
  PSD187          01.01   88/07/08  88/07/08 18:59    543   543    0 CSCJGJ
  PSD200          01.00   88/07/08  88/07/08 18:58     16    16    0 CSCJGJ
  **END**
```

FIGURE H.1 TSO/ISPF member list screen presenting member statistics, stored as "user information" in a partitioned data set directory

```
-------------------------- RESET ISPF STATISTICS --------------------------
OPTION  ===> r

    R - Create/update ISPF statistics, conditionally reset sequence numbers
    N - Create/update ISPF statistics, no reset of sequence numbers
    D - Delete ISPF statistics

NEW VERSION NUMBER ===> 2        (Required for option "R")
NEW TSO USERID     ===>          (If userid is to be changed)

ISPF LIBRARY:
    PROJECT ===> CSCJGJ
    LIBRARY ===> CSC
    TYPE    ===> C203CBL
    MEMBER  ===>                 (Blank for member list, * for all members)

OTHER PARTITIONED DATA SET:
    DATA SET NAME  ===>
    VOLUME SERIAL  ===>          (If not cataloged)

DATA SET PASSWORD ===>           (If password protected)
```

FIGURE H.2 TSO/ISPF 3.5 screen providing the means to reset or delete statistics information for members of a TSO/ISPF library; as completed here the version number will be changed to 2 and a member list for selection of affected members will be presented

N   create or change member information statistics without affect-
    ing any member line numbers

D   delete optional member user information, eliminating all but
    the member name from TSO/ISPF member list screens.

Resetting Member Version Number

A common use of the TSO/ISPF 3.5 screen is the resetting of the
"version number" on members. An IBM convention, maintained
for software it distributes, identifies software with version and
modification numbers. Release 1.0 of a product—version 1, modification 0—is the first edition of it. Release 1.1 or 1.01 indicates
that minor changes and updates have been inserted in the software,
but that it is still essentially the same product. Releases 1.02, 1.03,
and upward represent a further gradual enhancement of the software.

When major changes in software operation or functionality are
evolved, IBM will customarily increment the version number, and
begin the modification numbering with zero once again. Thus the
first release of the PC-DOS operating system was known as 1.0, followed by releases 1.1 and 1.25. When major functionality was
added, the product was called release 2.0, followed shortly thereafter by release 2.1. More recently, this software product was up-
graded to release 3.0, then 3.1 and in 1988 to release 4.0.

TSO/ISPF automatically maintains an individual modification
number for each library member, beginning with modification
number 00. Both a version number and a modification number are
carried for each member as items of user information within the
directory. During edit, these numbers are presented at the top of
the screen. The modification number is increased by TSO/ISPF
every time a change is made in a member and it is saved at the end
of an edit session. The maximum value of modification number is
99. Once this is attained, it remains at this value.

The version number of one, several, or all members in a library
can be changed using the TSO/ISPF 3.5 function. If the screen is
completed as shown in Figure H.2, the version number on selected
members can be changed to 2. Since no member name is filled in
on this screen, the member selection list of Figure H.3 is presented.
Candidate members for version number change can be selected by
placing S in front of them. When the ENTER key is pressed, the

member list returns with the version number changed, as indicated in Figure H.4

Changing the version number updates most of the other statistics. The modification number is automatically reset to zero, and the current date is placed into the creation date and last changed date. The current number of lines becomes the "original" number of lines, since this figure represents the original size of the current version. The quantity of modifications value, MOD, is set to zero.

Other ways exist to specify members for version number and/or TSO user id change. To reset a single member, enter the member name on the initial TSO/ISPF 3.5 screen. To reset all members, enter an asterisk at the member name field.

Changing the version number may be desirable when a program under development has been completed and is being shifted into a different status, such as user acceptance or production. Alternatively, if a program development effort is shifted from one person to another, the reassigned work might be identified with a new version number. Another reason for version number change could be that members were created or modified on another system, or by another party. While TSO/ISPF automatically creates statistics for a member when it is modified and saved, changing the version number for all members creates statistics for them en masse.

Changing the Origin ID Field

If the NEW TSO USER ID field of the TSO/ISPF 3.5 screen is filled in, the ID field of user information can also be changed in the member information, with or without changing the version number. Figure H.5 depicts the entry of a new TSO user id and the request of a member list. Figure H.6 illustrates the selection of two members from the member list, while Figure H.7 shows how the member list appears after the ID field modification has been processed.

Difference Between N and R Options

The N and R options of the TSO/ISPF 3.5 screen accomplish almost the identical processing. The only difference between these options is the treatment of line numbers.

The R option is used to create statistics for members that do not have them and to update existing statistics. Under option R, each

```
RESET -- CSCJGJ.CSC.C203CBL -------------------------------------------------
COMMAND ===>                                              SCROLL ===> PAGE
      NAME           VER.MOD  CREATED    LAST MODIFIED  SIZE  INIT  MOD   ID
  s AGNES4           01.64    88/04/18   88/07/08 16:03  543   114    0 CSCJGJ
  s CSC001           01.05    88/03/27   88/07/08 16:04   39    25   39 CSCJGJ
    PROG1            01.05    88/01/25   88/03/27 22:20  104   101    0 C203A00
    PROG2            01.00    88/04/04   88/04/04 09:58  104   104    0 C203A00
    PSD187           01.01    88/07/08   88/07/08 18:59  543   543    0 CSCJGJ
    PSD200           01.00    88/07/08   88/07/08 18:58   16    16    0 CSCJGJ
    **END**
```

FIGURE H.3 Selection of two members for resetting of the version number as indicated on the TSO/ISPF 3.5 screen depicted in Figure H.2

```
RESET -- CSCJGJ.CSC.C203CBL -------------------------------------------------
COMMAND ===>                                              SCROLL ===> PAGE
      NAME           VER.MOD  CREATED    LAST MODIFIED  SIZE  INIT  MOD   ID
    AGNES4  *RESET   02.00    88/07/15   88/07/15 18:13  543   543    0 CSCJGJ
    CSC001  *RESET   02.00    88/07/15   88/07/15 18:13   39    39    0 CSCJGJ
    PROG1            01.05    88/01/25   88/03/27 22:20  104   101    0 C203A00
    PROG2            01.00    88/04/04   88/04/04 09:58  104   104    0 C203A00
    PSD187           01.01    88/07/08   88/07/08 18:59  543   543    0 CSCJGJ
    PSD200           01.00    88/07/08   88/07/08 18:58   16    16    0 CSCJGJ
    **END**
```

FIGURE H.4 Effect of resetting the version number on two members; the CREATED, LAST MODIFIED, and INIT information items are also affected

247

```
------------------------- RESET ISPF STATISTICS ----------- 2 MEMBERS RESET
OPTION  ===> n

   R - Create/update ISPF statistics, conditionally reset sequence numbers
   N - Create/update ISPF statistics, no reset of sequence numbers
   D - Delete ISPF statistics

NEW VERSION NUMBER ===>         (Required for option "R")
NEW TSO USERID     ===> ccpq00  (If userid is to be changed)

ISPF LIBRARY:
   PROJECT ===> CSCJGJ
   LIBRARY ===> CSC
   TYPE    ===> C203CBL
   MEMBER  ===>                 (Blank for member list, * for all members)

OTHER PARTITIONED DATA SET:
   DATA SET NAME   ===>
   VOLUME SERIAL   ===>         (If not cataloged)

DATA SET PASSWORD ===>          (If password protected)
```

FIGURE H.5 TSO/ISPF 3.5 screen as completed to change the originating ID field of member statistics to CCPQ00; since no member name is entered, a member selection list will be presented.

```
RESET -- CSCJGJ.CSC.C203CBL -------------------------------------------------
COMMAND ===>                                              SCROLL ===> PAGE
   NAME        VER.MOD  CREATED    LAST MODIFIED  SIZE  INIT  MOD   ID
   AGNES4      02.00    88/07/15   88/07/15 18:13  543   543    0  CSCJGJ
   CSC001      02.00    88/07/15   88/07/15 18:13   39    39    0  CSCJGJ
 s PROG1       01.05    88/01/25   88/03/27 22:20  104   101    0  C203A00
   PROG2       01.00    88/04/04   88/04/04 09:58  104   104    0  C203A00
 s PSD187      01.01    88/07/08   88/07/08 18:59  543   543    0  CSCJGJ
   PSD200      01.00    88/07/08   88/07/08 18:58   16    16    0  CSCJGJ
   **END**
```

FIGURE H.6 Selection of members for resetting of the origin ID field of statistics information

```
RESET -- CSCJGJ.CSC.C203CBL -------------------------------------------------------
COMMAND ===>                                                      SCROLL ===> PAGE
   NAME              VER.MOD  CREATED    LAST MODIFIED  SIZE  INIT  MOD    ID
   AGNES4            02.00    88/07/15   88/07/15 18:13  543   543    0 CSCJGJ
   CSC001            02.00    88/07/15   88/07/15 18:13   39    39    0 CSCJGJ
   PROG1    *RESET   01.05    88/01/25   88/03/27 22:20  104   101    0 CCPQ00
   PROG2             01.00    88/04/04   88/04/04 09:58  104   104    0 C203A00
   PSD187   *RESET   01.01    88/07/08   88/07/08 18:59  543   543    0 CCPQ00
   PSD200            01.00    88/07/08   88/07/08 18:58   16    16    0 CSCJGJ
   **END**
```

FIGURE H.7   Effect of changing the ID field of statistics information, as initiated in the screens of Figure H.5 and H.6

selected member is scanned to determine if it contains valid ascending line numbers. If so, the member is renumbered as a part of reset processing and the last two digits of each standard line number, in positions 73 through 80, are changed to zero. If a member does not contain valid ascending standard line numbers in columns 73–80, it is assumed to be unnumbered and is not renumbered.

The N option is also used to create or update statistics, as with option R. With the N option, however, member line numbers are not scanned and no line renumbering action is included in reset processing.

Deleting Statistics

Option D on the TSO/ISPF 3.5 screen allows the removal of statistics information from one, several, or all members of a partitioned

data set. This option may be selected by placing D at the COM-
MAND ===> line, as illustrated in Figure H.8.

The deletion of statistics from a member collapses the information storage in its directory record from the 42 bytes normally
maintained by TSO, to 12 bytes, the minimum necessary for partitioned data set operation. The minimum 12 byte entry contains the
up to eight character member name and the TTRC pointer. If statistics information is deleted, nothing will appear on any TSO member list for the partitioned data set except each member name.
Figure H.9 illustrates the effect of statistics deletion on member
lists.

The deletion of statistics information for members or whole libraries is reversible in that statistics can be reapplied if eliminated,
but the actual values of the old user information statistics cannot
be recreated. If statistics are deleted and then reset, all member
creation dates and last modification dates will appear as the current date. Little reason ordinarily exists to delete member statistics.

INTERNAL COMPOSITION OF A PARTITIONED
DATA SET DIRECTORY

The directory of a partitioned data set exists within the file making
up the PDS as unblocked records. Each record of the directory is
256 bytes in length regardless of the length or format of records in
the PDS; each such record constitutes a "directory block." The
number of directory blocks is specified for the PDS at the time of
its creation, and cannot be changed thereafter. Following the last of
the directory block records of a PDS is a delimiting mark similar
to a normal "end of file" indication, which separates the directory
from the PDS data space.

Listing and Dumping Directory Blocks

IBM provides the utility program IEHLIST, which can read the PDS
directory and provide a paper listing of directory contents in hexadecimal. Figure H.10 illustrates the job control language and control statement necessary to execute IEHLIST. Figure H.11 depicts
the output of IEHLIST, and compares it to the TSO/ISPF member
list rendition of member information. The TSO/ISPF member list

```
---------------------------- RESET ISPF STATISTICS ----------------------------
OPTION  ===> D

   R - Create/update ISPF statistics, conditionally reset sequence numbers
   N - Create/update ISPF statistics, no reset of sequence numbers
   D - Delete ISPF statistics

NEW VERSION NUMBER ===>          (Required for option "R")
NEW TSO USERID     ===>          (If userid is to be changed)

ISPF LIBRARY:
   PROJECT ===> CSCJGJ
   LIBRARY ===> CSC
   TYPE    ===> C203DAT
   MEMBER  ===>                  (Blank for member list, * for all members)

OTHER PARTITIONED DATA SET:
   DATA SET NAME   ===>
   VOLUME SERIAL   ===>          (If not cataloged)

DATA SET PASSWORD ===>           (If password protected)
```

FIGURE H.8   TSO/ISPF 3.5 screen completed to delete member statistics; lack of member name entry will cause a member selection list to be presented

```
EDIT --- CSCJGJ.CSC.C203DAT --------------------------------------------------
COMMAND ===>                                              SCROLL ===> PAGE
   NAME          VER.MOD  CREATED   LAST MODIFIED  SIZE  INIT   MOD    ID
   CMRIDATA
   DATC
   DATM
   PAYROLL          ┌──────────────────────────────────────────────┐
   P1TEST           │ No statistics information is displayed because│
   UNREAL3          │ TSO 3.5 has been used to delete from this library│
   **END**          └──────────────────────────────────────────────┘
```

FIGURE H.9   Appearance of a TSO/ISPF member list for a partitioned data set library after member statistics have been deleted; no information except member name is stored or provided

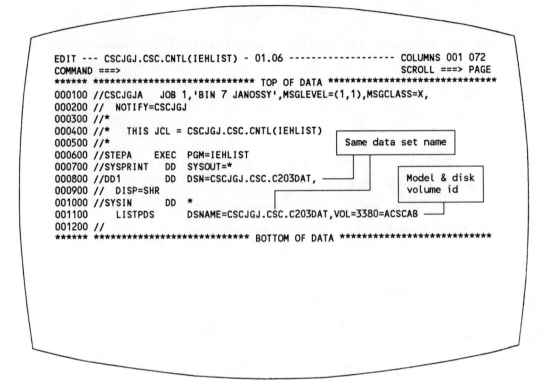

```
EDIT --- CSCJGJ.CSC.CNTL(IEHLIST) - 01.06 ----------------- COLUMNS 001 072
COMMAND ===>                                                SCROLL ===> PAGE
****** *************************** TOP OF DATA ******************************
000100 //CSCJGJA    JOB 1,'BIN 7 JANOSSY',MSGLEVEL=(1,1),MSGCLASS=X,
000200 //  NOTIFY=CSCJGJ
000300 //*
000400 //*    THIS JCL = CSCJGJ.CSC.CNTL(IEHLIST)
000500 //*                                               Same data set name
000600 //STEPA     EXEC  PGM=IEHLIST
000700 //SYSPRINT    DD   SYSOUT=*
000800 //DD1         DD   DSN=CSCJGJ.CSC.C203DAT,           Model & disk
000900 //  DISP=SHR                                         volume id
001000 //SYSIN       DD   *
001100    LISTPDS      DSNAME=CSCJGJ.CSC.C203DAT,VOL=3380=ACSCAB
001200 //
****** *************************** BOTTOM OF DATA **************************
```

FIGURE H.10   Job control language to execute the IEHLIST utility to list the contents of partitioned data set directory blocks

cites the statistics information in the same field sequence as it is stored in the directory blocks.

Utility programs and in fact any program, even those written in COBOL or other general purpose programming languages, can read a PDS directory directly as data using JCL that identifies the data set as a sequential one, rather than as a partitioned data set. When a data set is read, the operating system ordinarily obtains information about it from its entry in the system catalog and its data set label. But entries in JCL override information in the catalog and data set label; when DCB = DSORG = PS, for "physical sequential," is coded, the PDS will be processed as if it were a simple sequential data set containing unblocked 256 byte "directory block" records. Reading of the file will be limited to the directory records only; this processing does not access the data space of the partitioned data set.

Figure H.12 depicts the job control language to execute the

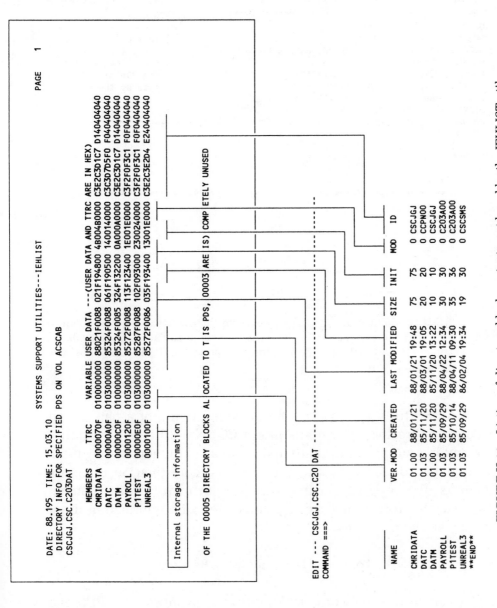

FIGURE H.11 Listing of directory block contents produced by the IEHLIST utility, compared to the appearance of the same directory entries as formatted by TSO/ISPF for a member list

253

```
EDIT --- CSCJGJ.CSC.CNTL(DUMP) - 01.02 --------------------- COLUMNS 001 072
COMMAND ===>                                                 SCROLL ===> HALF
****** **************************** TOP OF DATA ****************************
000100 //CSCJGJA   JOB 1,'BIN 7 JANOSSY',MSGLEVEL=(1,1),MSGCLASS=X,
000200 //  NOTIFY=CSCJGJ
000300 //*                                           This DCB overrides
000400 //*   THIS JCL = CSCJGJ.CSC.CNTL(DUMP)        the data set label
000500 //*                                           and allows reading
000600 //STEPA    EXEC  PGM=IDCAMS                    the PDS directory
000700 //SYSPRINT  DD  SYSOUT=*                       records themselves
000800 //DD1       DD  DSN=CSCJGJ.CSC.C203DAT,
000900 //  DISP=SHR,
001000 //  DCB=(RECFM=F,LRECL=256,BLKSIZE=256,DSORG=PS)
001100 //SYSIN     DD  *
001200     PRINT       INFILE(DD1) -
001300                 COUNT(50) -
001400                 DUMP
001500 //
****** **************************** BOTTOM OF DATA ****************************
```

FIGURE H.12   Job control language to execute the IDCAMS utility to obtain a dump of a partitioned data set directory; the DCB parameter overrides the data set label and the DSORG = PS specification forces treatment of the directory blocks as sequential 256 byte records

IDCAMS utility to request a hexadecimal dump of a partitioned data set directory. The limitation of COUNT(50) is not a requirement, it is simply a safeguard to prevent a voluminous listing if the input partitioned data set directory has more than 50 directory blocks. Figure H.13 illustrates the output of IDCAMS when requested to provide such a dump, annotated with information about the material presented.

Format of Directory Block Records

The length of the records making up the members of a PDS can range from 18 characters to 32,760 characters, the same range as for any records. Fixed length records or variable length records can be housed; JCL and program source code is stored in 80 byte fixed

```
RECORD SEQUENCE NUMBER - 1                     Member name

000000  00FEC3D4 D9C9C4C1 E3C10000 070F0100  00000088 021F0088 021F1948 004B004B  *..CMRIDATA......................*
000020  0000C3E2 C3D1C7D1 40404040 C4C1E3C3  40404040 00000A0F 01030000 0085324F  *..CSCJGJ    DATC    ...........|*
000040  0088061F 19050014 00140000 C3C3D7D5  F0F04040 4040C4C1 E3D44040 40400000  *...........CCPN00    DATM    ..*
000060  0C0F0100 00000085 324F0085 324F1322  000A000A 0000C3E2 C3D1C7D1 40404040  *........|...|.......CSCJGJ    *
000080  D7C1E8D9 D6D3D340 0000120F 01030000  0085272F 0088113F 1234001E 001E0000  *PAYROLL ........................*
0000A0  C3F2F0F3 C1F0F040 4040D7F1 E3C5E2E3  40400000 0E0F0103 00000085 287F0088  *C203A00    P1TEST  ..........."..*
0000C0  102F0930 00230024 0000C3F2 F0F3C1F0  F0404040 E4D5D9C5 C1D3F340 0000100F  *..........C203A00   UNREAL3 ....*
0000E0  01030000 0085272F 0086035F 19340013  001E0000 C3E2C3E2 D4E24040 40400000  *...........^.......CSCSMS    ..*

RECORD SEQUENCE NUMBER - 2

000000  000 FFFF FFFFFFFF FFFF 000 00000100  00000088 021F0088 021F1948 004B004B  *................................*
000020  000                    040 C4C1E3C3  40404040 00000A0F 01030000 0085324F  *..CSCJGJ    DATC    ...........|*
000040  0088061F 19050014 00140000 C3C3D7D5  F0F04040 4040C4C1 E3D44040 40400000  *...........CCPN00    DATM    ..*
000060  0C0F0100 00000085 324F0085 324F1322  000A000A 0000C3E2 C3D1C7D1 40404040  *........|...|.......CSCJGJ    *
000080  D4D3C9E2 E3F0F4F4 00001400 D7C1E8D9  D6D3D340 0000120F 01030000 0085272F  *MLIST044....PAYROLL ............*
0000A0  0088113F 1234001E 001E0000 C3F2F0F3  C1F0F040 4040D7F1 E3C5E2E3 40400000  *...........C203A00    P1TEST  ..*
0000C0  0E0F0103 00000085 287F0088 102F0930  00230024 0000C3F2 F0F3C1F0 F0404040  *........."...........C203A00    *
0000E0  00000000 00000000 00000000 00000000  00000000 00000000 00000000 00000000  *................................*
```

Contents of one 256-byte directory block record (info on six PDS members)

Displacement of the first byte listed in line from start of record, in hex; generated by IDCAMS dump and not part of the directory block.

HIGH-VALUES in a location where a PDS member name would be found indicates the end of information for members. The remainder of directory block content is not predictable or informative, consisting of the residue of BPAM (Basic Partitioned Access Method) space management actions.

FIGURE H.13 Hexadecimal dump of a partitioned data set directory produced by IDCAMS as a result of executing the JCL illustrated in Figure H.12

length records, while CLIST commands can be stored in variable length records with a maximum length of 255 bytes. The record length is established at the time the PDS is allocated, as is the block size for records in the data area. The format of the directory of the PDS is always the same, consisting of unblocked 256 byte records.

A given directory block can hold entries for 6 to 18 members, depending on how extensive a set of user information is maintained for each member. TSO/ISPF statistics add 30 bytes to the bare minimum 12 bytes of "location with the data space" information that a PDS directory entry must house.

When TSO/ISPF creates members in a partitioned data set, each member is uniformly accorded a 42 byte entry in the directory. Six of these entries can be accommodated in one 256-byte directory block, with some extra bytes before and after the entries. The format of a directory block of this type is illustrated in Figure H.14, using a COBOL record description. As denoted on that figure, Julian format is employed for date fields, while highly unusual unsigned packed decimal and single-digit binary formats are used for certain other fields.

Since the formation and storage of user information in directory entries is customizable by an installation and dependent on the software in use, it would be incorrect to assume that all partitioned data sets maintain their directory records in the TSO/ISPF format illustrated in Figure H.14. Load module libraries and libraries in which one or more members do not carry TSO/ISPF statistics will not exhibit this regular six members per directory block format. Figure H.15 illustrates an IEHLIST of the beginning of one partitioned data set directory, that of SYS1.LINKLIB, which does not follow the TSO/ISPF format. Figure H.16 is an IDCAMS hexadecimal dump of this same directory, which shows the irregular placement of member entries within the 256-byte directory blocks of the data set. As annotations on Figure H.15 describe, processing an irregularly formatted PDS directory block involves complex decoding not necessary if a directory block maintained by TSO/ISPF is to be accessed.

Listing a TSO/ISPF Library Directory With a COBOL Program

It is unusual to read a TSO/ISPF library directory as data, but it does provide a means of building customized programs to produce

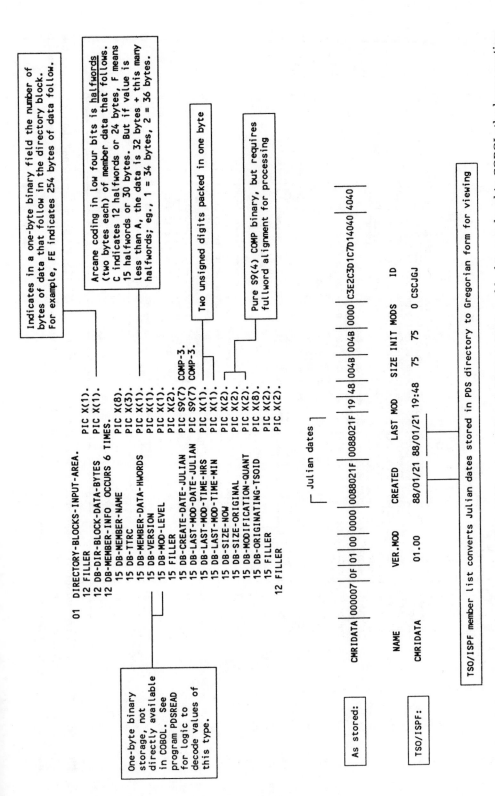

FIGURE H.14 Record definition for a TSO/ISPF library partitioned data set directory block as rendered in COBOL; the lower portion depicts a 42-byte member entry as stored compared to the way TSO/ISPF decodes it for presentation in a member list

```
DATE: 88.196  TIME: 17.33.48       SYSTEMS SUPPORT UTILITIES---IEHLIST                    PAGE    1
DIRECTORY INFO FOR SPECIFIED PDS ON VOL ACSRES
SYS1.LINKLIB

  MEMBERS      TTRC      VARIABLE USER DATA ---(USER DATA AND TTRC ARE IN HEX)
  ACCOUNT      00992D2C  009A010000 000000C2E2 0010701070 0000008800 0101000
  AD           012411B1  0125010000 00000002E2 00BA803000 0000008800 0100000C9 C3C8C3C1C4 F0F00101
  ADDGROUP     011C1CB1  011D010000 00000002E2 0038802680 0000008800 0200000C9 C3C8C3C1C7 F0F00101
  ADDSD        012411B1  0125010000 00000002E2 00BA803000 0000008800 0100000C9 C3C8C3C1C4 F0F00101
  ADDUSER      011E13B1  011F010000 00000002E2 00549830C8 0000008800 0300000C9 C3C8C3C1E4 F0F00101
  ADRDSSU      01E40E2E  01E5010000 0000000C2C2 05C1A032E0 02BAF09800 0100506404 520101
  ADRRELVL     01E40EB3  01E5010000 00000000C2C2 05C1A032E0 0431109800 0102BAF0C1 C409C4E2E2 E440506404 520101
  AG           011C1CB1  011D010000 00000002E2 0038802680 0000008800 0200000C9 C3C8C3C1C7 F0F00101
  AHLCWRIT     00690D2C  0069130000 00000002E2 0020A820A8 0000008800 01010100
  AHLGTF       0067082C  0068010000 00000002E2 006C282FA0 0000008800 02010100
  AHLIWRIT     0069042C  00690A0000 00000002E2 001A681A68 0000008800 01010100
  AHLTMON      0068132C  0069010000 00000002E2 000B380B38 0000008800 01010100
  AHLTASK      00680A2C  0068100000 00000002E2 000C400C40 0000008800 01010100
  AHLWRIT      0069162C  00691C0000 00000002E2 0022202220 0000008800 01010100
  ALD          01220781  01220E0000 00000002E2 009E203208 0000008800 0400000C9 C3C8C3C3C4 F0F00101
  ALG          011D07B1  01100D0000 00000002E2 004C102F88 0000008800 0300000C9 C3C8C3C3C7 F0F00101
  ALTDSD       01220781  01220E0000 00000002E2 009E203208 0000008800 0400000C9 C3C8C3C3C4 F0F00101
```

These four bits indicate the number of halfwords of user data
that exist in the member entry. A hexadecimal letter indicates
the number of two-byte halfwords, while a number indicates the
number of halfwords + 16. For example, F indicates 15 halfwords
or 30 bytes of user data, which added to the 12 bytes of member
name and TTRC data equal 42 bytes per member entry. This is the
standard for TSO library data sets. But 1 indicates 16 halfwords
plus 1, or 17 halfwords, which equals 34 bytes of user data.
Different members can carry different amount of user data; this
is a listing from SYS1.LINKLIB, a system load module library.

FIGURE H.15 IEHLIST presentation of the member entries in the directory of a non-TSO/ISPF library partitioned data set, that of the common system load module library SYS1.LINKLIB. Not all member entries contain the same quantity of user information, making the directory block content irregular and not consistent in format.

LISTING OF DATA SET - SYS1.LINKLIB

RECORD SEQUENCE NUMBER - 1

```
000000  00DEC1C3 C3D6E4D5 E3400099 2D2C009A  01000000 0000C2E2 00107010 70000000  *..ACCOUNT .........BS......*
000020  88000101 0000C1C4 40404040 40400124  11B10125 01000000 000002E2 00BA8030  *........AD.............S...*
000040  00000000 88000100 0000C9C3 C8C3C1C4  F0F00101 C1C4C4C7 D9D6E4D7 011C1CB1  *.........ICHCAD00..ADDGROUP....*
000060  011D0100 00000000 02E20038 8026B000  00008800 02000000 000002E2 C1C7F0F0  *.....S............ICHCAG00*
000080  0101C1C4 C4E2C440 40400124 11B10125  01000000 000002E2 00BA8030 00000000  *..ADDSD .........S........*
0000A0  88000100 0000C9C3 C8C3C1C4 F0F00101  C1C4C4E4 E2C5D940 011E13B1 011F0100  *........ICHCAD00..ADDUSER ........*
0000C0  00000000 02E20054 9830C800 00008800  03000000 C9C3C8C3 C1E4F0F0 01010000  *.....S....H......ICHCAU00.....*
0000E0  00000000 00000000 00000000 00000000  00000000 00000000 00000000 00000000  *..........................*
```

RECORD SEQUENCE NUMBER - 2

```
000000  00F6C1C4 D9C4E2E2 E44001E4 0E2E01E5  01000000 0000C2C2 05C1A032 E002BAF0  *.6ADRDSSU .U...V......BB.A.....0*
000020  98000100 50640452 0101C1C4 D9D9C5D3  E5D301E4 0EB301E5 44405064 0000C2C2  *........&.....ADRRELVL.U...V......BB*
000040  05C1A032 E0043110 98000102 BAF0C1C4  D9C4E2E2 E4405064 04520101 C1C74040  *.A.........OADRDSSU &......AG*
000060  40404040 011C1CB1 011D0100 00000000  02E20038 8026B000 00008800 02000000  *.........S...............*
000080  C9C3C8C3 C1C7F0F0 0101C1C8 D3C3E6D9  C9E30069 0D2C0069 13000000 000002E2  *ICHCAG00..AHLCWRIT.........S*
0000A0  0020A820 A8000000 88000101 0100C1C8  D3C7E3C6 40400067 082C0068 01000000  *..y.y.....AHLGTF ........*
0000C0  000002E2 006C282F A0000000 88000201  0100C1C8 D3C9E6D9 C9E30069 042C0069  *...S.%........AHL1WRIT......*
0000E0  0A000000 000002E2 001A681A 68000000  88000101 01000000 00000000 00000000  *.......S......*
```

Different members have differing quantities of user data similar to TSO statistics, so the format of the directory block need not be as uniform as for programmer TSO/ISPF library PDSs.

FIGURE H.16 IDCAMS hexadecimal dump of the same directory blocks as listed in Figure H.15 with IEHLIST; SYS1.LINKLIB is a system load module library containing members created by various linkage editing or assembly processes. This results in varying amount of directory-stored user information.

member lists. It also allows programmatic examination of member creation and change dates, and the formation of control statements to be processed by a utility to affect the PDS. A program that reads a directory can, for example, identify any members in a load module library that were created before a certain date, and use the information to form control statements for a subsequent run of IDCAMS, to delete each member meeting a specified age-since-update criteria.

Figure H.17 illustrates a COBOL program named PDSREAD that can be used to read and list TSO/ISPF-maintained library directories. This program employs the record format defined in Figure H.14, as well as creative use of a two-byte field redefined to serve as a conversion mechanism between different data formats. The program moves various unsigned packed decimal fields and single-digit binary fields through this conversion field to decode them.

Figure H.18 illustrates the output of program PDSREAD. Since the program does not convert Julian dates to Gregorian format, its simple listing presents each member creation date and last modification date as a Julian date. Figure H.19 illustrates the output as

```
000100 IDENTIFICATION DIVISION.
000200 PROGRAM-ID.     PDSREAD.
000300 AUTHOR.         J JANOSSY.
000400 INSTALLATION.   DEPAUL UNIVERSITY.
000500 DATE-WRITTEN.   JULY 1988.
000600 DATE-COMPILED.
000700*REMARKS.        READ AND DISPLAY CONTENTS OF PDS DIRECTORY.
000800*
000900 ENVIRONMENT DIVISION.              ┌─────────────────────────────┐
001000 CONFIGURATION SECTION.             │ Program reads a TSO/ISPF PDS │
001100 SOURCE-COMPUTER.  IBM-4381.        │ directory with statistics   │
001200 OBJECT-COMPUTER.  IBM-4381.        │ only, and decodes it.  Can be│
001300 INPUT-OUTPUT SECTION.              │ modified to output it as data│
001400 FILE-CONTROL.                      │ records for further processing.│
001500     SELECT DIRECTORY-BLOCKS        └─────────────────────────────┘
                                   ASSIGN TO DIRBLOCK.
001600*
001700 DATA DIVISION.
001800 FILE SECTION.
001900 FD  DIRECTORY-BLOCKS
002000     LABEL RECORD ARE STANDARD
002100     BLOCK CONTAINS 0 RECORDS
002200     RECORD CONTAINS 256 CHARACTERS.
002300 01  DIRECTORY-RECORD          PIC X(256).
002400*
002500 WORKING-STORAGE SECTION.
002600 01  WS-EOF-FLAG               PIC X(1)  VALUE 'M'.
002700 01  WS-SUB                    PIC S9(4) COMP.
002800 01  WS-MEMBER-COUNT           PIC 9(5)  VALUE 0.
```

FIGURE H.17 Source code for program PDSREAD, a COBOL program that can read normal TSO/ISPF library partitioned data set directory blocks and decode the unusual storage formats of their fields

```
002900*
003000 01  DIRECTORY-BLOCKS-INPUT-AREA.
003100      12 FILLER                          PIC X(1).
003200      12 DB-DIR-BLOCK-DATA-BYTES          PIC X(1).
003300      12 DB-MEMBER-INFO  OCCURS 6 TIMES.
003400          15 DB-MEMBER-NAME               PIC X(8).
003500          15 DB-TTRC                      PIC X(3).
003600          15 DB-MEMBER-DATA-HWORDS        PIC X(1).
003700          15 DB-VERSION                   PIC X(1).
003800          15 DB-MOD-LEVEL                 PIC X(1).
003900          15 FILLER                       PIC X(2).
004000          15 DB-CREATE-DATE-JULIAN        PIC S9(7) COMP-3.
004100          15 DB-LAST-MOD-DATE-JULIAN      PIC S9(7) COMP-3.
004200          15 DB-LAST-MOD-TIME-HRS         PIC X(1).
004300          15 DB-LAST-MOD-TIME-MIN         PIC X(1).
004400          15 DB-SIZE-NOW                  PIC X(2).
004500          15 DB-SIZE-ORIGINAL             PIC X(2).
004600          15 DB-MODIFICATION-QUANT        PIC X(2).
004700          15 DB-ORIGINATING-TSOID         PIC X(8).
004800          15 FILLER                       PIC X(2).
004900      12 FILLER                           PIC X(2).
005000*
005100 01  WS-HALF-WORD                         PIC S9(4) COMP.
005200 01  WS-PACKED-FIELD-2BYTES   REDEFINES
005300      WS-HALF-WORD                        PIC S9(3) COMP-3.
005400 01  WS-HALF-WORD-X   REDEFINES WS-HALF-WORD.
005500      12 WS-HALF-WORD-HI-BYTE             PIC X(1).
005600      12 WS-HALF-WORD-LO-BYTE             PIC X(1).
005700*
005800 01  DISPLAY-LINE.
005900      12 DL-MEMBER-NAME                   PIC X(8).
006000      12 FILLER                           PIC X(1)  VALUE SPACE.
006100      12 DL-VERSION                       PIC 9(2).
006200      12 FILLER                           PIC X(1)  VALUE '.'.
006300      12 DL-MOD-LEVEL                     PIC 9(2).
006400      12 FILLER                           PIC X(1)  VALUE SPACE.
006500      12 DL-CREATE                        PIC 9(5).
006600      12 FILLER                           PIC X(1)  VALUE SPACE.
006700      12 DL-LAST-MOD                      PIC 9(5).
006800      12 FILLER                           PIC X(1)  VALUE SPACE.
006900      12 DL-LAST-MOD-HRS                  PIC 9(2).
007000      12 FILLER                           PIC X(1)  VALUE ':'.
007100      12 DL-LAST-MOD-MIN                  PIC 9(2).
007200      12 FILLER                           PIC X(1)  VALUE ' '.
007300      12 DL-SIZE-NOW                      PIC ZZZ9.
007400      12 FILLER                           PIC X(1)  VALUE ' '.
007500      12 DL-SIZE-ORIGINAL                 PIC ZZZ9.
007600      12 FILLER                           PIC X(1)  VALUE ' '.
007700      12 DL-MODIFICATION-QUANT            PIC ZZZ9.
007800      12 FILLER                           PIC X(1)  VALUE ' '.
007900      12 DL-ORIGINATING-TSOID             PIC X(8).
008000/
008100 PROCEDURE DIVISION.
008200 0000-MAINLINE.
008300      PERFORM 1000-BOJ.
008400      PERFORM 2000-PROCESS UNTIL WS-EOF-FLAG = 'E'.
008500      PERFORM 3000-EOJ.
008600      STOP RUN.
008700*
008800 1000-BOJ.
008900      OPEN  INPUT DIRECTORY-BLOCKS.
009000      DISPLAY 'START OF PDSREAD DIRECTORY BLOCK DECODER PROGRAM'.
009100      DISPLAY ' '.
009200      DISPLAY
009300       ' NAME     V.M   CRE  -LAST-MOD-- SIZE INIT MODS ORIGIN'.
009400      DISPLAY ' '.
009500      PERFORM 2700-READ.
009600*
009700 2000-PROCESS.
```

> This format defines the nature of the entries in a 256-byte directory block record when TSO/ISPF statistics are kept.

> This work area is necessary to decode one-byte binary and unsigned packed decimal fields

FIGURE H.17 (continued)

```
009800        PERFORM 2100-DECODE-DISPLAY
009900           VARYING WS-SUB FROM +1 BY +1
010000             UNTIL WS-SUB > +6
010100               OR WS-EOF-FLAG = 'E'.
010200        IF WS-EOF-FLAG NOT = 'E'
010300           PERFORM 2700-READ.
010400*
010500 2100-DECODE-DISPLAY.
010600        IF DB-MEMBER-NAME(WS-SUB) NOT = HIGH-VALUES
010700           PERFORM 2110-LIST-IT
010800           ADD +1 TO WS-MEMBER-COUNT
010900        ELSE
011000           MOVE 'E' TO WS-EOF-FLAG.
011100*
011200 2110-LIST-IT.
011300        MOVE DB-MEMBER-NAME(WS-SUB)  TO DL-MEMBER-NAME.
011400*
011500        MOVE DB-VERSION(WS-SUB)         TO WS-HALF-WORD-LO-BYTE.
011600        MOVE LOW-VALUES                 TO WS-HALF-WORD-HI-BYTE.
011700        MOVE WS-HALF-WORD               TO DL-VERSION.
011800*
011900        MOVE DB-MOD-LEVEL(WS-SUB)       TO WS-HALF-WORD-LO-BYTE.
012000        MOVE WS-HALF-WORD               TO DL-MOD-LEVEL.
012100*
012200        MOVE DB-CREATE-DATE-JULIAN(WS-SUB)    TO DL-CREATE.
012300        MOVE DB-LAST-MOD-DATE-JULIAN(WS-SUB)  TO DL-LAST-MOD.
012400*
012500        MOVE +0 TO WS-PACKED-FIELD-2BYTES.
012600        MOVE DB-LAST-MOD-TIME-HRS(WS-SUB)  TO WS-HALF-WORD-HI-BYTE.
012700        COMPUTE DL-LAST-MOD-HRS =
012800           WS-PACKED-FIELD-2BYTES / 10.
012900*
013000        MOVE DB-LAST-MOD-TIME-MIN(WS-SUB)  TO WS-HALF-WORD-HI-BYTE.
013100        COMPUTE DL-LAST-MOD-MIN =
013200           WS-PACKED-FIELD-2BYTES / 10.
013300*
013400  .     MOVE DB-SIZE-NOW(WS-SUB)        TO WS-HALF-WORD-X.
013500        MOVE WS-HALF-WORD               TO DL-SIZE-NOW.
013600*
013700        MOVE DB-SIZE-ORIGINAL(WS-SUB)   TO WS-HALF-WORD-X.
013800        MOVE WS-HALF-WORD               TO DL-SIZE-ORIGINAL.
013900*
014000        MOVE DB-MODIFICATION-QUANT(WS-SUB) TO WS-HALF-WORD-X.
014100        MOVE WS-HALF-WORD                  TO DL-MODIFICATION-QUANT.
014200*
014300        MOVE DB-ORIGINATING-TSOID(WS-SUB)  TO DL-ORIGINATING-TSOID.
014400*
014500        DISPLAY DISPLAY-LINE.
014600*
014700 2700-READ.
014800        READ DIRECTORY-BLOCKS INTO DIRECTORY-BLOCKS-INPUT-AREA
014900           AT END
015000             MOVE 'E' TO WS-EOF-FLAG.
015100*
015200 3000-EOJ.
015300        DISPLAY ' '.
015400        DISPLAY 'END OF MEMBER LIST'
015500        DISPLAY 'MEMBERS LISTED = ', WS-MEMBER-COUNT.
015600        CLOSE DIRECTORY-BLOCKS.
```

Decodes one-byte binary value

Decodes an unsigned packed decimal value stored in a one-byte field; requires the computation shown

These MOVEs insure appropriate treatment of binary values, which must be aligned on word boundaries for proper handling

FIGURE H.17 (continued)

```
START OF PDSREAD DIRECTORY BLOCK DECODER PROGRAM

NAME      V.M    CRE   -LAST-MOD-- SIZE INIT MODS ORIGIN

CMRIDATA 01.00 88021 88021 19:48   75   75    0 CSCJGJ
DATC     01.03 85324 88061 19:05   20   20    0 CCPN00
DATM     01.00 85324 85324 13:22   10   10    0 CSCJGJ
PAYROLL  01.03 85272 88113 12:34   30   30    0 C203A00
P1TEST   01.03 85287 88102 09:30   35   36    0 C203A00
UNREAL3  01.03 85272 86035 19:34   19   30    0 CSCSMS

END OF MEMBER LIST
MEMBERS LISTED = 00006
```

> The decoded directory block fields
> are listed here in an order much like
> a TSO/ISPF directory list just for
> familiarity sake. Once decoded, the
> fields can be listed or used in any
> desired way.

FIGURE Figure H.18 Output of program PDSREAD when run on the TSO/ISPF library partitioned data set directory listed in Figure H.11 and dumped in Figure H.13

```
SDSF OUTPUT DISPLAY CSCJGJA  JOB 1098 103 LINE     1  COLUMNS   2  81
COMMAND INPUT ===>                                    SCROLL ===> PAGE
START OF PDSREAD DIRECTORY BLOCK DECODER PROGRAM

NAME      V.M    CRE   -LAST-MOD-- SIZE INIT MODS ORIGIN

CCPZ001  01.20 87047 87067 07:16  319  276    0 CCCPZ00
CCPZ002  01.04 87067 88190 15:41  912  915    0 CSCJGJ
CCPZ003  01.13 87052 87067 07:21  673  600    0 CCCPZ00
CCPZ004  01.06 87066 87067 00:36  234  216    0 CCCPZ00
CHDS4001 01.00 87043 87043 12:03  222  222    0 CSCJGJ
CHDS4012 01.00 87043 87043 12:05  559  559    0 CSCJGJ


. . . . . . . . . . . . . . . . . . . . . . . . . . . . . . .

EDIT --- CSCJGJ.CSC.COBOL --------------------------------------------
COMMAND ===>                                         SCROLL ===> PAGE
   NAME            VER.MOD  CREATED   LAST MODIFIED  SIZE INIT  MOD   ID
   CCPZ001          01.20  87/02/16  87/03/08 07:16  319  276    0 CCCPZ00
   CCPZ002          01.04  87/03/08  88/07/08 15:41  912  915    0 CSCJGJ
   CCPZ003          01.13  87/02/21  87/03/08 07:21  673  600    0 CCCPZ00
   CCPZ004          01.06  87/03/07  87/03/08 00:36  234  216    0 CCCPZ00
   CHDS4001         01.00  87/02/12  87/02/12 12:03  222  222    0 CSCJGJ
   CHDS4012         01.00  87/02/12  87/02/12 12:05  559  559    0 CSCJGJ
```

FIGURE H.19 Output of program PDSREAD as viewed using SDSF, and compared to a TSO/ISPF member list of the same library; PDSREAD does not convert Julian format dates stored in the directory to Gregorian format as presented in the member list

```
EDIT --- CSCJGJ.CSC.CNTL(CLINKGO) - 01.11 ----------------- COLUMNS 001 072
COMMAND ===>                                                 SCROLL ===> PAGE
****** **************************** TOP OF DATA ******************************
000100 //CSCJGJA   JOB 1,'BIN 7 JANOSSY',MSGCLASS=X,MSGLEVEL=(1,1),
000200 //  NOTIFY=CSCJGJ
000300 //******************************************************************
000400 //*                                                                *
000500 //*    CLINKGO      COMPILE, LINK, AND RUN WITH CCP PROC CLINKGO    *
000600 //*                                                                *
000700 //******************************************************************
000800 //STEPA   EXEC  PROC=CLINKGO,
000900 //       PDS='CSCJGJ.CSC.COBOL',
001000 //  MEMBER='PDSREAD'
001100 //GO.DIRBLOCK   DD DSN=CSCJGJ.CSC.COBOL,
001200 //  DISP=SHR,
001300 //  DCB=(RECFM=F,LRECL=256,BLKSIZE=256,DSORG=PS)
001400 //
****** **************************** BOTTOM OF DATA ***************************
```

FIGURE H.20 Typical job control language to compile, linkage edit, and run program PDSREAD on a TSO/ISPF library using a cataloged procedure; the procedure cited here is similar to VSCOBCLG

viewed using the SDSF function on one portion of a split screen, and the actual TSO/ISPF member list on the other portion of the screen.

If a person is technically inclined and curious as to the composition of TSO/ISPF partitioned data set directory blocks, program PDSREAD can be used as a base to explore them. Figure H.20 illustrates typical job control language that can be employed with a compile, linkage edit, and go cataloged procedure to execute program PDSREAD. The program itself is available in machine readable form on diskette, for uploading to a mainframe, as described in Appendix E.

DETAILED
INDEX

The most frequently referenced items are listed in **bold letters;** when multiple page references for an item exist, the most informative page references are listed in **bold numbers.**

A

Account, TSO, 10
Allocate a data set, 137–43, 197
ALT key, 6, 7
AUTOLIST, 219
AUTOSAVE, 70, 75, 220

B

B14 error, can't end edit, 237
Background function, 21
BOUNDS, 220
BROWSE (1), 24, 42
BUILTIN, 221

C

CANCEL, abandon edit, 70, 77, 221
CANCEL, terminate job, 70, 114, 221, 240
CAPS, 75, 221
Catalog a data set, 147
CC/CC block line copy, 60, 63
Change password, RACF, 12–13
CHANGE text string in edit, 82–84, 221
CICS, log on interference, 16
CLIST (TSO command list):
    allocating CLIST library, 196

disk block size calculation, 200, 203–06
editing and submitting a job, 210, 212–215
executing from library, 119, 201
message to multiple parties, 209, 211
message to single party, 207
syntax, 197–202
tape block size calculation, 198, 201
CLASS, and TSO 3.8 Outlist, 98, 100–01
CLEAR key, 5, 17, 175, **182, 185**
COLS column ruler, 61, 68, 222
COMMAND line, 54, 55, 73
Copy data set, 149–57
COPY library member, 46, 86–88
Copying lines during edit, 60, 63
CREATE members with copy-out, 88–90, 222
Creating a new member, **50–51,** 57–59

D

D37 error code, see E37 error code, 236

Data set (library):
    allocating with JCL, 39, 196
    allocating with TSO/ISPF, 137–43, 197
    cataloging, 147
    copying, 149–57
    default editing columns based on name, 38
    deleting, 143–45
    directory, 39–49
    directory block format, 252, **257**
    dumping and decoding directory, 250–64
    information screen, 131, 135, **145–47,** 148
    moving, 153–57
    names, 9, 37–38
    partitioned, 35–42
    recovery during edit, 74
    renaming, 143
    reorganization, 40, 132, **187–93**
    sequential, editing, 71
    space, monitoring, 72, 146
    uncataloging, 148
DD/DD deleting blocks of lines, 60, 62, 69, 223
DEFINE a macro or alias, 223
Delete a data set, 143–45
DELETE excluded/nonexcluded lines, 223

265

Deleting a member, 129–30, 136
Deleting output, 97, 100, 105
DEV CNCL key, unlock keyboard after failed print, 6
Directory, see also Data set, 39–41, 250–64

E

E37 error, can't end edit, 40, 236
EDIT (2), 24, 46, 47, **49–51, 54–72,** 223
Edit, abandoning with CANCEL, 70
END key, PF3, 8, 176
ENTER key, special role, 4
Error codes:
    B14 error, can't end edit, 237
    D37 error, see E37 error code, 236
    E37 error, can't end edit, 40, 236
    522 error code, timed out, 238
    80A error code, insufficient memory, 238
EXCLUDE lines from view, edit, 223
Excluding (X) lines in edit, 61, 67, 223, 232
EXEC, executing CLIST, 119, 200–01
Expired password, RACF, 12

F

FIND text string in edit, 80–81, 223
Foreground function, 21

H

Held output, 95, 100, 102, 105
HELP facility (PF1), 120–23
HEX hexadecimal edit display, 91, 92, 224
HyDra ASCII protocol converter, 183–85

I

IBM-7171 ASCII protocol converter, 183–85
IDCAMS character/hexadecimal dump, 254–55

IMACRO, 228
Input queue, 106
INSERT key, 5, 175, 185
Inserting lines in edit, 58, **60**

L

Label (.XXXXX), 233
LEVEL, 224
Library, see Partitioned Data Set, 35–42
LINE FEED key, 6
LISTCAT, data set list, 115–116
Load module library, 41
LOCATE line by label, 78–79, 225
Log and list data sets, 29–30, 180
Log on problems, 16–18
Logging on to TSO, 9
LOGOFF command, 15, 112

M

Main menu structure, 20, 21
MASK, 225
Member, library:
    copying, 46, 86–88
    creating, **50–51,** 57–59
    deleting, 129–30, 136
    editing, 24, 46, 47, **49–51, 54–72,** 223
    member list, 41, **51–54**
    moving, 60–63, 225
    promoting, 157
    removing line numbers, **85–86,** 231
    renaming, 129–31
    renumbering, 46, 86, 227
    repeating lines, 61, 65
MM/MM block line move, 60, 63
MODEL library, 225
MOVE a library member, 225
Moving lines in edit, 60, 63
MSGCLASS and SYSOUT, 95–96

N

NEWLINE key, 4
NOTE, 226
NOTIFY (JCL), 47
NUMBER mode, setting, 226

O

Origin ID field, member list, 246
Out of space when ending edit, 40, 236
Outlist (3.8), 24, 47, 95–101
Output queue, 103–104

P

PA keys, "program attention," 6, **181–82**
PACK member in storage, 226
PANELID screen identifier, 121–123
PARMS (0), 23, 25
Partitioned data set reorganization, 40, 132, **187–93**
Partitioned data set, 35–42
Passthrough, native mode TSO commands, 113
Password, changing, 12–13
PDS, Partitioned Data Set, 35–42
PF keys, "program function," 4–5, 8, 31–32, **118–19, 175–79,** 184
PF3 END key, 7–8, 176
Print a member, 127–30, 167–72
PRINT key, 6, 179
PROFILE, 74–77, 227
Promoting a member, 157
Protocol converter, ASCII, terminal emulation, 183–85
Purging output, 105, 114

R

RACF security, 11, 12, 240, **242**
READY prompt, native mode TSO, 14
RECONNECT, 16
RECOVERY, 74, 76, 94, 227, 238
Removing COLS and messages, 69
Rename a data set, 143
Rename a member, 129–31
RENUM applying line numbers, 46, 86, 227
Reorganization, see also Space, library, monitoring, 40, 132, **187–93**
Repeating lines, 61, 65
REPLACE a member with copyout, 88–90, 228

RESET command, 69, 84–85, 228
RESET key, 6, 7
RETURN key, 4, 6
RMACRO, 228
RR/RR repeat block of lines, 60, 65

SAVE a member being edited, 91, 93, 228
Scrolling the display, 57, 59, 112
SDSF (S), Spool Display and Search Facility, 23, 24, 47, **101–09**
SEND a message, 116–117
Sharing access to a TSO library (RACF), 240
Shifting columns, 61, 66, 232
SHOW portion of excluded lines, 228
SORT, TSO/ISPF command, 229
Source code diskette for book, 217
Space, library, monitoring usage, 72, 146
Split screen (PF 2), 107–109
Stacking commands, 120–22
Statistics, information in member list, 243, 249
STATS, 229
STATUS, checking submitted job, 113, 114
SUBMIT, submitting jobs, 77–78, 229
SYSOUT and MSGCLASS, 95–96

TABS line in profile, 229–30
TE (Text entry), 231
Terminal emulation, 183–85

Terminal setup (0.1), 25–28
Terminate submitted job, 70
TF (Text flow), 231
Transfer feature (=), 28, 111
TS (Text split), 231
TSO account, 10
TSO functions, overall diagram, 22
TSO user id, 9
Tutorial, TSO/ISPF, HELP, 120–123

UNNUM removing line numbering, 85–86, 231
Utilities (3)
  allocate a data set, 137–43
  catalog a data set, 147
  compress library, 132
  copy a data set or member, 149–57
  data set list (3.4), 159–65
  delete data set, 143–45
  delete member, 129–30, 136
  information about data set, **72,** 131, 135, **145–47,** 148
  monitoring data set space usage, 72, 146
  move a data set or member, 153–57
  print a member, 127–30, 167–72
  print all library members, 133–34
  print a library member list, 133
  promote a member, 157
  rename a data set, 143
  rename a member, 129–31
  renumber a member, 46, 86, 227
  uncatalog a data set, 148

Unlock 3270 keyboard after failed print, 6

VER, changing version number, 231
Version numbers, member list, 231, **245–46**
VT-100/3270 terminal emulation, 183–85

Wrong columns, shifting to correct, 237
Wrong length record in library, 240

XX/XX excluding lines, 61, 67

Symbols and numbers

& ampersand in CLIST syntax, 199
* asterisk in TAB line, 229–30
- hyphen in TAB line, 230
- hyphen and + plus sign in CLIST syntax, 199
= TSO/ISPF transfer feature, 28, 111
⟩⟩ and ⟨⟨ data shift, 232
)) and)) shift columns, 61, 66, 232
3270 terminals, 4, 5
B14 error, can't end edit, 237
D37 error, see E37 error code, 236
E37 error, can't end edit, 40, 236
522 error code, timed out, 238
80A error code, insufficient memory, 238

SUMMARY
INDEX

Items here are keyed to this reference symbol in the text:

3.1	R
	RENAME

Allocate a data set   137
CANCEL, abandon editing a
  member   77
CANCEL a submitted job   114
CHANGE a text string   82
Copy a library member   149, 151
COPY within edit   86
CREATE, copy lines to new
  member   88
Delete a data set   143
Delete a library member   129
Edit an item   49, 73
EXEC a command list **(CLIST)**   119
FIND a text string   80
HEXadecimal screen display   91
Info on library space condition   131,
  135, 148
KEYS, seeing/redefining PF keys   118,
  176

LISTCAT, list data set names   115
LOCATE by line number or label   78
Move a library member   149, 153
Output from a job; view it   95
Print a member   127, 167
PRINT the screen   167
PROFILE, edit session controls   74
Rename a data set   143
Rename a library member   129
RENUM member line numbers   86
RESET the edit screen display   84
SAVE an edited item manually   91
Scroll the screen   112
SDSF, view output   95, 101
SEND a message   116
STATUS of submitted jobs   114
SUBMIT a job   77
UNNUM, remove line numbers   85
View output from a job   95